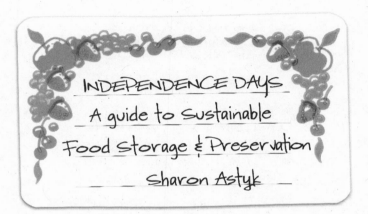

INDEPENDENCE DAYS

A guide to Sustainable

Food Storage & Preservation

Sharon Astyk

NEW SOCIETY PUBLISHERS

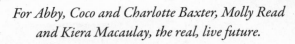

For Abby, Coco and Charlotte Baxter, Molly Read
and Kiera Macaulay, the real, live future.

And in affectionate memory of Carla Emery,
who did it all first, better and wiser.

Cataloging in Publication Data:
A catalog record for this publication is available
from the National Library of Canada.

Cover design: Diane McIntosh.
Cover photo: © iStock/Natalia Siverina

Printed in Canada by Friesens.
First printing August 2009.

Paperback or Hard cover ISBN: 978-0-86571-652-0

Inquiries regarding requests to reprint all
or part of *Independence Days* should be addressed to
New Society Publishers at the address below.

To order directly from the publishers,
please call toll-free (North America) 1-800-567-6772,
or order online at www.newsociety.com

Any other inquiries can be directed by mail to:

New Society Publishers
P.O. Box 189, Gabriola Island, BC V0R 1X0, Canada
(250) 247-9737

New Society Publishers' mission is to publish books that contribute in fundamental ways to building an ecologically sustainable and just society, and to do so with the least possible impact on the environment, in a manner that models this vision. We are committed to doing this not just through education, but through action. This book is one step toward ending global deforestation and climate change. It is printed on Forest Stewardship Council-certified acid-free paper that is **100% post-consumer recycled** (100% old growth forest-free), processed chlorine free, and printed with vegetable-based, low-VOC inks, with covers produced using FSC-certified stock. Additionally, New Society purchases carbon offsets based on an annual audit, operating with a carbon-neutral footprint. For further information, or to browse our full list of books and purchase securely, visit our website at: www.newsociety.com

NEW SOCIETY PUBLISHERS
www.newsociety.com

Mixed Sources
Cert no. SW-COC-001271
© 1996 FSC

FSC

Advance Praise for *Independence Days*

Be warned! *Independence Days* will change the way you eat. It is not just a guide to storing food but a manual for living in a changing world. This is truly one of the best books I have read on this subject and I have read them all.

— Kathy Harrison, author of
Just In Case: How To Be Self Sufficient
When The Unexpected Happens

While making us fully aware of the the rocky road of food chaos opening up in front of us, Sharon Astyk takes our hand and guides us, fretting and nervous, to a calm garden we can safely begin working from. With generous and needed detail, and a gentle recognition of our resistence, she builds a sturdy path to a full larder, a safe family and a more secure community.

— Robin Wheeler, author of
Food Security for the Faint of Heart
and *Gardening for the Faint of Heart*

If you have any interest at all in where your food comes from, *Independence Days* is the perfect book to start with. Sharon Astyk makes a compelling argument for taking charge of your food security and is thorough in her coverage of food storage and preservation techniques including delicious recipes to get you started. But, make no mistake about it, this well thought out resource is more than just a food storage and recipe book—it is a call to arms to really think closely about the food that gives us sustenance and how it gets to us.

— Deanna Duke,
writer/publisher,
TheCrunchyChicken.com

Contents

Old Ways and New

The Barn in Winter

Acknowledgments

This book was the endpiece of two year marathon of writing that resulted in three books and me nearly losing my mind. That any of it remains is a testament to many people, most of whom I have probably forgotten to name, because of aforementioned loss of mind.

First, the readers of my blog, and the participants in my six online food storage classes, who all helped advise, clarify, critique and who asked the right questions and helped me find the write answers. Thank you all so much.

To Ingrid Witvoet and New Society for being willing to take a third crazy risk on an unknown author, before the first book was even published—I'm so grateful. To Ginny Miller for tireless reassurance and enthusiasm, and Sue Custance, for the shiny cool cover. Also profuse thanks to Murray Reiss for improving this manuscript enormously, and putting up with me.

Thanks to those who led the way on some piece of this—I learned a lot from so many people, including many participants over the years on various newsgroups and in person classes. Particular thanks to those I stole ideas from: Bob Waldrop, Dmitry Orlov, Matt Mayer, Miranda Edel, Chile, Robyn Morton; Kathy Harrison; Deanna Duke; Robin Wheeler; Pat Meadows (who deserves more than thanks—she should get royalties!); and all the people we thanked in *A Nation of Farmers* who helped me better understand our food system.

Thanks to those who kept me company along the journey, among them, Alexandra, for berries and the prettiest jam jars ever; Susan, Joe and Steve for never rolling their eyes where I could see; Bess, for always wanting to try the next thing; Deanna for knowing that liquor always makes jam better; Jesse for always chopping onions; Miriam for stretching my cooking skills; Alice for practically being my agent for free; Sandy for endless support and babysitting; and Aaron, who is the best co-author on earth, even on books he doesn't have to write.

Thanks to Susie, who was my first jam-making role model, to Dad who made my first sourdough, to Mom who taught me that cheap is a virtue; to Rachael, who still makes better preserves than I do; and to Vicki who can feed more people, more gracefully. Thanks to my wonderful brothers in law, Billy and Sander as well, and to Luana for pickles. Thanks to Nancy and Marty for all the times you forgave my absence and entertained my kids so I could get this done.

I am most of all blessed in my children and husband, who are full scale participants in our food preservation project, and who love me despite my limitations. Eli taste-tests everything, Simon is my most devoted berry picker, Isaiah watches and waits and is my cooking companion and Asher won't stop until all the work is done. I am so grateful to them. And, of course, to Eric, who I could never thank enough, who knows the difference between me on paper and me in the real world, and who still loves me anyway. I'll be paying that debt, gladly, until the end of time.

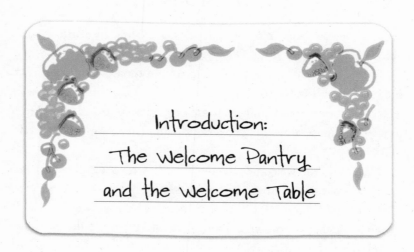

Introduction:
The Welcome Pantry
and the Welcome Table

I'm going to sit at the welcome table, hallelujah!
I'll sit at the welcome table one of these days.
I'm going to feast on milk and honey, hallelujah!
I'll feast on milk and honey one of these days.
All God's children gonna sit together, hallelujah!
All God's children gonna sit together one of these days.

— "River Jordan," traditional spiritual. —

I DON'T THINK IT IS OVERSTATING the case to say that a lot of us are feeling powerless right now. Most of what's going on in the world is not something we can control. Most of us rightly try not to let that stop us — we try to claim what power we can as often as we can. So even though we know it might not help, we talk to our representatives, we give money, we demonstrate. But at some level, most of us are living a history that is sweeping us along with it. This is not always fun.

All of us need to devote some energy to fighting battles that will probably be lost, simply because we have an obligation to fight the good fight. But most of us can't live on a steady diet of tilting at windmills. We also need to do work where we know we can accomplish something, and where we know we matter. That's why I think food preservation and storage matter so much. Ultimately, we are talking not only about the fairly manageable question of what to have for dinner, but also about transforming our society, our use of energy, our culture.

One battle we can win is the recreation of the welcome table and the full pantry. One of the things we can do to tie ourselves to others is to share food with them, with those in need of food and with those in need of companionship, conversation and friendship — that is, all of us.

What does the welcome table have to do with the full pantry? A reserve of food means that our pantry is never so empty that we cannot share a little. Our table is not bare because we have preserved and stored a season's overflowing abundance and captured the richness of summer in our kitchens. A little of that warmth can be passed on, neighbor to neighbor, as we sit down together, or as we bring a pot or a jar of something to someone in need. We think of the pantry as a measure of personal security — and it is — but it is also a measure of our capacity for generosity.

One of the reasons we so rarely sit down with others is that we are so terribly intimidated by the idea of "entertaining" or "cooking" in the fancy sense shown to us by countless TV shows and magazines. All you have to do is read the magazines in the supermarket check-out line to realize that "entertaining" is one heck of a project. You have to have little bits of smoked salmon in cream puff shells with lemon-thyme crème fraîche. You are supposed to have fancy dishes and multiple courses and serve meals that cost enough that you have to take out another mortgage on your house.

Now there is a real place for the occasional lavish feast. The idea that you might save up the best foods for a celebratory display has a long history. But so too does something other than "entertaining." Sitting down together at a meal with others to whom you are tied — just a plain, ordinary meal — is celebratory not because of what's in it, but because of who is at it. And the more we watch famous people show off their homes, cleaned by underpaid minions, and their elaborate buche de buttercreams, the harder it becomes for a lot of people to imagine eating a simple meal together from their pantries. And yet, the lentil soup, the loaf of bread, the baked potato, the jar of jam...these are the comforts that we need most, the things we most need to offer one another, and that we most need for the daily, but never wholly ordinary work of feeding ourselves, both body and soul.

We live in a world of need. In 2008, more than one hundred million more people went hungry due to rising food prices, while one out of every nine US families now requires food stamps. The world is full of hunger — hunger for food, security, hope, companionship, community and joy. And that rising tide of unfed hungers makes us see the world in terms of scarcity, of what we don't have and what we aren't sure of. The welcome table and the welcoming pantry run contrary to this. They remind us that summer comes round again, and that we have on hand sufficient to share, even if our sharing is plain.

The welcome table can be as simple as inviting an elderly neighbor to dinner, or making sure that you really sit down with your sister-in-law once in a while and drink tea and eat something. It can be welcoming an army of neighborhood children in for milk and cookies, or setting the church table for an army of people in need. It can be dropping that extra casserole or pie over at the family that just had a baby or lost their job. It can be taking the risk and asking someone to come eat with you — that step in a casual friendship that opens you up, perhaps frighteningly, for more.

The welcome pantry feeds the welcome table. It ensures that there's enough when the children come, when the guests arrive and there are two more. A little more rice in the pot, a little more broth in the soup, a jar of pickles to stretch it all, and there is enough for everyone. When the pantry is full you need not run to the store in order to give a little, share a little, or simply feed your family.

We've lost the habit of the welcome table and the welcome pantry. I once taught a Hebrew School class of fifth graders about Passover, and I asked how many of them, when the Haggadah commands them to cast open their doors and call out "Let all who are hungry come and eat," actually do so? What, I asked them, would they do if someone actually tried to come in and sit down? Overwhelmingly, these children in a comfortable suburb told me that they would never really open their doors, and that if a stranger tried to enter and eat, they would be afraid. There are, perhaps, some legitimate reasons for fear — but some even greater reasons for overcoming it. We are people who have learned to fear the idea of casting open our doors to others.

There are things we can only understand about one another by sitting together for a meal, or by cooking and preserving together. Seated together, we learn about each other's food culture. In fact, we create a food culture. Standing at the chopping block or the stove, we learn about the traditions that bind us, the history of how we have filled our pantries and secured our future. Until we eat together, there are intimacies we cannot share. Cooking and eating together are powerful ways of tying our lives together. Building community depends upon them. Because so many of us are too busy, or too afraid or intimidated or simply not in the habit, we lose community and intimacy in precisely the measure that we do not share food. Food is a starting point for most human connections.

Every faith that I know of has elaborate laws of hospitality and generosity. It is worth remembering that these faiths — and secular movements that share these ideals — grew up not in worlds of wealth and privilege but in times of vulnerability and uncertainty, when we were far poorer than we are now. These moral systems do not emphasize hospitality because they are concerned with minutiae, but because these are not minutiae. The welcome table is the basis of strong communities and a humane society. The welcome pantry makes the welcome table possible, and creates the food culture that we live within. Both together give us a hand on the reins of our future.

PART ONE

Independence Days

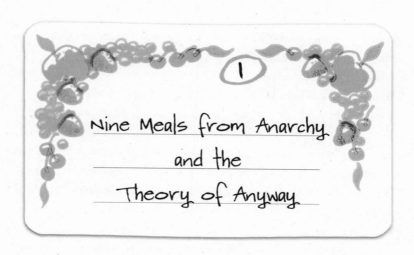

1

Nine Meals from Anarchy and the Theory of Anyway

I went to a restaurant that serves "Breakfast at any time."
So I ordered French toast during the Renaissance.

— Steven Wright —

Real Independence Days

THE RHUBARB IS UP. And it has me thinking about democracy, justice and what to have for dinner. If that seems like a strange line of thought, rather on the order of Steven Wright's surrealist breakfast order, that's because we rarely ask ourselves what our food has to do with power, with democracy, with justice. And yet, through most of human history "Who eats?" and "What's for dinner?" have, in fact, been the central questions about justice. If we've forgotten that, I think part of the reason is that we've been kidding ourselves in our conviction that dinner is only dinner.

I don't think there's any doubt that food security is one of the central issues of our time. Our food system is inextricably tied to our energy system. Over the last 75 years, a smaller and smaller percentage of Americans have been involved in agriculture while human power has been replaced by the heavy use of fossil fuels. Our long-term energy crisis is also a food crisis; nearly 20 percent of all fossil energies are used in the food system. Meanwhile, more than 30 percent of all global-warming emissions are tied in some way to our agricultural system. As biofuels have grown in popularity, whether a crop is food or fuel is now often uncertain: human beings and cars compete for grains and legumes. Global agribusiness represents a huge and powerful government lobby, which now holds an increasingly large portion of our political power. And of course, "Who eats?" remains one of the central questions of justice in our society, an increasingly urgent one to ask in a nation where one out of every nine families depends on food stamps. Worldwide, this isn't just an issue of social justice, but one of national security, as more and more nations are destabilized by hunger. So yes, food matters a lot.

Follow the lines of the major issues of our day — energy, economy, environment, globalization, disenfranchisement, a growing sense of powerlessness among the people — and most of the lines track back to basic questions of food and energy. If all these issues are so tightly intertwined, might we also find that personal action in one corner reverberates throughout the system?

I was lucky enough to know one of the people on the earth who knew the most about the ties between a good life, a decent world and good food — Carla Emery, author of *The Encyclopedia of Country Living: An Old-Fashioned Recipe Book*. Before her death in 2005, Carla was travelling the nation trying to help people get ready for the tough times she knew were coming. She'd done almost everything in her book (and it is a big book) at least once, and knew more about food than anyone I've ever met. Here's what she says about how she made sure her family was fed:

> All spring I try and plant something every day — from late February, when the early peas and spinach and garlic can go in, on up to mid-summer, when the main potato crop and the late beans and lettuce go in. Then I switch over and make it my rule to try and get something put away for the winter every single day. That lasts until the pumpkins and sunflowers and late squash and green tomatoes are in. Then comes the struggle to get the most out of the stored food — all winter long. It has to

be checked regularly, and you'll need to add to that day's menu anything that's on the verge of spoiling, wilting or otherwise soon becoming useless. Or preserve it a new way. If a squash gets a soft spot, I can gut it out and cook, mash, can or freeze the rest for a supper vegetable or pie, or add it to the bread dough.

You have to ration. You have all the good food you can eat right at arm's reach and no money to pay...until you run out...

People have to choose what they're going to struggle for. Life is always a struggle, whether or not you're struggling for anything worthwhile, so it might as well be for something worthwhile. Independence days are worth struggling for. They're good for me, good for the country and good for growing children.

— Emery, 493–494

Carla's words inspired this book. Right now, we stand at a crisis point. We are increasingly struggling financially, while also facing major energy and environmental crises that demand a fundamental shift in our way of life. An increasing number of climate scientists now agree we're very near an ecological tipping point, after which it may not be possible to address global warming. As I write this, more and more mainstream economists have stopped speaking of a recession and changed their language to "depression." Meanwhile, even the International Energy Agency, while refusing to actually use the words "peak oil" has admitted we're expecting year-over-year declines in oil supply that mean that current low prices can't last. So while we're all struggling just to keep dinner on the table, we also have to find ways to ameliorate climate change and address higher energy prices. These are daunting problems.

Are all the solutions to these daunting problems vast ones, best left in the hands of political leaders and scientists? We are often told this is the case, that we should accept the limited power of our vote and our occasional activism, accept the fact that our daily actions are less important than most lobbying efforts. We are told that what "we the people" do in our ordinary lives is comparatively unimportant and that our importance emerges only during election years. But this isn't true. What we buy, how we eat, how we live — these things indirectly shape agricultural policy, fund the corporations that undermine our political power and decide the future of our children and our planet.

Taken in isolation, none of our personal actions probably matter that much. Not our individual votes, and not our decisions to eat peas we put up over the summer instead of those frozen and shipped from far away. But collectively, a movement of ordinary people shifting their ordinary activities — moving their dollars away from corporations and towards home, not eating food grown with artificial nitrogen or shipped from far away, living more simply, using less energy — can cut off the economic lifeline of the corporations that both undermine our political power and try to force us to depend on them.

Carla's "Independence Days" were the ones in which her family ate food they grew themselves, or got from their neighbors and local farmers. They were the days they were able to rely on their own stores and preserves to feed their family. She was absolutely right that this kind of independence is worth struggling for. In fact, it isn't just worth struggling for, it is one of the most powerful tools we have to secure our future.

More and more of us are aware of how important food is. Perhaps you've already taken steps to eat locally and more sustainably. Perhaps you belong to a Community Supported Agriculture (CSA) farm or shop at a farmer's market, or grow food in your yard or in containers. Perhaps you are among the millions of new "locavores" who are working hard to reconnect to their food system by both buying locally and growing their own.

Each of those things does a host of good. If we are buying local, small-scale and organic, we reduce the fossil fuels involved in the food system. We are subsidizing a food system that can work for us even if the just-in-time industrial delivery system that brings food into the supermarkets fails us in some way. If you grow your own wisely and carefully, you can sequester carbon in soils, making your home part of the solution, not part of the problem. Eating direct from the soil means eating more vegetables, and usually much better.

But most of us who live in cold climates, or in regions where there is a hot, dry season where not much grows also find ourselves frustrated by the limitations of our local food systems. We've gotten accustomed to the delicious, fresh and ethical food that pours out of our CSA baskets, overflows at the farmer's market and bursts from our gardens. But now, we find ourselves back at the supermarket, picking up limp spinach that has been sprayed with who-knows-what. What a loss.

It isn't just a loss of flavor, texture, connectedness with our local farms and nutritional value — it is a loss of power. The dollars you spend at the supermarket, or even at Whole Foods, generally go back to large-scale industrial corporations. Kraft Foods is part of the Altria corporation, which among other things, owns the cigarette company Phillip Morris. Even many organic companies are now subsidiaries of large industrial food producers. These corporations influence political policy — not just agricultural policy, but environmental and land use policies, carbon targets and economic policies. Moreover, dollars that were enriching our neighbors and farmers directly are now enriching corporations like Altria, Monsanto and ConAgra. The dollars that were spent in our communities and brought local prosperity now go to multinationals.

Moreover, each dollar we spend in a food system that requires ten calories of oil to produce a single calorie of food leaves us vulnerable. As long as our food is inextricably tied to oil, our food prices depend on volatile energy prices, leaving families hungry when oil and natural gas prices jump. At its most extreme, this model puts us at risk of hunger. If energy systems fail us, and we're dependent on a just-in-time delivery system that keeps only three days worth of food on the shelves, and leaves us, as one British writer put it, "nine meals from anarchy" — only three days, that is, from the civic disruption that follows watching our children go hungry — then we are helpless. But with stores of food in our pantries, and investments in local agricultural systems that can feed our communities, we need not be tied to foreign oil markets. We need not be so terribly, terribly vulnerable.

This book, then, is about two linked and equally important projects. The first is taking the next step in local eating — that is, finding ways to keep local food through the cold or dry season, so that we can enjoy the pleasures and benefits of local eating all year round. The tools we need to do this are the tools of food preservation. Sometimes they are as simple as finding a cold spot to store our apples; or they may be slightly more complex, involving learning the work of canning or dehydrating. Just as eating seasonally comes with a host of new recipes and tricks, so does eating home or locally preserved food.

The second, related project is protecting and insulating ourselves from the limitations of our fossil-fueled, ecologically damaging and uncertain food system. Besides avoiding a crisis by building local food systems, we can also recognize that right now, the industrial food system is in crisis, and that food supply disruptions of all types are increasingly likely. Thus, all of us need to build up a pantry of foods, ideally foods acquired directly from farmers or from sustainable sources, but that also provide a reserve against disasters small and large, whether a hurricane that prevents food from being trucked in, a job loss that means we have little money for food, or a disruption in energy supplies that empties supermarket shelves.

The former is nominally "food preservation," while the latter is "food storage," but of course, the two are intertwined and it is hard to sort out which one we are actually talking about at any given moment. Those jars of green beans and jam are preserved, of course, but they are also hedges against hunger if your local food system is disrupted. You might associate food storage with survivalists with crates of Meals, Ready-to-Eat (MREs) — but for most of human history, stored food was simply everyday food, packed carefully away when there was an abundance, and eaten in times when food was scarce.

Whether in the cycle of seasons, where summer's bounty is preserved for winter's scarcity, or in the cycle of human events, where the surplus from the years of good harvest and plenty are carefully reserved for the inevitable hard times to come, this is how human beings lived for most of human history. Living and eating cyclically meant recognizing that some measure of our abundance must be put forward for days to come. But we have lost the habit. Most of us no longer save money or put food by in summertime. We've come to believe — and corporations and even the government have gone a long way to convince us — that our due is now an endless season of bounty, abundant times that never stop.

So why should *we* preserve foods and build reserves? Because no one else is. Your supermarket, as mentioned before, has only three days worth of food on the shelves, and less in many urban areas. At one time, the US established grain stockpiles and held large reserves of food. Those days are gone — like most nations that have eaten down their stockpiles, the US has very little food available for a crisis.

But more importantly, right now we are seeing that the idea of endless bounty, in which no one need save or think ahead for a dry time to come, is wrong. We are entering a time of great economic trouble. The rapid rise and sudden crash of energy prices has undermined the food system in fundamental ways. One major industrial producer, Pilgrim Foods, producer of much of the US's chicken, is already bankrupt. Food prices remain high even as wages fall because farmers had to buy their feed, seed and fertilizer during boom times.

Carla was right — not only are Independence Days worth striving for because they are good for us, our nation and our families in all the ways I've just described, but also because we may need the food we grow or buy locally and put in our pantry simply to keep fed. That's an increasingly difficult project for many of us.

Every spring, I sit down and inventory our food stores, particularly the things I put up the previous year. At the back of my mind is this question: "If we had to live on what we grow and put up and have stored in case of a bad year, how would we do?" And the answer is that it would be tough — but that every year we do a little more.

Now, even after years of practice I still don't have feeding ourselves down to a perfect science. But even if we never achieve perfection, there's a great deal of satisfaction in putting by and getting better at it. Because even right now, every bite of food we don't purchase is a gift. It represents money we don't have to spend on groceries and can devote to other things. Every bite closer we get to feeding ourselves means we eat better, tastier food, food we know is safe and hasn't been contaminated in the increasingly dangerous industrial food system.

Americans tend to believe that hunger could never come their way. They forget that just two generations ago, during the last depression, as many as 25 percent of urban schoolchildren were malnourished and people stood in bread lines. They forget that the experience of privilege we've known in the wealthy nations is a historical anomaly. That pretty much all human beings going back from our grandparents knew periods of food insecurity and that the majority of people in the world right now know hunger at some point in their lives. Should we bet the farm on the notion that this magical immunity to the plague of hunger will go on forever? I certainly hope it will, but we already have millions of hungry people in America, millions who can't afford food for their kids, but who might be able to grow some and preserve a little of summer's bounty.

All the little pieces in the food puzzle suggest an overall structural problem. It isn't just the climate impact, or just the rising number of hungry kids, or just the fact that our industrial supply is increasingly contaminated. In fact, as journalist Paul Roberts writes in his superb book *The End of Food*, the problems are interrelated:

> On nearly every level, we are reaching the end of what may one day be called the "golden age" of food, a brief, near-miraculous period during which the things we ate seemed to grow only more plentiful, more secure, more nutritious, and simply *better* with every passing year. Thus, even as we struggle to understand why the safety of our food is becoming so much harder to assure, it's clear that safety is only one of a cluster of concerns and that we need to asking a much broader set of question: What is happening to our food? How could our immensely successful food system have become so overextended? How close are we to the point of breakdown?

I spent much of 2007 and 2008 researching and writing a book called *A Nation of Farmers* that added to a growing consensus of journalists, agricultural scientists and public intellectuals who recognize that our food system is extremely vulnerable, that all the assorted problems we are seeing in the system are part of one large crisis.

On the first day of 2009, Michael Chertoff, director of the US Department of Homeland Security (DHS) issued this call to national preparedness, acknowledging that we are not a secure food nation:

> All too often, people take this assistance [Of FEMA and the American Red Cross] for granted. They assume that first responders will routinely ride to the rescue, arriving in time to meet human needs. Unfortunately such a benign outcome cannot be guaranteed. For one thing, disasters are unpredictable. Responders can't always reach the beleaguered in time. A host of obstacles can delay their arrival. News accounts of coordination lapses between fire and police departments in the aftermath of the terrorist attack in Mumbai, India, highlight what can go wrong in the aftermath of a disaster.
>
> Thus, preparedness should not be left to organizations alone. Individuals and families must engage in it as well. They must take preparedness measures of their own ahead of time, measures that can enable them to respond safely and faster when an emergency occurs.
>
> That is why DHS, through its Ready Campaign, is now launching a nationwide effort, "Resolve to be Ready," to persuade individuals and families, as well as businesses and communities, to take decisive steps to prepare for emergencies in the coming year.
>
> — myrtlebeachonline.com/opinion/story/727428.html

Even the head of an agency designed to provide mitigation admits that we simply cannot rely on others. We must begin to rely primarily on ourselves and our own preparations.

But this book is not merely about the disasters we're facing — it is about how to heal our food system. Most of all, it is about how preserving and storing food allow us to eat locally and sustainably all year round, and how that ability can shift our whole food culture.

Preservation—Wherever You Live

Carla Emery lived on a farm most of her life, and while I grew up in the city, I now live on a small farm in upstate New York. It would be easy to think that this book is only for farmers. But in fact, preserving and storing food can and should be part of everyday life in all sorts of environments, whether city, country or suburb. I'll talk more about how that works in each kind of home, but generally speaking, the more self-sufficient we can be, the more secure we are. Self-sufficiency is not only for country dwellers.

Being involved with your food means being really seriously involved with your food. It means changing the way we've come to think about the world back to the way we once did—revisiting a life of seasonality, with a time to plant, a time to sow, a time to harvest and a time to rest. It isn't just a song, or a Bible verse, it becomes a way of life. That link to nature may be the thing we've been missing in our lives. There's growing evidence that people who work in the dirt, live with the seasons and connect to nature are happier and healthier than those who live in more artificial circumstances.

So in spring my job is to figure out how many cucumbers I need to plant next year, so that this time, the pickles (devoured by my three pickle-fiend sons) make it all the way until July, when I can make more. As nature's abundance starts to pour out upon us, we start thinking back to the last year—what did we have enough of? What did we want to do differently? And we think forward into the future, around through the season (remember, after the strawberries come the blueberries, the cherries and the raspberries...) and into the winter when the berries are gone again. We live in the fusion of past, present and future. But of course, that is how human beings have lived for most of their history.

This is how life was in city and country, and how it can be in the suburbs. Cities are at the center of food culture. It is in cities that people demand the best, the freshest, the most wonderful foods. And it is city people who can ensure, by preserving food, by sharing knowledge, that the culture of food evolves in the direction of the welcome table and pantry. A culture of food preservation cannot exist without urban participants — food trends arise not in rural areas but in San Francisco, New York and Miami.

Preserving food is everyday work. It begins with the first rhubarb that will be dried or canned or made into sauce (and a reminder that I still have a bit left of last year's to eat). Next come the strawberries and asparagus, and then the cycle begins in earnest. It really doesn't take much time, once you get into a routine, and is well worth it. There are always some busy days in the summer, but it isn't too hard to put berries in the dehydrator after work or mix up pickle brine while making dinner.

Even if you don't grow your own, preserving what is seasonal and fresh can provide you with a great deal of economic and food security. If you go to the farmer's market at the end of the day, you may be able to get bushels of produce for almost nothing. Then comes the work of dehydration, or canning, or pickling. The work is worth it, both because it enables you to eat a local diet and frees you from dangers in the food supply, but also because it means you don't depend on corporations to provision you.

That last point may be the most important. Food preservation and food production are keys to democracy. We accept that a politician who is dependent on the money special interests provide cannot be wholly independent in their thought. We know that no matter how much personal integrity they may have, their intentions are fundamentally corrupted by being beholden to others.

The same is equally true of individuals. We cannot simultaneously call for an end to multinational monoliths and also pay them to feed us. As long as we are dependent on corporations, any attempt at reform or culture change will fail, because we ourselves are corrupted by that dependence. We cannot deplore McDonalds and then complain because poor people cannot buy their food from the equally troubling industrial organic producers who sell through Whole Foods. We need to recognize that our food dependence affects not just what we eat, but the fundamentals of our democracy and our political power.

We should not owe our lives to entities we deplore. The only possible escape from this bind is to declare food independence — to meet as many of our basic needs as possible ourselves, and through small, sustainable farms with which we have real and direct relationships. And that means not just growing food, but ensuring a stable food supply, reasonable reserves and a dinner born of ties to things we value. Worth struggling for indeed!

The Theory of Anyway, Peach Jam and Why We Do Too Have Time for This

The Theory of Anyway is not my idea. It is the creation of a woman I've known for many years on various Internet venues but, for a host of reasons, I've never met in person. She is disabled, in her sixties and lives with her disabled husband in a tiny house in rural Pennsylvania. At home, she grows much of her own food and writes and inspires tens of thousands of people. She never gets paid a penny for her long hours of work guiding people through the mysteries of growing food in containers and reducing their energy impact. If anyone in the world has an excuse to be caught up in dealing with her own difficulties it is Pat, who is both very poor and in pain much of the time. And yet, she never takes the easy way out, she never ceases to try to do what is right rather than what is easy. I think it is fair to say that she finds in a life lived well a comfort and ease she could never find in a life lived without consideration.

I wrote about the Theory of Anyway in my first book, *Depletion and Abundance: Life on the New Home Front*, and I will quote what I wrote here, because I think it applies very much to the whole project of preserving and storing food — we are seeking here, a way of eating well, of doing right three times a day, when we sit down to eat. It seems, in some ways, a daunting project. How do we know that this is the right way to spend some of our precious time and energy? And is the victory we might achieve in doing so too small, compared to the magnitude of the problems that beset us?

To me, the Theory of Anyway shifts the structure of the discussion. Instead of asking "Do we have time to make the peach jam?" It asks the question as it should be asked: "Do we have time to live rightly?" And the funny thing is that when asked that way, it is hard to say no, isn't it?

My friend Pat Meadows, a very smart woman, has a wonderful idea she calls "The Theory of Anyway." She argues that 95 percent of what is needed to resolve the coming crisis is what we should do anyway, and when in doubt about how to change, we should change our lives to reflect what we should be doing "anyway." Living more simply, more frugally, leaving reserves for others, reconnecting with our food and our community — these are things we should be doing because they are the right thing to do on many levels. That they also have the potential to save our lives is merely a side benefit (a big one, though).

This is, I think, a deeply powerful way of thinking because it is a deeply moral way of thinking. We like to think of ourselves as moral people, but we tend to think of moral questions as the obvious ones: Should I steal or pay? Should I fight or talk? But the most essential moral questions are the ones we rarely ask of the things we do every day: Should I eat this? Where should I live? What should I wear? How should I keep warm/cool? We think of these questions as foregone conclusions — I should keep warm a particular way because that's the kind of furnace I have, or I should eat this because that's what's in the grocery store. Pat's Theory of Anyway turns this around, and points out that the way we live must pass ethical muster first. We must always ask the question, Is this choice contributing to the repair of the world, or its destruction?

So if you told me tomorrow that Peak Energy had been resolved, I'd still keep gardening, hanging my laundry and trying to find a way to make do with less. Because even if we found enough oil to power our society for a thousand years, there would still be Climate Change, and it would be wrong of me to choose my own convenience over the security of my children and other people's children.

And if you told me tomorrow that we'd fixed Climate Change, I would still keep gardening and living frugally. Because our agriculture is premised on depleted soil and aquifers, and we're facing a future in which many people don't have enough food and water if we keep eating this way, and to allow that to happen would be a betrayal of what I believe is right.

And if you told me that we'd fixed that problem too, that we were no longer depleting our aquifers and expanding the dead zone in the Gulf of Mexico, I'd still keep gardening and telling others to do the same, because our economy and our reliance on food from other nations impoverishes and starves billions of poor people and creates massive economic inequities that do tremendous harm.

And if you told me that globalization was over, and that we were going to create a just economic system, and we'd fixed all the other problems, and that I didn't have to worry anymore, would I then stop gardening?

No. Nurturing and preserving my small slice of the planet would still be the right thing to do. Doing things with no more waste than is absolutely necessary would still be the right thing to do. The creation of a fertile, sustainable, lasting place of beauty would still be my right work in the world. I would still be a Jew, obligated by my faith, to "the repair of the world." I would still be obligated to live in a way that prevented wildlife from being run to extinction and poisons from contaminating the earth. I would still be obligated to reduce my needs so they represent a fair share of what the earth has to offer. I would still be obligated to treat poor people as my brothers and sisters, and you do not live comfortably when your siblings suffer. I am obligated to live rightly, in part because of what living rightly gives me — integrity, honor, joy, a better relationship with my deity of choice, peace.

There are people who are prepared to step forward and give up their cars, start growing their own food, stop consuming so much and stop burning fossil fuels — just as soon as Peak Oil or Climate Change or government rationing or some external force makes them. But that, I believe, is the wrong way to think. We can't wait for others to tell us or the disaster to befall us. We have to do now, do today, do with all our hearts, the things we should have been doing "anyway" all along.

For me, storing and preserving food, so that I eat all year round the way I eat in summer — locally, sustainably, deliciously, healthfully, pleasurably, peacefully — is one of the most basic things we should be doing "anyway." But of course, that doesn't magically make more hours in a day, or prevent me from feeling that I'm tired, and couldn't it just be someone else's responsibility to do right today.

There are people who will find it impossible to do many of the things in this book. It would be easy to say that because of that fact, preserving and storing food "isn't realistic" for most people. A single mother in a poor neighborhood, for example, might find it very hard to find the money to build up even a small reserve of food, much less take an evening to put up fresh food from a farmer's market miles from her neighborhood.

All of that is, of course, perfectly true. At the same time, the single mother has less time to shop than most people, and is probably more vulnerable to economic tough times than a family with more earners. She desperately needs a reserve of food in her pantry, so that she can spend the little free time she has with her kids, rather than running errands, and so that she can keep her kids fed in hard times. Her small food budget and lack of time mean that the food she does buy is often of poor quality. She's more vulnerable to food contamination in the industrial system, she's less likely to get the nutritional benefits of food that hasn't been held in shipping for weeks. She can least afford to pay extra for someone to cut up the peaches and make them into jam. If she can find time and energy to do it herself, perhaps with her kids at her side, she can insulate them from poor quality food, and get much better tasting food for much less money.

Her neighborhood is the one most likely to be left to fend for itself when hard times hit. Perhaps it isn't "realistic" for her — perhaps she won't be able to make the jam. But the Theory of Anyway requires that we ask why this woman should be having so much trouble getting decent food for her kids. It isn't just about asking, "Can she make jam?" but also, "Why is it that we should have a system that makes it so incredibly hard for ordinary working people to meet basic needs?" and "How can those of us who have a little more money and a little more time connect with those who do not, but most need the benefits of local food?"

My feeling is that discussions of realism rarely take into account the fact that we spend an average of four hours a day watching television and, according to Juliet Schor's *The Overworked American*, more than an hour and a half a day shopping. They rarely take into account the fact that fast food costs us billions a year in health and nutritional costs we can ill afford — more if you count the health costs of one in every three Americans eating in a fast food restaurant every single day. It becomes a question of whether we can afford *not* to do what we should "anyway."

Sleeping Beauty and Why You Should Prepare for Hard Times (Even If It Seems Much Nicer Not To)

When I wrote my first book, I had to overcome skepticism that energy, food and financial stability were really issues. As I write this, the global economy is falling apart, we've just thrown 700 billion dollars at it without even a bump in the markets, most of the people living in my neck of the woods are scared to death that they won't be able to afford to heat their homes, and food prices have become increasingly unstable. We've seen oil rise to nearly $150 a barrel and fall back to $38 — the definition of volatility. Now I think we have to worry less that people won't understand than that dealing with all of this will seem so overwhelming and terrifying that it will be easier to just say, "There's nothing we can do." But we need people to screw up their courage and look hard at difficult stuff, because the problems caused by our financial crisis, climate change and peak oil are not something any of us can afford to ignore.

My guess is that most people reading this have some investment in the future — maybe in their own personal future, maybe in the future of their children or grandchildren, or the children of someone they know and care about, maybe in their dedication to the good of humanity. The truth is that you are needed, right now, to safeguard your own future, and the future of our posterity. That's not campaign rhetoric or storytelling, that's simple truth. If you don't participate in creating a decent future, we won't have one. We need you, and you need you to take as hard-edged a look as you can.

This is when I remind people of the story of Sleeping Beauty. You see, a King and Queen wanted something desperately, a blessing that filled their every prayer. Finally, bounty was showered down upon them, a wonderful daughter, one they named Beauty. And in their delight and joy, they forgot something important. They forgot that with gifts come responsibilities. When they were planning a vast celebration of their good fortune, they forgot the unpleasant job of inviting the one fairy no one liked very much to the christening.

This fairy, who is the embodiment of all that's been left undone, she noticed that they'd left that one small thing undone. And she came to the christening, after almost all the invited fairies had given their wonderful gifts, and took from the King and Queen what mattered most to them — their posterity. At just the moment that Beauty was coming into her full potential, at just the moment her parents were most proud, she would prick her finger on a spinning wheel, and die.

Well her parents began to keen their grief, and all the guests did too. It was so terribly unfair, they had never intended this consequence, it was all just a mistake, they would never have done it if they'd realized the price was so high. The King, in denial, began to order all the spinning wheels in the kingdom burned, believing that he could control any situation — even one so obviously out of his control.

But over the cries of grief, up spoke one voice. It was the very last fairy godmother, the one who had not yet given her gift. She said, "I cannot break the curse, but I can soften it a little. I can make it so that you don't lose everything. Instead of dying, Beauty will fall asleep for a hundred years."

I think this story is remarkably analogous to our present situation. We received this enormous bounty of fossil fuels and the wealth that came with it, and while we did not mean or intend it, while we did not know what the consequences were, we still face consequences for what we have left undone. We neglected to put resources aside to prepare for the day when those resources ran out. We neglected to consider the impact of our energy usage. We can't make the curse go away — those consequences are peak oil, climate change and the ending of the economic growth cycle brought on by endless supplies of energy.

But despite these curses, it is also true that each of us is a little like that last Fairy Godmother. We can soften the curse a little, we can make it possible, if we have strength and courage, that we who are now adults can take on the burden of changing our society and our lives, and give our children and grandchildren, if not a perfect happy ending, a great deal more hope.

How often, in this world, do you get to be the Fairy Godmother? How often do you get to do so much, for something most of us value so deeply?

Depression Cuisine

Ok, I'm going to talk bad financial news. Now for all I know, by the time you read this, perhaps bought used or borrowed from your sister five years after publication, the biggest problem we face may not be the economy. But for now it is, and I think it is important to begin with the assumption that our current financial crisis may be lasting and seriously undermine everyday people's food security. Because then we can begin talking about the ways people adapted their cuisine to tough times in the past.

A lot of folks keep saying we aren't in a depression, that all will be well soon. My own take is that as I write this, at the end of 2008, the problem is that we are in the early stages of a depression, and the reassuring comments we keep getting — that this isn't as bad as it was then, that during the Depression unemployment was 25 percent and now it is only nearing 9 percent — are missing the fact that this is the start of something serious.

The statistics that the commentators are citing are figures from deep in the middle of the Depression. Observing that the dire situation of 1933 — when 25 percent unemployment was a reality — isn't upon us isn't very helpful, because at the comparable stage of the Great Depression, those things weren't upon us either.

For example, when the stock market crashed in October of 1929, a news report observed that "the vast majority of Americans remain unaffected." Two months after the stock market crash, Secretary of the Treasury Andrew Mellon said, "I see nothing in the present situation that is either menacing or warrants pessimism."

Unemployment rose gradually. In 1930, a year after the stock market crash, it was at 8.7 percent, just a little lower than ours is as I write this. It took nearly two years to double to 16 percent. Meanwhile, those who were lucky enough to keep their jobs found themselves at first in a decent position, as Don Lescohier reports in John R. Commons's *History of Labor in the United States*: "The first impact of the Depression of the 'thirties did not affect the wages structure. It cut the earning of millions through unemployment and part-time work before it affected wage rates. It was not until the last quarter of 1930 that appreciable downward changes in manufacturing wages occurred."

Yet again, the first ripples in the financial centers didn't actually translate right away. But by 1932, wages in Ohio had fallen by nearly 60 percent. It is worth remembering that unemployment isn't the only consequence of economic crisis.

In that sense, the current system may be worse than the Depression — while wages haven't declined, buying power has declined much more precipitously than it did in a parallel period during the Depression. And we are certainly further removed from our food system than we were then. It should worry us that even during periods of record harvest in the Depression years, economic instability rose so fast that farmers and urban dwellers were both radically impoverished. This is how you can have hunger in a nation of plenty. Consider this testimony given by Oscar Ameringer before Congress in 1932.

During the last three months I have visited…some 20 states.…
In the state of Washington I was told that the forest fires raging
in that region all summer and fall were caused by unemployed
timber workers and bankrupt farmers in an endeavor to earn

a few honest dollars as firefighters. The last thing I saw on the night I left Seattle were numbers of women searching for scraps of food in the refuse piles of the principal markets of that city. A number of Montana citizens told me of thousands of bushels of wheat left in the fields uncut on account of its low price that hardly paid for the harvesting. In Oregon I saw thousands of bushels of apples rotting in the orchards because of the cost of transporting them to market.... At the same time there are millions of children who, on account of the poverty of their parents, will not eat one apple this winter.

While I was in Oregon, the Portland Oregonian bemoaned the fact that thousands of ewes were killed by sheep raisers because they did not bring enough in the market to pay the freight on them. And while Oregon sheep raisers fed mutton to the buzzards, I saw men picking for meat scraps in the garbage cans of New York and Chicago. I talked to one man in a restaurant in Chicago. He told me of his experience in raising sheep. He said he had killed 3,000 sheep this fall and thrown them down the canyon, because it cost $1.10 to ship a sheep to market and then he would get less than a dollar for it. He said he could not afford to feed the sheep and he would not let them starve, so he just cut their throats and threw them in the canyon.

The roads of the West and Southwest teem with hungry hitchhikers. The camp fires of the homeless are seen along every railroad track. I saw men, women and children walking over the hard roads. Most of them were tenant farmers who had lost their land and been foreclosed. Between Clarksville and Russellville, Ark., I picked up a family. The woman was hugging a dead chicken under her ragged coat. When I asked her where she had procured the fowl, first she told me she had found it dead in the road, and then added in grim humor, "They promised me a chicken in every pot, and now I got mine."

As a result of this appalling overproduction on one side and the staggering underconsumption on the other side, 70 percent of the farmers of Oklahoma were unable to pay the interest on their mortgages. Last week one of the largest and oldest mortgage companies in that state went into the hands of the receiver. In that and other states we have now the interesting spectacle of farmers losing their farms by foreclosure and mortgage companies losing their recouped holdings by tax sales that could never meet the value of the land.

The farmers are being pauperized by the poverty of the industrial population and the industrial population is being pauperized by the poverty of the farmers. Neither has the money to buy the product of the other."
— David Shannon, *The Great Depression*, 26–28

This, I think, is particularly haunting in the face of our present disconnect between farm and table. The only way for us to prevent the nightmare scenario here taking place in our lives is to rebuild our food supplies — to have stores in people's houses, the knowledge of how to grow and preserve food in our lives, and to help people buy direct from farmers when times are good, and preserve and store something to tide them through tough times. This is why I have written this book.

Depression Recipes

This recipe appears anonymously in an online collection of Depression-Era recipes. Do not can — put in the fridge and eat within two weeks.

Sunshine Strawberries and Cherry Preserves

Use equal weight of sugar and fruit. Put fruit in the preserving kettle in layers, sprinkling sugar over layers. The fruit and the sugar should no be more than 4 inches deep. Place the kettle on the stove and heat slowly to the boiling point. When it begins to boil, skim carefully. Boil 10 minutes, counting from the time the fruit begins to bubble. Pour the cooked fruit into platters, having it about 2 or 3 inches deep. Place the platters in a sunny window in an unused room for 3 to 4 days. or put fruit in a shallow pan, cover with a sheet of glass and set out of doors in a sunny place.

The fruit will grow plump and the syrup will thicken almost to a jelly. Put the preserves, cold, into jars or glasses. Note: if cherries are used, and not seeded, add 1 or 2 tablespoons water to each layer of sugar.

Scalloped Corn

Recipes for scalloped corn are common in Depression-era cookbooks. I've modified this one a little bit, to include things like oven temperatures and baking times—I guess you were just supposed to know.

- 3 eggs
- 2 cups milk
- 1 teaspoon sugar
- 1 can corn or 12 oz. fresh corn cut off the cob

- 2 tablespoons butter
- ½ cup cracker or bread crumbs
- 1 teaspoon salt

Separate eggs, and beat yolks and whites separately. Put 1 teaspoon of butter in baking dish and 1 tablespoon melted butter into crumbs. Add egg yolks, milk, salt and sugar to corn, fold in whites of eggs. Bake in casserole dish for 50 minutes at 350°. Serves four as a side dish or a generous two as a main course.

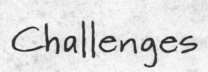

Challenges

In the spring of 2008 I decided that I wanted to try and get better about preserving and storing food. I took as my mantra Carla Emery's wonderful passage about Independence Days quoted in Chapter 1, the idea that you should do something every single day.

Her words about choosing what we should struggle for rang out to me like the Declaration of Independence rings out. Or perhaps the Constitution of the United Food Sovereign People of the World. We so desperately need to declare our independence from the globalizing, totalitarian, toxic agriculture that is destroying our future, our power and our democracy.

And so, when in the course of human events it becomes necessary for people to divorce themselves from a system that has become destructive, thus:

> We the people, in order to form a more perfect union of human and nature, establish justice and ensure food sovereignty, provide for the common nutrition, promote the general welfare and ensure the blessings of liberty for ourselves and our posterity, do ordain and establish this constitution for the United Food Sovereign People of the World.

Well...something like that.

I challenged myself to not allow myself to be intimidated by the whole idea, but to do one little bit every day or week. I decided this was worth struggling for, and I opened my challenge to other people, asking all of those who were reading my blog to do one thing every day to create Food Independence. In each day or week, we might try to:

1. **Plant something.** You should plant all week and all year, as long as you can. That beet you harvested left a space — maybe for the next one to get bigger, but maybe for a bit of arugula or a fall crop of peas, or a cover crop to enrich the soil. Independence is the bounty of a single seed that creates an abundance of zucchini, and enough seeds to plant your own garden and your neighbor's. Whether you grow in a pot or a thousand acres, plant something.

2. **Harvest something.** From the very first nettles and dandelions to the last leeks and parsnips dragged out of the frozen ground, harvest something from the garden or the wild every day you can. I can't think of a better way to be aware of the bounty around you than to realize that there's something — even if it is dandelions for tea or wild garlic for a salad — to be had every single day. Independence is appreciating and using the bounty that we have.

3. **Preserve something.** Sometimes this will be a big project, but it doesn't have to be. It doesn't take long to slice a couple of tomatoes and set them on a screen in the sun or hang up a bunch of sage for winter. And it adds up fast. The time you spend now is time you don't have to spend hauling to the store and cooking later. Independence is eating our own, and cutting the ties we have to agribusiness.

4. **Minimize waste.** Can you cut down on packaging by ordering in bulk? Make sure that the kids aren't wasting food? Do more with your leftovers? Compost? Feed your scraps to some critter, whether chickens or worms? Glean the fallen apples in your neighbor's yard? Make sure the leftovers from your work lunches get to the food pantry? Cut back on your junk mail?

5. **Want not.** Hit a yard sale and pick up an extra blanket. Purchase some extra legumes and oatmeal. Sort out and inventory your pantry. Make a list of tools you need. Find a way to give what you don't need to someone who does. Fix your bike. Fill that old soda bottle with water with a couple of drops of bleach in it. Plan for next year's edible landscaping. Make back-road directions to your place and send it to family in case they ever need to come to you in an emergency — or make them for yourself for where

you might have to go. Clean, mend, declutter, learn a new skill. Independence is being ready for whatever comes.

6. **Cook something new.** Try a new recipe, or an old one with a new ingredient. Sometimes it is hard to know what to do with all that stuff you are growing or making. So experiment now. Can you make a whole meal in your solar oven? How are stir-fried pea shoots? Stuffed squash blossoms? Wild morels in pasta? Independence is being able to eat and enjoy what is given to us.

7. **Manage your reserves.** Check those apples. Take out the ones starting to go bad and make sauce with them. Label those cans. Clean out the freezer. Ration the pickles, so you'll have enough to last to next season. Use up those lentils before you take the next ones out of the bag. Find some use for that can of whatever it is that's been in the pantry forever. Sort out what you can donate, and give it to the food pantry (in Canada these are called food banks). Make sure the squash are holding out. Independence means not wasting the bounty we have.

8. **Work on local food systems.** This could be as simple as buying something you don't grow or make from a local grower. It could be as complex as starting a co-op or a farmer's market, creating a CSA or a bulk store. You might give seeds or plants or divisions to a neighbor, or solicit donations for your food pantry. Maybe you'll start a guerilla garden or help a homeschool co-op incubate some chicks. Maybe you'll invite people over to your garden, or your neighbors in for a homegrown meal, or sing the praises of your local CSA. Maybe you can get your town to plant fruit- or nut-producing street trees or get a manual water pump or a garden put in at your local school. Whatever it is, our Independence Days come when our neighbors and the people we love are food secure too.

I'm not suggesting you do all these things on any day (heck, that's impossible), but try to do one of them every day — or every week, or every weekend, if that's what your schedule allows. It takes practice to live and grow and eat this way. So let's do it now while we've got the time and energy and each other for support.

2

Local Eating, Pantry Eating

When you cook it should be an act of love.
To put a frozen bag in the microwave for your child is an act of hate.

— Raymond Blanc —

THERE IS, I THINK, a typical order of things for people who discover local eating. They start with a CSA share, the farmer's market or maybe a home garden. The first venture is to find or grow local, familiar produce during the growing season to use in day-to-day meals, like the fresh, ripe-to-bursting tomatoes and the sweet corn. Then the CSA or the beautiful displays at the market introduce them to new produce, vegetables they haven't tried, and all of a sudden they are eating fava beans and chard in season. They begin to look for recipes for these new foods.

After that, comes the question of how to get local and ethically raised meat, dairy and eggs. There might be eggs in the CSA basket or a local cheesemaker at the market, and from the vegetables comes the question of what else they might be able to get locally. It is a delightful exploration, the sudden realization that one's cookies can be made with local honey and the Thanksgiving turkey might come from over the hill.

And if people do these things, they begin not just a shift in where their food comes from, but in how they eat. Instead of thinking,

29

"Wednesday is spaghetti night" they are looking into their CSA baskets and thinking, "What can I make with peas?" This also means a shift from a kind of cooking that assumes you can always get everything you want to one that is genuinely seasonal.

Often people are enticed by the food and serious about it — and sorry when the season ends. And thus, the question begins to arise in peoples' minds: what do we do when the CSA season ends? Sometimes the CSA itself raises these questions, when it sends, for example, large quantities of garlic from some exuberant producer and eaters are forced to ask, "Why would they send me six months worth of garlic? And what do I do with it?"

Many people become aware that even animal products have seasons. Milk is flush when grass is lush and eggs naturally proliferate and are cheap in spring and pricey in winter. Even meat has a season. Autumn, when it is time to use precious reserves of hay, is a good time for butchering and the time when hunting is permissible.

For many, the next step is to start looking for grains and beans, particularly for the budget conscious, who can't afford large quantities of local meats, and for vegetarians. This is easy in some grain-producing areas and harder for many of us that aren't close to them. Finding producers of staple foods can be as easy as buying a 50-pound sack of potatoes in the fall, or as difficult as mail-ordering from far away. And as part of this shift in priorities comes the awareness that it is less expensive, more efficient and more environmentally sound to get all one's bread flour or cornmeal or rice in one fell swoop, directly from a farmer, than to buy small packages repeatedly.

In short, Food Preservation and Food Storage are logical steps in locavore life. Many new local eaters haven't made them yet, and some people haven't yet realized that they *are* steps in a process. But the truth is that if we want to eat sustainably, and build the kinds of food systems that we're going to need in the future, the first step is eating locally while in season. But the season ends, and we're either back to eating mealy, oil-drenched supermarket tomatoes, or we've begun to think about how to keep the links going all year around.

Food Preservation and Food Storage are two slightly different things. Food Preservation is home- or community-level preservation of locally produced foods. It includes freezing, canning, pickling, lactofermenting, dehydration, root cellaring, preservation in salt, wine and sugar, and smoking. The idea is to preserve at home or at local food processing facilities the foods you will need during the season in which they are not available.

Food Storage involves the bulk purchase of staples (and also sometimes the purchase in smaller quantities of an additional reserve), ideally from local farmers. When we can't buy directly from local farmers, we should seek out ways to get our food from farmers outside our region, in ways that mean that most of our dollars go to them rather than middlemen. Many of us will never be able to fill our pantry locally, so purchasing directly from farmers or through co-ops that pay them well puts our dollars into positive food systems. To minimize energy costs, it is easiest to buy larger quantities — a bushel, 50 pounds, 25 pounds at a time. Right now we use an increasingly costly, environmentally destructive and unsustainable just-in-time delivery system to get food to our store shelves, and then private cars to get it home as we need it. This can't last. Our homes have to take the place of the supermarket in many cases for a host of reasons. The best way to ensure a reliable food supply and safe food sources is to preserve your own (and support community food preservation efforts and local small producers and preservers) and to buy staple food direct from farmers or through co-ops whenever possible.

It is possible to eat mostly local all year round, even in the harshest of climates, but eating this way is fundamentally different than eating out of the supermarket. Eating a mostly local diet, based on staple foods and local sources, with preserved foods added is really, deeply different than the way the average American eats. Not only different, but radically *better* than a processed diet in a host of ways — better nutritionally, better tasting, better for the environment and often cheaper — almost certainly cheaper when health costs are calculated in.

But local eating and CSA support is just a start. We have to begin to think in terms of a fundamental change in diet, and in terms of food storage and preservation as fundamentally integrated into local eating.

Why do you have to change your diet now? Think back to the last time something really awful happened to you—someone close to you died, you were in a car accident, you lost your job. Think about what you ate. Not much, maybe. Or maybe just comfort foods. You certainly didn't try new recipes. You didn't have the emotional energy, nor would you even have bothered to eat if you had to try a lot of new foods. Now think about the last family celebration you had. What did you eat? Traditional foods of your community, your family, your culture. How much pleasure and satisfaction did you get from eating those things? How much is your sense of family, community, celebration, joy, love tied up in what you eat? For many of us, food is a significant repository of our memories. Do you want to take those things away from your family at exactly the time they struggle the most?

We need to make the dietary changeover now to ensure that our elderly, our children and the ill will not suffer or even die from a sudden shock of dietary change, and to make sure we are all able to keep strong and healthy when we need it the most. We need to establish new fundamental foods for our family and culture or adapt the old ones to the new conditions of energy scarcity. The changes involved strike me as taking place in two ways. The first is building a food storage and eating from that. The second is preserving locally produced, seasonal food so we can eat it all year round. These are separate but interrelated issues.

In a time of crisis, we may well have a period in which we cannot eat fresh, local foods, and we need to find ways to make nutritious, balanced, tasty, enjoyable meals from our food storage, probably from limited ingredients. Eating seasonal foods may not seem difficult, but it is. If you've ever produced a lot of food from your garden and animals, you'll realize how disconnected from seasonality our culture is—how many food combinations simply don't go together in nature (carrots and peas, the ubiquitous frozen duo, for example), or are impossible to replicate (I love sushi, but it isn't going to be a major feature of my diet here in upstate New York). Eating seasonally usually involves eating a *lot* of something for a short while, and then either not eating it again for a year, or eating it in a different preserved form—eating tomatoes every day during the warm season, and then canned or dried tomatoes for the winter and spring. So for every major crop we produce, we need both ways to take the greatest advantage of it during its fresh season, and, if possible, a tasty way to preserve it and its nutritional value for the rest of the year.

That doesn't necessarily mean you need to preserve a hundred different crops. Most cultures that rely on their own produce and meat have a staple starch and a staple protein that are the mainstay of their diet and then add other ingredients as flavorings. Whether rice and fish, corn and beans, pork and corn, potatoes and milk, etc., every peasant culture is based around easily grown starches and protein foods. In the first world, we've moved away from this habit, both in our culture's tendency to over-emphasize the protein above the staple starch and in our endless demand for variety. But eating this way doesn't have to be unpleasant. While appetite fatigue is a real phenomenon, most people *like* and enjoy their staple foods, and are aware of subtleties and flavors within them that can't be perceived by outsiders.

So one of the first steps is to figure out what you are realistically going to eat if you have to live on what is grown in your climate, by you or by local farmers. If you live in upstate New York, like I do, as much as you may like rice, it isn't going to be your primary grain. Potatoes, corn, oats or wheat are much more likely. Look around at the native peoples in your area — what did they eat? Check out the farmers in your area. While small farmers may grow sweet potatoes, for example, if no one grows them on a large scale, they will probably not be available unless you grow your own.

Whatever you do, think *now* about food, and start finding ways of making basic foods delicious and part of your daily diet.

I write a lot about how to integrate food storage into your daily life. Because honestly, not only am I not that interested in foods you buy and put in a bunker for 20 years, I think that is a really bad way to go about this. You lose almost all the advantages of food storage if it's not integrated. You lose the advantage of saving money, you lose the nutritional value over the years, you lose the knowledge that in a crisis you won't have to adapt psychologically or physically to a new diet, you lose the advantage of not having to make trips to the store and the advantage of having your comfort and ritual foods be made from things you can always get and afford. It simply doesn't make sense to buy food, preserve food or grow food and not eat it.

And yet, it happens all the time. People buy a big reserve for an emergency, but don't know how to make it tasty or to use it well, or it isn't familiar, and somehow, they look up and five years have passed with no disaster compelling enough to get them to eat things they don't like anyway, and they are wondering whether the canned chicken is still edible post expiration, and they've lost all the time and energy and money they put into this. No wonder people who did this once don't really get excited about doing it again.

The thing is, the kind of eating you do if you rely on food storage is fundamentally different than the way you eat when you rely on supermarkets and radically different than buying food you don't actually eat for a hypothetical time when you'll be desperate enough to consider eating surplus MREs. You are generally using whole grains, because they have the maximum nutritional value and storage ease. Most Americans don't use grains in their whole form. For many people, this kind of eating will mean eating fewer animal products because most of the reasonably priced options are low quality (usually industrially processed) and because storing a lot of meat by any mechanism other than "on the hoof" or freezing is expensive and/or time consuming. Freezing itself is increasingly expensive and sometimes unreliable. It is a good way to keep meat, but you risk the loss of a lot of high-value meat in a power outage. It is simply easier to store more beans and eat a bit less meat than it is to can 200 chickens. You can definitely do it, but you might not want to.

For people who have been used to eating all their produce "fresh," this involves changing menus a bit (by the time most produce reaches the supermarket it is often well over a week old and sprayed with waxes and preservatives, so calling it "fresh" is only a technicality here). During the time when things don't grow, you'll be eating food grown by season extension, root-cellared or long-lasting fresh foods, and preserved foods. The balance depends on you. Our family, for example, doesn't eat that many canned vegetables. We'd rather eat cabbage from the root cellar, but people who like canned green beans might prefer that to stir-fried cabbage.

The easiest way to get started is simply to start making menus. You start thinking "Ok, what can I make with what I've got?" Come up with as many things you like, and things you think you might like, as you can. Look at cookbooks — if you are going to have a lot of squash to deal with, check out the squash recipes. Hit the library and check out their choices, and make use of the Internet.

Can you make familiar recipes while changing ingredients slightly so they become "pantry" meals? Our family always has the ingredients for certain meals in the house. We automatically stock up on these as our stores get depleted, because then we're never out of ingredients if someone suddenly stays for dinner.

Think about substitutions. Most classic recipes already contain a history of substitutions written into them. The cake you make with vanilla? It was probably flavored with rosewater when your great-grandmother made it, since vanilla was expensive and tropical. Great-grandma probably often substituted one kind of flour for another, used vinegar instead of lemon and a host of other techniques. Many recipes grew up in regions where they were constantly adapted to one place or another. Paella in one region might have used freshwater frogs and snails, along with meats available in that region, while coastal paellas used fish. Because you can make pancakes out of almost anything, and people have, there are hundreds of recipes for pancakes in the world. Anyone who says that there's only one way to make something is just plain wrong (unless they are talking about clam chowder, when there really is only one way to make it, and anyone using tomatoes is evil… OK, sorry, I grew up in Massachusetts and inherited my prejudices honorably). I avoid cookbooks and recipe sites that speak of "the one true way" to make food. That's not to say some things don't taste better than others, but with the exception of some fundamentally uneuphonious combinations, often things can be made to taste just fine with a bit of work, even if you change things around quite a bit.

This is one of those practicing things — getting familiar with new food and new ways of cooking it, gradually integrating it into your diet and family life. It does take work and practice. It is also worth it.

Making the Best Use of What We Already Have to End Hunger

The power of our food system is this. Up to 12 percent of our total fossil fuel use is linked to the food system. More than 35 percent of our total greenhouse gas emissions are linked to our food system. Our hope of controlling climate change or avoiding a world in which many, many people die from lack of food depends on creating a system that can withstand the coming shifts in climate, energy costs and availability and a worldwide depression. Without basic food security, we can expect radical political change — people looking for scapegoats, governments overthrown, acts of war, violence. Without basic food security we can expect to see a lost generation. People all over the world will be stunted developmentally, their children dead and their anger rising. They will be too weakened by hunger to have learned about citizenship or be able to address their crisis. As Gandhi said because they are too hungry, angry, and hopeless, they can see God only in the form of bread. Dinner is that important.

And why focus on cooking, food preservation and storage? Why not emphasize growing food? There are a couple of reasons. The first is that many people and organizations already focus on that end of things. The production and distribution of food have the attention of many groups — community gardeners, victory garden groups like Kitchen Gardens International, food and farming experts, and millions of ordinary people are starting to see how important it is that we focus on the agricultural system. Michael Pollan and Barbara Kingsolver and a host of others have written important books about the ways that food production needs to be at the forefront of our policy initiatives. And I've already written a book about growing food myself.

The other reason is that we have enough food. It is true that we need to increase yields in some of the poorer places of the world, but increased access and not wasting or losing what we have is as central a project as producing more — perhaps more so.

That's why I'm focusing on the quieter end of this, the one that hasn't as yet gotten the attention it so desperately needs. Worldwide, nearly one third of all the food we produce is lost before it can be consumed — whether it is lost in the field because there is no one to harvest it (as in some US states this year due to a decline in migrant labor) or because of transport delays and shortages, pest damage or lack of the right tools for low-energy food preservation.

In the US, millions of people suffer food insecurity in part because they do not know how to cook low-cost staple foods, or how to make use of leftovers and parts of vegetables not commonly eaten. Our food security may well come to depend on local food systems, but most Americans who "eat local" do so only during the harvest season because they have no idea how to preserve food or minimize loss. In the poor world, children suffer from malnutrition and hunger because the food their parents grow cannot be preserved. They have no access to basic tools, or fuel for cooking and preserving due to deforestation. In the rich world, children suffer malnutrition and hunger because so few people know how to cook, preserve, or feed themselves, so they eat cheap, toxic fast food and processed food at high cost.

I want to draw attention to the urgent problem of making the best possible use of the food we do have — to minimizing waste, to supporting the local food systems we will depend on in the new economy and to cooking, that most ordinary work of human beings, which makes the difference between decent nutrition, good health and the normal development of children and the disastrous loss of a healthy future.

This is one of the places where everyone can act. We can all learn to store and preserve food, to take local foods and put them up to bridge seasons where little is grown, be they hot and dry or cold and snowy. We can all learn to cook. We can learn to use basic staples as our primary source of food, leaving rich foods like meats for festivals, increasing both pleasure and health. We can share food with our neighbors, and strengthen local communities when we sit down for a meal together.

We can save a bit of money on our grocery bills by eating what is local, abundant and basic, and give that money to the increasing number of people in our neighborhoods and the world who need a helping hand just to eat. We can share our knowledge and our techniques with others, and help them out of a growing poverty. We can take the appalling quantity of wasted food and eat more of it, creating greater equity in the world and reducing methane in landfills. We can come closer to the use of a fair share, and leave more for others.

Clean Plate Club: Food Waste and Its Relationship to Food Storage and Preservation

In one sense, in our house there really is no food waste — between the chickens, the dogs, the worms and the compost pile, nearly everything gets eaten. On the other hand, it does behoove me to ask myself, "Is there a less expensive way to feed chickens than on potato-leek soup and asparagus that I really meant to eat before it got icky? Is it possible that I could reduce the sheer quantity of fuzzy things that are not peaches in my life?" Sure, composting is great, but wouldn't it be better if I did a little less of it?

Americans waste 100 *billion* pounds of food a year collectively. Food is wasted everywhere in the food system, from rotting in the fields, to rotting in warehouses, to rotting in our fridges. The average American spends fifteen percent of their food budget on food they will simply throw away. According to the USDA, nearly one sixth of what they throw out was still edible. We throw out enough food every year to feed 49 million hungry people — about the same number of new starving people the world welcomed in 2008.

So if you remember your mother telling you to clean your plate because children are starving in India, and you wondered what the connection was (obviously you weren't going to mail your leftovers to them), this is the link between what you eat and that they do. The food that we waste and lose at various points in the system costs us money we can't afford, it absorbs food needed by others, it creates greenhouse gas in landfills, and it destroys our hope of food security.

Now what on earth does this have to do with food preservation and storage? Well, the reason we call it preservation is this: it stops or slows spoilage. So food preservation is one of the primary tools we have to reduce food waste, and to ensure that there's enough food to go around.

It works the other way around as well — our stores of food can be built up by minimizing waste and food loss. This is especially important for those who struggle financially to build up a supply of stored food. We can't afford to throw away the equivalent of $600 worth of food every year — and yet that's what the average American household simply tosses out. Six hundred dollars is more than a month's worth of food for every American. Can you afford to throw away an entire month's groceries? Six hundred dollars could feed a hungry child in the poor world for an entire year.

Pantry eating, food storage and preservation are tools to reduce hunger. We need to learn to preserve the food we can't eat immediately, and to rescue supplies of food that are simply going to waste. We need to cut back our losses. This means preserving those apples as applesauce when they start to get wrinkly, or freezing that pepper with a soft spot so we can enjoy it in spaghetti sauce in winter.

Pantry eating means eating more foods that are stored in their whole forms or already preserved in appropriate sizes, so there's less waste. Emphasizing stored foods means having foods that don't go bad as often. There are fewer rotting things in the back of the fridge.

One study found that when they shop primarily for one particular recipe, people tend to overestimate what they are going to do and a lot of the ingredients go to waste. But pantry eating is different. Food storage means emphasizing foods that keep well and taking care of them, but it also means emphasizing adaptive foods. Instead of odd ingredients that you only use once in a while, you rely on primary staples that can be used in many ways and that don't decay rapidly. So pantry eating really does cut down on food waste.

What Can Food Storage and Preservation Do?

For a lot of us, the idea of storing food is a fraught one. Will it make us survivalists? Do we have time? Isn't it expensive? Where will I put it all? Doesn't it mean eating MREs? Won't someone just take our stores away?

Before we get down to the nitty gritty of how to build up stores and preserve food, it is important to think about how we might look at our reserves. I know some people reading this don't think an extended, widespread crisis is possible or likely, and they may wonder whether they really need a store of food at all. I know other people think that a crisis is immanent. I don't pretend to know the answer. I only know that I will be a lot happier in an extended crisis if I have a food reserve than if I don't. I also know that it is possible to have a purely personal extended crisis — a sudden major illness or extended job loss.

In a true emergency, food storage *can* provide a cushion or a hedge, allowing you to go for an extended time without depending on stores, or to extend limited food dollars by relying primarily on stored food. Depending on how much reserve you have, it might be enough to get you through a short-term crisis. If, for example, a crisis occurs during a dormant season (cold in the north, hot and dry in some parts of the south), it can help you get from one planting season to another.

Food storage *can't* get most of us through a long-term crisis lasting years. We will have to find some way to refill our stores and meet present needs. Food storage *does not* obviate the need for gardening, preserving or supporting safety nets and local food systems.

Because you are eventually going to have to rely on local food systems that means food storage *can not* and probably *should not* reproduce the food you get from the grocery store. That is, if we're going to preserve food, buy in bulk and eat out of our pantries, our meals will be different than when we were shopping several times a week and eating from our fridges. In order to make the adjustment as pleasant as possible, we should start eating this way now, first with one meal a week, then two, then four.

It is possible to eat an extremely high quality, nutritious, good tasting diet out of your food storage. But this is different than how most Western people eat now. It relies on whole grains, roots and legumes at its base, with some preserved foods, fresh foods from the garden and root cellar and lots of herbs and flavorings. Meals based on these foods take advantage of things that don't lose quality in storage, that do taste good when kept dry. *Instead of forcing things that don't store well into the shape of your diet, this centers your diet around foods that do store well.*

Meat, milk and eggs, if you include them in your food storage, *can be used* as supplements, but generally not as centerpieces (I am speaking here only of storage, not of home-produced versions of these foods). The reason for this is that meat, milk and eggs simply don't preserve all that well except by freezing — and freezing means risking the loss of your stored food in a power outage. Freezers are fine, but they are not a substitute for foods that don't require electricity.

You will have to decide for yourself how important these foods are to you. But as you do so, think about how your food storage integrates with the diet your region is likely to provide when your food storage runs out. All of us enjoy some foods from far away. But if you don't know how to cook what does grow well in your region, and how to eat and enjoy it, you will have to adapt to a difficult dietary change at a difficult time.

Many people in the US do actually go hungry because they don't know how to cook and eat the foods that they have access to. That is, many poor people in the US don't stretch their food dollars in part because they do not know how to cook inexpensive staples. (This is not bigotry towards the poor; this inability to cook transcends economic status, but it most hurts the poor because they have few good options.) So it isn't enough to say, "OK, if we ever get reduced to corn and beans, I'll learn to cook with them." The truth is that if corn and beans are what grows well in your region, your family needs to learn to cook and eat them now. Eating out of your food storage now *can* prevent real hunger and illness later.

Food storage *can* help you make that transition. It can ease you over to a diet heavy on root crops and peas, while still allowing you some rice and salmon to smooth things over. But you can't live on food storage forever. That's not to say it doesn't have value, but *food security* depends on creating local food systems — systems that start at your garden, but go outwards, across your local foodshed. Your "foodshed" is the land that produces the food you eat, just as your watershed is the land that directs, filters and supplies your water. It may be a vast, wide area or a very small one indeed.

Thus, food storage *should* as much as possible be built on a foundation of supporting your local food systems. Some of us may not have much choice about where we get our food. But those of us who do have some leeway in our budgets and do have choices should build our food storage as much as possible from local farmers — or, at worst, direct from farmers that help build someone else's local food system. Dollars spent building up your food storage at the supermarket or Costco are dollars that are working *against* the local food producers that we most need to rely on in the long term. I'm not suggesting that we won't buy some things that support the industrial food system. We're all bound up in it to a degree. But every dollar we can spend locally on food that our region grows well, or everything we can grow, can and dry ourselves, makes possible not just your short-term food security (that is, the stuff you've got in storage) but the long-term possibility of security in a crisis.

So what's the gist of this? We should be thinking about what food storage can and can't do for us, what it should and should not do for us. Yes, it can save our lives — in the short term. But it's best to think of it as a bridge to the local food systems that are our long-term security and hedge against disaster.

Recipes

Salmon Cakes with Chipotle Mayonnaise

Salmon Cakes

These delicious, cheap, quick-and-easy-to-make patties are a frequent staple on our dinner table, and an easy pantry meal. Add a green vegetable on the side and you have a complete meal. If you use matzo meal in the recipe, they are an ideal kosher-for-Passover entrée. With breadcrumbs, you can use up your stale bread. You can use either pink or red canned salmon. The red is a bit more flavorful, but the pink is considerably less expensive. We try to purchase salmon that was wild-caught and that benefits small communities in Alaska.

• 1 15-oz can salmon (pink or red)	• 2 eggs
• ½ cup bread crumbs or matzo meal	• 1 medium or 2 small potatoes, quartered
• vegetable or olive oil for frying	

Cover the potatoes with water in a small saucepan and boil until soft. (You can peel them first if you wish, but we leave the skins on.) Mash them with a fork or potato masher until reasonably smooth (some small lumps are fine). Drain the salmon and add to the potatoes, mixing with a fork. Add the eggs and the bread crumbs or matzo meal. If the mixture is still too wet to make patties, add a little bit more of the bread crumbs or matzo meal. Shape the mixture into patties. Bake or fry, as preferred. Can be served with chipotle mayo (below), ketchup or cocktail sauce.

Makes 4 patties; serves 2.

Mayonnaise Dipping Sauces

Generally speaking we are not "mayonnaise people." We tend to prefer mustard or hot pepper relish on our sandwiches. There are, however, certain dishes to which mayonnaise-based sauces seem to be the perfect complement. We use chipotle mayonnaise with salmon cakes. Chipotles are smoked jalapeno peppers, and these days can be found in many supermarkets in the Mexican/Hispanic section in the international foods aisle, and are a great addition to your pantry. If you don't do spicy, garlic mayonnaise works very well too, and is also the perfect accompaniment for steamed artichokes.

• ¼ cup fresh lemon juice or cider vinegar	• 1 tbsp sugar
• ½ cup purchased mayonnaise, or you can make mayonnaise (recipes for vegan and egg- based mayonnaise below)	• Your choice: 2 chipotles in adobo sauce, finely chopped (for chipotle mayonnaise), *or* 2 cloves raw garlic, finely minced

Mix together all ingredients, and then portion into small bowls for dipping or else spoon directly on top of your salmon cakes or whatever it is you're eating it with.

Makes a little under 1 cup.

Homemade Mayonnaise

This is much better than any commercial option—by a long shot. It does, however, require a supply of fresh eggs, and there is some risk of salmonella from eggs. But oh, the difference!

- 3 egg yolks
- 1 cup good quality olive or sunflower seed oil
- 3 tsp good quality Dijon mustard
- 1 clove fresh garlic, minced
- 3 tbsp fresh lemon juice or good wine vinegar

Whisk all ingredients except oil together, and whisking steadily, gradually add the oil until completely emulsified. Alternately, you can do this in a food processor, and process until the oil is absorbed and the texture is what you want.

Makes many servings, keeps 3 days in the fridge.

Tofu Mayonnaise

- 1½ tsp vinegar
- 1 tsp sugar
- 1 clove garlic, minced
- 10 oz silken tofu, either homemade or purchased (shelf-stable tofu is fine)
- 1 tsp salt
- 1 tsp mustard powder

Puree all ingredients together until smooth, serve as desired. This is great with dill on sandwiches.

Makes many servings, keeps one week.

wealth

I can't say when the sight of my pantry full of food started to make me feel richer than money in the bank. It was a process of unlearning all the things that my society told me. Money is wealth, I was told, because it will always enable me to buy whatever I need. But as I learned more about the complex connections required to transform oil, seed, natural gas, a farmer's time and a corporation's packaging into a bag of "baby" carrots on the store shelf, I was struck by both how wondrous, and how unlikely those connections were.

Despite the environmental costs, it is in some ways wonderful and astonishing that a processor in California can take oil pumped from the ground by a Saudi Arabian, fertilizer manufactured from Canadian natural gas, seed grown by a farmer in China, a refrigerator truck driven by a man from Georgia and a processing company in Colorado that scrapes full-sized carrots into "baby" form, put them together, pack them into another truck, driven by a man from Indiana, and haul them to a shelf in upstate New York, where my husband, in a car fed by Venezuelan oil and Iowan corn-based ethanol, can drive them home.

At the same time however, that such fragmented pieces have been drawn together should also remind us of how easily the connections can become unwound as things change. Things, as William Butler Yeats reminds us, fall apart. But what is disturbing is not just the complexity, it is the way in which each step in the process degrades the ability of the system to continue. The natural gas-based fertilizers and the chemical pesticides and herbicides used by the farmer degrade the soil and the water, killing off beneficial life forms and contaminating water for the humans who depend on it. The oil we burn, the nitrogen fertilizer in the carrots and the corn ethanol in the trucks warm the planet — warming and drying California, and reducing the mountain snows that the carrots depend on for irrigation. Using gas and oil at so many stages — for the plastic packaging, in the tractor, the refrigerated truck, and our car — all of that burns a depleted resource, one whose price is increasingly volatile, and ties the price of something as basic as food to the price of energy.

Complexity is all very well, but 2009 showed a lot of us that the money that enabled the complex fulfillment of basic needs can easily disappear — the 401K, the college fund, the family savings that we hoped would be turned into food, heat and a home simply evaporated into the mist that is the money supply, and many of us were left wondering what we would rely on to get by now. An economy that has to grow all the time requires us to believe that the laws of physics are not in place. So what's the alternative? One answer is to feed ourselves from the pantry. The price of beans may go up and down, but the price of dinner in my children's mouths remains forever the same — priceless.

The taxman and the mortgage company still don't take canned carrots or sacks of potatoes. It is not my claim that my pantry is all the wealth that ever was. And even if the Wall Street Journal did recently suggest that people buy food instead of stocks, since it seemed a more reliable investment, I've yet to find anyone who will pay interest on my chickens. Or maybe that's wrong — the chickens pay dividends, in the form of eggs. The garden multiplies exponentially. From the tiny carrot seeds, nearly invisible in my hands, come pounds and bushels of orange roots, sweet and crisp. My time and effort multiplies. Two hours become a dozen quarts of applesauce waiting to be served on a dozen winter nights when I am tired and need a quick side dish.

The value of Independence is not all the truth that ever was. It is not sufficient to mend all ills or fix all problems. It is merely — and thus, wondrously — a way of creating a wealth we can hold onto.

3

How Much Food Should You Store?

Our lives are not in the lap of the gods,
but in the lap of our cooks.

— Lin Yutang —

I THINK THERE'S A TENDENCY, when we talk about food storage, to leap immediately to the end of the world, or if you don't buy those scenarios, to dismiss the value of food storage along with the apocalypse. But that's not the primary merit of food storage. The primary merits of food storage are that it saves your family money, gets you better quality food than you could for the same expenditure, and is environmentally sound. I also think the fact that it can insulate you from a crisis — whether purely personal or national — has merits. And that's where many of us start, and where I'm starting in this chapter. But I do want to remind everyone that food storage is as much or more about your day-to-day diet than about your opinion about the likelihood of any particular crisis.

When I first started teaching food storage, I wrote an essay that discussed the bare minimum for food storage — the two weeks recommended by both the US Department of Homeland Security and the American Red Cross. I noted that two-week periods in which we are unable to shop or get supplies are actually not at all uncommon. They have occurred many times in rich-world nations including the US because of floods, earthquakes, blizzards and hurricanes, and all of us should, as simply commonsense preparedness, have a two-week supply of food. I then went along trying to get my readers to store much more food than that, but I didn't want to push too hard on that, because I know that for some people, the idea that you might not be able to get food at the store for more than a couple of weeks due to a short-term disaster is just plain crazy talk. For other people, the idea of dealing with large quantities of food is so overwhelming that their brain goes numb when we start talking about the quantities involved, and they begin to immediately assume that they could never do that.

But when it came time to write this book, I looked over that material and knew that I'd be lying if I said that two weeks was really sufficient. I'm a little worried that when I use the words "months" people will be frightened or turned off, but it is the truth, and it is better not to shy away from the truth. Everyone who reads this who still has the ability to build up a food reserve really needs a minimum three-month supply. Now before you panic, I promise, it doesn't have to be that overwhelming—and yes, you are going to have two weeks before you get to three months. But I don't think you should stop, if at all possible, until you've got a larger reserve.

Why three months? Five reasons, all of them important.

1. Disasters don't always fit neatly into two-week periods, unfortunately. Longer periods of large scale crisis and limited supplies are well within the realm of the possible, and government planning scenarios include many events where two weeks wouldn't be enough. For example, the US government's pandemic planning estimates quarantines might be necessary for as long as 12 weeks or more, while the Australian government recently recommended that everyone have a full three months worth of food stored.

   Hurricane Ike knocked out power in the city of Houston on September 13, 2008. Two weeks later, almost half a million people were still without power. Almost three weeks later, nearly 5,000 Houston residents still remained without power, according to one news report. In Kentucky in January 2009, many residents were without power for more than three weeks.

2. People planning for very short-term storage actually are at a disadvantage in several ways. First, they may end up paying more because for as little as two weeks, they may not investigate bulk purchasing. But the other reason is that if you think that two weeks is the longest you are likely to go in a difficult situation, you are likely to limit your preparations to short-term solutions. But short-term solutions don't always work very well, and sometimes are more costly than long-term ones.

What do I mean by that? Well, let's say you were preparing for up to two weeks without power. One logical outcome might be to go get a generator. But a generator is very expensive, it requires correct installation, which also costs, and if there are very widespread power outages, you probably won't be able to get gas for it after a few days because the gas pumps require electricity too. Even if you can get gas, you won't have enough electricity to run everything you need. This is what happened in Houston.

On the other hand, the same money spent with the assumption that you might need to live without power for as long as three months can get you better equipped for even a short-term power outage. The same goes for a range of strategies. Someone thinking in terms of a two-week supply might invest primarily in freeze-dried and instant foods, only to discover that their family doesn't really like to eat those foods, and that two weeks on them leads to health consequences because they are high in sodium and can be constipating. Imagining your situation as a lifestyle change, an experience long enough that you have to achieve a "new normal," allows you to think outside conventional lines.

3. It is mistake to view food storage and preservation as merely a hedge against a major, widespread national disaster. Personal disasters occur all the time, and can be just as devastating as a national supply crisis — often more so. Buying food now, and storing it in bulk means you can keep your family fed in a medical crisis, after a job loss, etc. I know many people who have already relied upon their stored food to preserve them in a family emergency when no one had time, energy or money to buy food. The most likely reason

you will need your food storage is that you have had a salary cut-back or a job loss in your family.

4. You may be caring for more than just yourself. It is easy to look around at your family right now and say, "OK, there's me, Mom and my brother, we need that times two weeks," but the truth is that a crisis in your region or your area may involve extended family who evacuate to your home, your neighbors coming to you to admit their pantry is completely empty, "and do you have anything at all for their hungry kids", someone coming and asking if you have anything at all to share with those who are worse off. Storing a reserve enables you to protect your own if your own expands, and to help people in need.

5. Those with the knowledge and ability to do so have the obligation not to drain resources needed for those who didn't have the capacity to prepare. Let's say that the disaster does only last two weeks, and that at the end of those two weeks, the Red Cross is out there with soup waiting. Is there enough soup for everyone? You don't know, and if the soup just arrived, it is probably watered down and stretched pretty thin. The mindset that says, "I just have to make it until the safety net picks me up," is the wrong one.

I believe in safety nets — but they work best when people can be trusted not to use them unless they really need them. There are almost certainly some people reading this who can't do anything else to protect themselves. They don't have the resources to buy more food, maybe don't have enough food now, or they are elderly, disabled or ill and can't make preparations. But if you aren't one of them — if you still have a job, can still afford the occasional treat — then you have enough money to stay out of the soup lines. Taking care of yourself is both a burden and a privilege. All of us have the obligation to keep the safety nets going for others.

So let's talk about possible scenarios in which you'd need more than two weeks of stored food. I know this is scary stuff, but the best way I know to manage fear is to address it — to reduce your vulnerability.

In the case of a flu pandemic, various government agencies estimate that an influenza wave might require quarantine periods of up to 12 weeks. The best possible way to reduce contagion in a pandemic is to keep people away from each other. People would be told to stay home, schools closed, employees laid off (and don't expect you'd be paid — another reason to keep that reserve). The last place you'd want to go would be the grocery store, even if it were open and had food on the shelves.

A flu pandemic is one possibility, but in general, the scenario planning that government agencies are doing tends to focus on a short-term, localized crisis — a tornado, a flood, wildfires. The assumption of the two-week theory is that there will be one big disaster, and the nation's response will be mobilized to get to you. Even when that's actually what happens, the two-week limit hasn't been adequate a number of times. In the ice storm that paralyzed much of the Northeast in the late 1990s, for example, areas of New York, Vermont and New Hampshire didn't have power back or road access for 16 days or more. In Kobe, Japan, during the last major earthquake, it took more than two weeks for rescue workers to reach some of the hardest hit suburbs — and Kobe was one of the best earthquake-prepared cities in the world. In Houston, in the fall of 2008, many stores were stripped of food shortly after a hurricane, and resupplies did not get to stores in many neighborhoods for more than three weeks. Power was out for more than one million customers for a minimum of three weeks.

We also could ask about our preparations for a non-localized crisis — either multiple natural disasters occurring simultaneously (not super-likely, but not at all impossible), or a dramatic, sudden disruption in energy supplies, a tsunami that affected many coastal areas simultaneously, or widespread electrical grid failures. In that case, everyone has needs that have to be answered simultaneously and there's simply no way for even the best organized response to meet everyone's needs. It would almost certainly be much longer than two weeks before basic resources were widely available.

Finally, the most likely disaster to befall you is this. You lose your job. Your spouse loses his or her job. You spend your savings on a medical crisis or two. You are stretched trying to keep your house/pay your rent/buy gas to get to work, and you don't have any money for food. Your kids are hungry, and the food pantry is, as at least one US pantry was in the summer of 2008, down to stale Doritos because of the huge demand. Maybe you get food stamps (assuming the program can still be funded after a radical drop in tax revenue), but they don't stretch to the end of the month. And two weeks worth of food won't save you. Neither will three months of stored food, but it gives you options, time to find other solutions, time to put the monthly food budget towards the mortgage, or rent on a new place.

I know that some of you can't buy extra food because you can't buy enough food. For the rest, you need to do what you can, both to protect yourself and to make sure that you don't compete for food resources with those who have no ability to protect themselves. Maybe you can drop a few cans at the food pantry, even when things get tough at home. That means a minimum of three months of food. Build it up gradually, write down what you eat, focus on meals based on staple foods like grains, dried beans, and locally produced and home preserved vegetables.

Project One: Getting Started

All of the first projects under this heading involve having something soothing to drink and having time to think. So wait until you've got them both, and can come into this not in a panic "I've got to get food now!" but calmly. So sit down with a cup of tea. I give you official permission to use another beverage if you prefer, but get a drink, tell the kids to go outside and play, the spouse that you are busy, get a pen and paper, and give yourself a little quiet time before you begin rushing madly off in all directions with food storage and preservation. Put on some music, breathe deeply, put your feet up and relax a little.

Now, you are going to do three things.

1. You are going to sit down and list four breakfasts, four lunches, four dinners and four snacks that use mostly ingredients that can sit on a pantry shelf or come out of your garden and *that your family likes.* They don't have to be complicated. In fact, ideally they won't be. If you can't think of enough of each, begin thinking through the reci-

pes you make regularly, and ask yourself, "Could I adapt this? Could it use shelf-stable tofu instead of the fresh stuff? Could I try it with kale instead of spinach in the late fall?" You can get seasonal about it, listing separate meals for different seasons, but if that seems overwhelming, just focus on four basic meals that everyone will eat — pasta with tomato-garlic sauce, your best spicy lentil soup recipe, tuna noodle casserole…whatever.

This will be the basis of your first food storage projects. You are going to build up enough of the ingredients to be able to make these meals easily, without going to the store. These are things you will eat anyway. These are things that will save you time, if you don't have to run out every time you need the ingredients. This is not a commitment to anything strange or weird — it is just shopping ahead. So figure out how many times you want to be able to make these meals. Let's say you get the ingredients to do each of them four times (and if money is tight, it may take some weeks to gradually add a little extra to your cart). By then, you'll have 16 days of food you like in the house without much extra worry. If you can get case or bulk discounts, you will probably even save some money. And it is food you are going to eat anyway. If you are ambitious, and no one has interrupted you, make the grocery list(s).

2. Now you are going to get up and walk around your house, because the next project is finding some space for food storage. Buying a few extra ingredients probably won't require you to do any major rearranging, unless you have a miniscule kitchen. Even then, you should be able to fit a lot of this food in the cupboards if you do some rearranging. Don't do it now (today we're still drinking tea) but put that on your "to do soon" list — to just sort through the cupboards, move the stuff you don't use that often, and consider getting rid of things. (You know how the nesting bowls always get cluttered because you only use the bottom two regularly, so the little ones are all over the place, and how your baking area has six little heart-shaped tart pans that you use once a year? Odds are you can move that stuff to a different place. We have the sense that all like things must go together in a kitchen, but this was not actually laid down as law anywhere I know of.)

If your goal is to get more food than just what's on your meal list, you'll need space for it. So now is the time to begin looking. How are you fixed for closet space? Could anything be packed up and moved around (remember, if you haven't used it in a while, you probably could move it). Are you storing any junk that could be given away or sold? And no, it doesn't count if all the "junk" belongs to your partner, and your stuff is "good stuff" that is absolutely needed — the first rule of decluttering is "you've got to get rid of some of your own stuff." What about under the bed? What about the basement? What about up along the top of the kitchen cabinets? What about your bedroom? Just because it is food, doesn't mean it has to live in the kitchen. Ideally, what you want is a pantry space — so now is the time to establish one. What will you need? Shelving? To rearrange furniture? To build something? To have a yard sale? Again, don't do it — make a list. There's still one more step.

The third thing you are going to do is make another cup of tea or other preferred beverage and answer some questions. You may want to run these questions by other members of your family, or you may not, but the idea is to help you figure out what you want. You don't have to write down the answers, although you might want to.

1. What am I storing food for? What are my concerns? What kinds of situations are likely in my region?

2. How much food do I want to store? For how many people? For how many pets? How much water do I want to store? Am I likely to have people outside my immediate household who are with us in a crisis? Are there other things I want to store? What are they? Clothing, medical supplies, tools?

3. How much time and energy do I have to devote to this? How much space do I realistically think I have to devote to this? How much money can I spend each week/month on this project? What are my biggest constraints — i.e., is my family not supportive, am I working long hours, are there no good sources of bulk food near me? How might I overcome them?

4. Where will my stored food come from? How much of it will I grow/produce? What are my goals for food preservation? How

much of my food will I buy, and from where? What can I get locally, and what do I have to get through the industrial food system? What's the best and most ethical source for my food? Remember, every dollar you spend is a vote. If you spend it at an industrial source, you say, "Great, do more of this." If you spend it locally, you say the same thing to your local farmer. It is safe to say that every one of us buys some food through the industrial system, and some of us don't have the money or the access to do more than get our food any way we can. Those people are off the hook. But if you have *any* discretionary food income, you need to think a little about the votes you are casting when you buy food. Also ask, how can I use my food storage to save money and time?

5. What do I imagine doing with my food storage? Do I want it mostly to provide a hedge against a crisis or for day-to-day use? Do I imagine myself eating regularly out of it and replacing it? Do I want to be able to share with others, or is my first priority protecting my own? How will I prevent loss of food to age, insects, mold? That is, what's my plan for making sure the older food gets eaten regularly and that I'm adding more food as I go? (Food is not like antiques, it doesn't get better with age.) How much am I and my family prepared to adapt our eating habits so that we get the most out of our food storage — save the most money, make fewer trips, and always have food to hand as well as having a reserve?

6. Finally, ask: Do I have to do this all alone? How can I get others — from my own family to my neighbors and my town or city — involved in the project of becoming more food secure? How can I see my own food security as part of a larger community project? Do I have neighbors who might be interested in forming a buying club, a co-op or simply in a "stocking up" club? Do I have friends who would like to share the work of preserving? Are there people in my community who could benefit from food storage? How can I get them involved? Should my community have a reserve of food on hand in case of a crisis? How can I bring this up with my municipality? What about water? Does my community have water pumping stations for when the power is out? Could they be established?

Are there community resources I don't know about — gleaning programs, bulk buying groups, community kitchens, food preservation classes, friends with the same interests? What's out there?

And what's in here? Is my family supportive? Neutral? Hostile? Are there ways to get them on board? How do I approach this issue, if they aren't interested in participating? Can I approach it differently, with a emphasis on saving money, or on likely short-term emergencies (hurricanes, blizzards, power outages) in ways that would be less scary? Can I involve my husband, my wife, my partner, my kids, my parents, my friends? Can I get them excited about helping with the menus, picking out things to store, building projects, saving money, working together as a family?

OK. Now that you are done drinking tea, you can stop. That's enough for today. I know you are all excited, and I can't stop you from running off to reorganize the kitchen and buy 60 cans of tomatoes, but I'd encourage you to stop here, and leave some stuff for tomorrow, so you'll remain enthusiastic, rather than getting exhausted and overwhelmed. Although if you really, really can't stand waiting to reorganize a kitchen, you are welcome to come over and do mine.

Getting Your Household Onboard with Food Storage

OK, I've convinced you. You need a reserve of food, you want to learn to can and dehydrate, you want to start eating more local foods. But you haven't done anything yet, because, well, the rest of your household isn't on board. Before you go there, you need to convince them. So I offer up this handy guide of answers to common protests about food storage and preservation. I also offer up some suggestions on what not to say, just in case you need them.

Protest #1: It will be too expensive!
Bad answer: "But honey, the world is going to come to an end soon, and male life expectancy is going to drop into the 50s, so you won't need your retirement savings anyway. Let's spend it on food so I have something to eat in my old age."

Good answer: "I'm glad you are so concerned about our finances, and I share your concern. I think in the longer term this will save us money, allowing us to buy food at lower bulk prices and when it is at its cheapest, and thus will insulate us from rising prices. But let's sit down and make a budget for what we think it is appropriate to spend on food storage."

Protest #2: No one has time to can and preserve food anymore! Isn't that a leftover from the bad old days when we women were barefoot, pregnant and chained to the stove?

Bad answer: "Of course you'll have time to do it, sweetie. Can't you get up before the kids do to make pickles? You already get four hours of sleep a night, so what's the problem? If you loved the kids, you'd make your own salsa."

Good answer: "What I think will end up happening is that we'll save time later from effort spent now — and we'll know that our food supply is nutritious and safe. I don't feel good giving the kids processed foods with all the recalls and contaminations. But let's definitely start slowly. I'll make some sauerkraut, and then if you think we should, we'll look into plans for a dehydrator. We'll work on it together."

Protest #3: Where are we going to put all that stuff? There's no way it will fit!

Bad answer: "On those shelves where you keep all your old vinyl records, silly. As soon as I get that stuff out to the trash, we'll be ready to build our pantry."

Good answer: "I think there's some unused space in that guest room, and if I clean out this closet, I know we could put shelves up and store some food. I guess I should think about cleaning out some of my junk, right?"

Protest #4: Storing food is for wacko-survivalist types. That's not us.

Bad answer: "Oh, didn't you read that stuff by Nostradamus that I gave you? Oh, and do you know how to use an Uzi?"

Good answer: "No, storing food is what my grandmother did to get through the Great Depression. It is pretty normal, actually. And the government says that everyone should do it as a basic part of being a citizen."

Protest #5: Nobody in our house is going to eat garbanzo beans. I'm certainly not going to. They make me want to puke!
Bad answer: "Oh, you'll eat those beans, young lady, or you'll spend the rest of your life in your room!"
Good answer: "Ok, you don't like chickpeas. That's OK—what do you suggest we get instead? Would you like to come with me to the bulk store and help me pick out some storage food?"

Protest #6: I don't want to think about bad stuff that might happen, or be reminded of it!
Bad answer: "Ok, you don't have to. But we're all doomed anyway."
Good Answer: "But remember, we're not just storing food for bad times, we're storing food so that we can save money, go shopping less, have more time for each other, and so we have to worry less about money."

Protest #7: Things will never get bad enough that we need our stored food, so what's the point?
Bad Answer: "I expect things to get so bad that we seriously consider whether or not to eat the hamsters—probably by next Friday. After Pookie and Herman, the neighbors will be next. Steve up on the corner looks pretty good."
Good Answer: "Well, this is really about a whole way of eating, not just storing food for an emergency. So no matter what happens, we come out ahead. We have the food, and it will get eaten."

Protest #8: Ok, I'm willing to think about some food storage, but storing water? That's for whack jobs.
Bad Answer: "Ok, well I'm storing water for me, and if anything bad happens, I'm just going to sit there watching you shrivel up."
Good Answer: "Remember the floods in the midwest this summer? A

lot of areas had contaminated water, and I don't really want to go for days with no water to wash my hands in or to cook with. All we've got to do is take these recycled soda bottles and fill them with water and a couple of drops of bleach, to know that we won't be in that position."

Protest #9: Home-preserved food isn't safe. I heard about someone who died from eating home-canned food.
Bad Answer: "Oh, you are right. Let's only eat industrially packaged food with lots of melamine in it."
Good Answer: "It is true that unsafe canning practices occasionally result in home-canned food hurting or killing someone. But think of all the trouble we've had with the industrial food system — the melamine in dog food, botulism in canned chili, salmonella and E. coli on tons of things. I agree we have to be very careful, especially when pressure canning, and I plan to be. But we can preserve our own in lots of ways that are completely safe, and overall, home-preserved food is actually safer, not to mention more nutritious, than commercially canned food."

Protest #10: There are so many things about this that are hard. It takes time, energy, new tools, money. It may be a good idea, but why would you want to take it on?
Bad Answer: "Because Sharon in this book says I should. She fed me the zombie paste, and now I have no will of my own."
Good Answer: "Because I think we deserve better food than we're getting. I want it to taste better, I want the money we spend to help do things we're proud of. I want to depend on ourselves more and on corporations less. I want us to be healthier, I want us to feel like when we are eating, we're doing something good.

What Does a Three Month Supply of Food Look Like?

In the next chapter I'm going to talk more about different ways of building up a supply, but for now, let's talk in broad generalities. I'm going to use a family of four, one adult man, one adult woman, two kids over seven as an example. Now this is very basic. You would want to personalize this much more than I have. But let's start here.

One possible model for three months' worth of food in a family that cooks from scratch, but doesn't have a grain grinder (we'll talk more about that a little later, so don't worry if you don't know why you'd want one) would look like this. It assumes that the folks involved eat a fairly basic American diet, and are shopping at the supermarket. Now this is not how I'd have most of us start out, actually, because it involves giving money mostly to big corporations. But this is at least mostly accessible stuff.

- 50 pounds brown rice
- 50 pounds white rice
- 50 pounds whole wheat flour
- 50 pounds rolled oats
- 30 pounds whole wheat pasta
- 10 pounds cornmeal
- 5 pounds pearl barley
- spices
- 5 pounds peanut butter
- 5 gallons olive or canola oil
- 25 pounds sugar
- 10 pounds brown sugar
- 5 gallons honey
- 60 pounds powdered milk
- 1 pound baking powder
- 1 pound baking soda
- 1 pound yeast
- 2 pounds raisins
- 24 cans of mustard greens
- 24 cans of diced tomatoes
- 12 cans of tuna fish
- 2 jars of bouillon cubes
- 3 pounds salt
- 1 gallon bleach
- 180 adult multivitamins
- 180 children's dose multivitamins
- 100 pounds mixed dry beans, lentils, split peas, etc.
- 50 pounds unbleached white flour
- ½ gallon vinegar (mix of wine and cider)
- 1 bottle each ketchup, mustard, Tabasco and soy sauce
- 5 pounds sprouting seeds (mix of wheat, alfalfa, mung bean, broccoli, radish)
- 24 cans of pureed pumpkin or sweet potatoes
- 12 cans of canned chicken, salmon or spam
- 5 pounds textured vegetable protein (tvp)
- 3-month supply tea, coffee, cocoa or vitamin C-rich fruit drink

Now that looks like a lot, until you break it down a bit. And I'm sure some of you are wondering where on earth you'd put it all. So one of the first steps when you decide you want to start storing food is to begin looking for space. It doesn't have to be space in the kitchen, though. All this food, properly stored, isn't going to attract pests or be a problem. It can go under a bed, in the back of a closet, in unused space on top of cabinets — anywhere reasonably cool and dry.

So let's imagine that the first week you cut back a little on your grocery budget — maybe give up the soda or the juice in favor of tea or water, and eat one less meal with meat. That should give you enough money to pick up five pounds of wheat flour, a package of yeast, two one-pound bags of lentils and a bottle of soy sauce. Look how much you've accomplished in just one week.

That's how it goes, week to week. Instead of trying to do everything at once, you do a little bit, spending $10 or $20 or whatever you can afford. So even people who don't go to farmers' markets and don't want to preserve any of their own food can get started.

What can you make with this food? Well, let's start with breakfast. From just this stuff (and this assumes you've got nothing else), you could make oatmeal with brown sugar, cinnamon and raisins, pumpkin biscuits or muffins, toast with peanut butter, pancakes with brown sugar syrup, vanilla rice pudding with dried fruit or cinnamon-raisin bread. For lunch you could have lentil soup with oatmeal-honey bread, tuna fish sandwiches with broccoli sprouts, pasta salad, jambalaya, hummus and pita bread or black bean-filled tortillas. For dinner there might be baked chicken and rice, tomato soup with cornbread squares, tuna noodle casserole, enchiladas, or pasta with spaghetti sauce.

It is a fairly basic menu, but it will keep everyone full, doesn't require anyone to eat a lot of unfamiliar foods and it will taste pretty good. It does have some limitations — it is very starchy and there are a lot of white grains. After a while the menu will get a little boring. And because the cornmeal, brown rice and wheat flour don't last long, the person storing them has to make sure he uses them up within six to twelve months, or he may lose some of his investment. And because it was all purchased from a supermarket, the money all goes to industrial food producers. And of course, there aren't a lot of fresh foods. Still, you'll live, and you'll eat.

But we can do better than this, better in a host of ways. First of all, we can get some of the food cheaper. Second, we can shift our dollars to the people we want to support. Third, we can get a more diverse menu and eat a healthier diet. So let's take another stab at a three-month supply of food for the same number of people. This time, however, let's focus on buying direct from farmers, on storing some fresh, local foods and on trying for a bit more balance.

Now this does require that you invest in a grain mill, because grains store best and taste best when they are freshly ground. This is a fairly substantial investment, and you can still buy directly from farmers without having one. But you can keep the food longer if you buy whole grains, and you'll be absolutely floored by how delicious fresh grains taste. If you can spend $150–$400 on a grain mill, you won't regret it. If you can't, OK, just buy and store the flours, and remember to eat up any ground whole grains or brown rice within a year.

So let's see what we can do now. What you might have will vary some by location; these are things I could get near me or by ordering directly from farmers. There are resources available at the back of this book and through my website, sharonastyk.com.

- 10 pounds of black beans
- 10 gallons of local honey
- 5 gallons of local maple syrup
- 50 pounds of Jacob's Cattle beans
- 100 pounds of whole wheat (ordered from a small farmer in Montana)
- 50 pounds rolled oats (ordered from a mill in Montreal)
- 50 pounds of whole dry corn (bought from a local farmer)
- 25 pounds of popcorn rice (from a farm in Louisiana)
- 50 pounds of potatoes (bought in a sack from a local farmer and kept in a cool place)
- 25 pounds of sweet potatoes (bought locally)
- 50 pounds of onions
- 20 pounds of sugar

- 25 pounds of popcorn (from a local farmer)
- 25 pounds of brown lentils (ordered from a farmer in California)
- 20 pounds of whole peanuts (for snacks and making my own peanut butter — many grain grinders can do this — ordered from North Carolina)
- 20 pounds of organic soybeans (ordered from Iowa)
- ⅛ pound of watercress and arugula seed
- 5 pounds of mixed sprouting seeds (broccoli, radish, lentil, onion, wheat, alfalfa)
- 5 gallons of good California olive oil
- 2 pounds of local dried cranberries and apples

The other items would remain mostly the same in this basic scenario. Remember, we're assuming that you haven't done any home preserving or sourcing of preserved foods from local farmers. This is just what you can store in its whole form.

Already the food is a lot healthier and a lot more appetizing. Taking out the white rice and white flour doubles the protein value of the grains. Now you can make an apple-cranberry pie, potato-fish cakes, a shepherd's pie, or a salad of sprouts, watercress and dried cranberries. You can make sweet potato pie and onion soup, the pancakes can have warm maple syrup on them and the kids can eat oatmeal cookies and popcorn. Plus, and perhaps most importantly, more than half the cost of your stores went either to local farmers or small farmers who sell grains and food directly to consumers. That is, the dollars improve local food systems, either in your area or someone else's. They didn't go mostly to corporate middlemen. You may have gone through a local co-op or followed the suppliers list on my website, but every dollar you kept out of the hands of agribusiness is a victory.

But even this has its limitations. And this is where the whole project of food preservation gets mixed in with food storage. Maybe you want some red meat in this diet and some jam, or maybe your family doesn't eat sweets. The question, then, becomes how do you adapt the diet to suit your tastes? And the answer to that is both simple and complicated. You start thinking about what you actually eat and how you might turn your favorite foods into pantry foods. And then, when you start looking around to find local sources — sometimes really local — you'll find options you never knew you had. If you add in home preservation, well, that's how you get exactly what you want.

It is also, in many cases, how you save a lot of money. Maybe you live somewhere where everyone has a citrus tree in their backyard. The lemonade you can, the marmalade you make, the preserved lemons you use to flavor your salad dressing — this is all free food. Or perhaps you hunt. If you can your venison, you've got the makings of a lovely stew with just what's in the pantry. Come autumn the rosehips and wild mint are there for the taking at the back of the park where no one sprays — and you have a winter's tea.

Even if you have to pay, you can still get some wonderful deals. The overripe peaches are perfect for fruit leather, the bruised apples make great apple juice, the stuff the farmer doesn't want to haul home from the market often come far more cheaply than they could ever be bought the rest of the time. When apples are ripe in our region, we can get them for 40 cents a pound — the rest of the winter the best price for non-organics is over a dollar a pound.

Your three-month supply of food probably won't look just like anyone else's. And it does take time and practice to learn what you can do with pantry staples. I'll talk more in the next chapter about what it means to eat from your pantry. It isn't as hard or as costly as it seems when you first consider the idea. We all go at it one step at a time, and each step gets us closer.

Now is three months enough? Personally, my recommendation is the same one that the Mormon church and a host of other groups make — that you store one year's worth of food for yourself, plus any family or friends you think might come live with you in tough times.

So why don't I start out with one-year quantities? Well, the truth is that for most of us, used to shopping every week, three months is scary enough. So we'll start with three months, and then we can do that again, and then again until we've got six months and nine months. Every journey starts with a single step.

Baby Steps

1. Make some space for food in your life. This can be as simple as taking the heart-shaped cake pans and bundt pans you use only three times a year and moving them to a back shelf, or it could involve getting rid of a bunch of stuff in a closet or building shelves into a basement area. You want it to be somewhere away from light, reasonably cool, ideally, not too moist and without critters in it. Stable temperature is more important than cooler temperatures. It is better that the place not swing between 20 and 90 degrees and that it be more like 65 degrees all year round. This applies to dry foods like beans, grains, spices and canned goods but not to root-cellared veggies, which we'll get to later in the book.

2. Inventory what you've got. Figure out what you already have in your pantry. I know, it is boring, but sit down and figure out how much food you have. You can then compare quantities roughly with the lists in the previous section.

3. Start eating from your pantry. Pick some recipes that rely primarily on storable ingredients and make them. Do you like them? Do they need jazzing up? Then do the jazzing. Then consider buying larger quantities of the components of this recipe. My family, for example, always has the ingredients for a Thai-style noodle dish we like: tofu (we make our own but you could buy shelf-stable), rice noodles, vegetarian oyster sauce, chili garlic paste, etc. The only thing we need to add are greens, and we usually have those either in the garden, in the root cellar (cabbage mostly), lactofermented, or as sprouts. Now try some more recipes. What do you like for breakfast? To drink? As a side dish? As you add pantry-compatible recipes, add some more of their ingredients to your stores.

4. Start to check out bulk resources. If you have a local co-op, buying club or bulk store, you can go through them. Don't forget local farmers. Even if you are part of a small household, consider dividing bulk purchases with others, since they minimize packaging and have a smaller environmental impact.

5. Begin experimenting with preservation techniques. Consider making a little apple butter out of those apples that are going mealy, or

lactofermenting some of your greens. And begin thinking about what foods, both home-grown and wild or gleaned, you can add to your stores. Remember, it isn't that big a project if you do just a little at a time. Now is also a good time to keep an eye out on freecycle and online for equipment like canning jars or dehydrators, or to start building projects.

That's really it — the baby steps! Not so bad, right?

Dry Goods: How to Sort Out What to Buy Locally and What Not to Worry About

First let's talk about the word "dry" here, because it is important. Globally, trucking and shipping are major contributors to climate change and heavy users of fossil fuels. And yet, the truth is that while some of us will be able to meet most or all of our needs in our local foodshed, others of us will not. We're going to have to get some of our staples from far away. So how do we make good choices in this regard?

Well, the first and most important way to do this is to restrict your long distance purchasing to dry foods — grains, beans, dry fruit, etc. Because when you ship fresh produce around the country, you are mostly shipping water. In many cases, we end up, as Joan Dye Gussow observes, shipping water from very dry places that grow food with irrigation to wet ones. This is both wasteful and, in the long term, reduces the ability of those dryer regions to continue to supply us. So it is especially important for us to get our fresh foods from near us. And while it is both important and useful for regions to start growing some of their staples, it is much more environmentally sound to buy bulk dry foods from far away than it is to buy bananas (not that most of us won't eat the occasional banana).

Now my first preference would *always* be that you get your staple foods from nearby local farmers. It is really important that we start producing local staple foods. So if you are seeking a staple food, the first place to look is in your immediate region. One good source is local harvest.com, and many more sources are listed on my website. Another good source is your local agricultural extension agent, who may know farmers that aren't online.

You might be surprised at what can be grown around you. I was surprised when I learned a farmer near me was growing barley, for example. There are a lot of small agricultural producers around and sometimes they are hiding.

But what if you can't get it locally? Well, expand your vision of "local" a bit. Cross a few borders. Maybe try a farmer in a nearby state. Check around. For example, I can get fairly local oats from Quebec, but not from any of the surrounding states.

If you have to get grains from far away, the least expensive way probably is to do it through your local co-op or bulk store. We have a co-op in Albany that we visit every couple of months, and a bulk store run by a friend about six miles from us. She can order things in bulk for me, because the trucks already come to her. The same is true of my local co-op.

But what if you don't have a co-op or bulk store? How about starting one? Co-ops are going to be desperately needed as a source of local food. On my blog I've suggested that everyone start stepping into the informal economy — a co-op is a good way to do this. Alternately, instead of doing it as co-op, you could do bulk buying as a for-profit home enterprise, like my friend does. For a long time, she did hers out of her home, although she eventually opened a store front. Delivery trucks and wholesalers will work with anyone who can order through them. If you repackage and sell smaller quantities, or get together with others and put together a bulk order, so much the better.

One category of items I don't worry much about are high value dry goods like spices, coffee, tea and chocolate. You see, while the raising of plantation coffee, for example, has plenty of ethical problems, generally speaking dry goods used in comparatively small quantities like this don't take a lot of shipping energy. And because they are expensive compared to beans and grains and certainly compared to "wet" foods like bananas and grapes, they are a good trade item for poor farmers all over the world. So buying your cinnamon or your tea, as long as you purchase it through a fair trade agency, is a really good way to help a poor farmer far away.

If none of these options is open to you, you'll need to do some research and start looking for direct sources to order from. I've listed many of these sources on my website, and an Internet search will help you find still more.

Storing vs. Hoarding: The Ethics of Food Storage

I get a lot of e-mails from nice, smart people who want to do the right thing. They want to protect themselves and their families, they want to store food for the benefit of their communities and their own peace of mind, but they are also worried that they might be doing something bad, something that the media calls "hoarding" if they buy a lot of food. So I thought it would be useful to discuss what hoarding is, and what the ethics of food and goods storage actually are.

First, a quiz!

Question 1: If James has a large group of Precious Moments figurines (those weird looking kids with big eyes in cutesy poses), including some that are very rare and scarce, and he has more figurines than anyone could possible use or appreciate (for me, that number would be one, but opinions on this subject vary), will people say James is hoarding Precious Moments figurines?

Question 2: If Laurie has more money than she needs to pay her expenses, and she takes this extra money, and puts it away where it earns interest and is available to her for future use, even though there are people in the world who could really use that money, will people say she is hoarding money?

Question 3: If Li goes to the grocery store only once every few months, purchases in bulk and in quantities he needs for a year, will people say he is hoarding food?

Question 4: If Gloria knows she is likely to lose her job soon, and takes her kids to the doctor, gets their teeth checked, and gets a three-month supply of her allergy medication while insurance will still pay for it, is she hoarding medical care?

Question 5: If Gloria knows she will lose her job soon and isn't confident about finding a new one, and goes to the thrift shop and buys clothes that are available in larger sizes for her oldest son and stores them, so that he'll have nice clothes for school even if they don't have money, will people say she is hoarding clothing?

Question 6: Laurie is also worried about affording clothes for her children. So she puts as much of her salary aside in a specific account marked for her daughter's clothing as possible. Will people say she is hoarding money for clothing?

Answers: 1. No, James is a collector. **2.** No, Laurie is saving. **3.** Probably many will. **4.** No, people will say she is exercising common sense. **5.** Probably, yes. **6.** No, Laurie is saving money.

I do this simply to point out the fact that we don't always look at having a lot of something, or storing for the future as a kind of hoarding. In fact, we can look at two different ways of dealing with precisely the same problem of not having enough money for clothes, and one is perceived as hoarding and the other isn't. We also tend to have a very visceral reaction to the idea that we would hold quantities of food or other basic staples — those, we're "supposed to" get through the just in time delivery system, and any other methodology is really strange to people. We tend to use the term "hoarding" for anything that seems strange to us.

Let's figure out what hoarding is, and what can be described with less emotionally laden language as "saving" or "storing." Hoarding is an attempt to disrupt an ethical, equitable and reasonably functional system of distribution by claiming widely needed scarce items in greater supply than you need. In order to have hoarding, you have to have two things. First, you need a system under which most people *can* get what they need, regardless of circumstances, and in the face of foreseeable consequences — that is, if the system is "just-in-time delivery to stores" most people have to be able to afford food, or subsidies have to be available, and food has to come into stores regularly. If any of those things falls apart, say, if the food stops coming in to stores regularly, the people who buy extra so they'll have something to eat when the food isn't there are not hoarding — they are using common sense and protecting themselves against hunger.

The other thing you need in order to hoard is scarcity of a necessity, or a conscious attempt to create scarcity. That is, you can buy up all the Beanie Babies you want, hoping that they will someday make you rich, but because Beanie Babies aren't necessary, this would be not hoarding. You can buy up all the dandelions you want, and transplant them all into your yard, and that's not hoarding either, because dandelions aren't scarce. You are only hoarding it you take something people really need, that is in short supply, and put it away, not for your own use, but either to manipulate markets or in excess of your ability to use it. For example, if you buy up 10 years of brown rice in a market that is short of rice in order to resell it at extremely high prices, that would be hoarding, unless, of course, you work for a major industrial food company.

The difficulty with the system I am expected to rely upon is that it won't work under a range of highly plausible situations. As noted above, the Centers for Disease Control in its avian flu preparations admits that in order to best avoid an epidemic, we need most people to have a three-month stockpile of food reserves, because otherwise the most effective means of controlling infection — avoiding contact with most people — can't be utilized at all. If we're all out grocery shopping because we've run out of food, no quarantine can be maintained. The just-in-time food delivery system also won't work in an extended depression, because in order to have food, you have to have money. The US government no longer has the substantial food reserves it once had set aside for distribution in an emergency. So if there are supply problems, we have no recourse but our own personal or community reserves.

Moreover, neither in the US nor the world is there an actual shortage of food. About twice as many calories per person worldwide as is actually needed was produced last year. The problems are distribution issues. Most US grains get used either in biofuels or in confinement livestock production, driving forces of the food price increases that have caused such misery worldwide. Undermining them by creating viable markets for whole grains for human consumption is a good thing.

Equally importantly, storing food is part of human culture. Just about every region on earth has a period of the year where less stuff grows than others. Every region on earth has experienced times of food shortfalls, or bad harvests. All through human history, our culture has grown up around the process of creating a reserve and a safety net to adapt to the fact that food systems are natural systems, not machines. Human food cultures grew up around food storage and stored foods are essential to those cultures — whether we're talking about Korean kimchi or southern American corn relish, the history of our storing has shaped our food culture. If we stop storing food, we are abandoning a large part of our heritage and our cuisines.

The truth is that we don't have an equitable system of distribution, we don't have a system that can withstand reasonably foreseeable shocks, and we don't have any intrinsic scarcity of food. The right response is to remove the subsidies for biofuels and to create a system in which cars can't compete with people for food. It is not to start feeling guilty that you need to be able to eat even if you lose your job.

Does that mean there are no ethical grey areas or problems in storing food? Of course there are — this is human life, not a sitcom. If we are going to store, we are obliged, if we can afford to act on these issues, to store carefully, to not buy foods that others are experiencing real shortages of, to buy and store foods that are as basic as possible (for example, prioritizing whole grains over animal products that were industrially produced with grain suitable for humans), and most of all, to spend our dollars in ways that increase the equity, quality and accessibility of the food system. Just like everything else, storing food has to be done as ethically as possible. The rules vary depending on your resources — those who have the money to buy locally and sustainably every time should, those who don't should do what they can.

It isn't possible for me to live as I do without storing both food and non-food items. I came to this not because I worry about the end of the world, but because my family of six has lived for the last seven years on between $20,000 and $40,000 per year, with minimal debt, mostly the mortgage, and while accumulating a reserve of goods, and expanding our farm. The fact is, there is no way we could run the farm, keep our trips as infrequent as they are, and feel ourselves comfortably well-off on that income (which to be fair has hovered closer to $40,000 for the last few years, but was much, much, much less for a long time before that) without these strategies.

Now it is true that I'm also buying stuff because I believe that hard times are coming. I'm concerned not as much that there won't be food in the stores, but that my husband might lose his job and I might not be able to keep my kids fed. That is, I am both concerned with keeping my food budget low and having good food, and also with the long-term impact of our society's choices.

To me the most likely result of peak oil and climate change, not to mention the economic situation we're in, is always this — we become poor. Our lives start looking more and more (and they already are looking that way for many) like the lives of the world's poor. The economy, energy prices and climate change make it more likely that I'll walk by a store and think, "I don't have enough to afford food or clothing for my family."

But this is one of those "theory of anyway" things. It makes sense if the world as we know it ends, but it also makes sense if it doesn't. And no, you can't store your way out of everything — but you don't have to. As long as you use your stores and use them wisely, you don't have to have enough to last you forever. The truth is that if the present system stops working, a new system will arise. We had shoes and food before peak oil and climate change, and people will make and grow them afterwards. But there will be a transitional period where there might not be enough food for sale, and where no one may be making shoes or distributing them, or where you can't afford either. And while we may have to get used to living without some of these things, it doesn't hurt anyone to make that a gradual transition, not a rapid one.

Black Bean Dip

This is terrific spread on cornbread, with homemade chips, or with pita squares. Yum!

- 1 tsp salt
- 1 small red onion, diced
- 3 tbsp chopped pickled jalapenos or hot sauce to taste, or both
- 2 tbsp lemon juice or cider vinegar

- ¼ cup vegetable stock
- 1 tbsp chopped cilantro
- 2 cups of black beans, cooked to tender (or 2 cans of black beans, rinsed and drained)

Mash beans, salt, broth and lemon juice or vinegar with a potato masher or a fork, or run through a food processor or blender. Stir in jalapenos, onion and cilantro. Devour. Serves six as an appetizer.

Very Basic Wheat Bread

If you've never baked bread before, or never tried whole wheat bread before, this is your recipe. It is very simple, and you won't screw it up. If you think your family only likes white bread, consider getting a "light" or "white" whole wheat. We like Prairie Gold but King Arthur sells a White Whole Wheat Flour. This recipe makes two loaves.

- 6 cups whole wheat flour
- 2½ tsp salt
- 2¼ cups very warm water (should feel warmer than body temperature, but not too hot)

- 2 tbsp yeast
- ¼ cup honey
- ¼ cup olive or canola oil or cooled melted butter

Mix dry ingredients in a large bowl. Meanwhile, mix yeast, honey and warm water together and let stand for five minutes. Pour liquids over flour and mix with a wooden spoon. Add oil and stir until smooth and mixed. It should still be sticky. If it is dry feeling, add more water. If very liquidy or runny, add a bit more flour.

Turn the dough out on a lightly floured board and knead until it is smooth. Kneading means folding, pressing down, folding over again, pressing hard and working the dough. Kneading is the key to developing the dough's stretchy gluten, so the dough will expand with the yeast-created gas bubbles, producing a high, light loaf, so you want to do it for about 10 minutes, and keep rotating the dough around.

Shape the dough into a ball; place back in the mixing bowl. Wet a cloth with warm water and wring it out. Use this to cover the bowl to keep the dough from drying out but allowing it to breathe.

Set the dough in a warm place, away from drafts (if you have an oven with a pilot light or a cookstove warming oven, this will be perfect, but a warm spot on a sunny windowsill or near the radiator is good too). Let the dough rise for about an hour, until it has about doubled in size. A little more or less isn't too big a deal, and it may take longer than an hour if the place is cool.

Push down until the dough deflates (this is called punching down) and knead again for a minute or two. Let it rise one more time for about ½ hour in a warm spot, until it doubles again. When it does, divide the dough in half, make two balls and put each in a loaf pan. Preheat oven to 350° and allow the bread to rise a little longer, maybe 20 minutes. Then bake until the bread is golden and sounds hollow when you tap it. Cool it and remove it from the pan. Don't forget to eat a slice hot out of the oven!

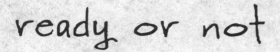

ready or not

When I was in college, I had no money. I don't mean the benign form of having no money common to college and graduate students, but a terrible and scary sort of poverty, gotten into mostly by accident and almost impossible to lever oneself out of. I remember the shame of going through the grocery line, realizing that I was a few cents short and having to put dinner back.

I mastered a host of skills for living cheaply, ate the ubiquitous ramen noodles, and most of all, I learned how to eat well while I ate cheaply. I have never had patience for bad food and fortunately have never been driven so far as to eat it. Instead, I decided that if I were going to eat cheaply, every one of my very limited pennies must be spent on good food. It wasn't worth buying cheap, sugary jam, and needing twice as much of it to get the taste of fruit.

I thought hard about what foods I really cared about, and learned to make them, or versions of them. I found that though I liked the taste of meat, it took only a small amount to lend richness and chewiness to stews and soups, and that miso paste and roasted onions made a stock nearly indistinguishable from good chicken soup. I learned the value of something sweet or salty or spicy as a condiment or complement to a meal of rice and beans or lentils — the difference, for example, that homemade pickles make. I learned that some of the best food was food I had to make myself. I could get overripe peaches and bruised apples at the market for nothing, but turning them into jam and sauce was my work.

Most of all, I learned that even though it was harder to build it, my pantry was my lifesaver. The 20-pound bag of rice, the sack of potatoes — they were cheaper per pound bought in bulk, and then,

75

when the month came that books had to be bought or expenses paid, there was rice in the kitchen and potatoes, pickles, and jam for bread. It wasn't perfect, but it was there, a measure of certainty and security at a time when my life was filled with worries.

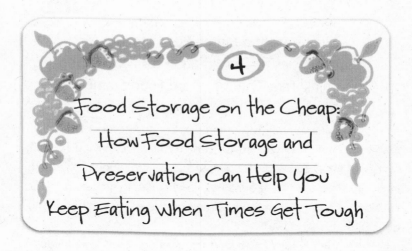

4
Food Storage on the Cheap: How Food Storage and Preservation Can Help You Keep Eating When Times Get Tough

If you can't feed a hundred people,
then just feed one.

— Mother Theresa —

THIS SECTION of *Independence Days* is designed for absolute beginners to food storage, who have felt they could not store food because they have no money. It was written by a friend of mine, a woman who has been extremely poor herself, and her strategies work. I think it is enormously valuable, because there are many people who will look at the lists in Chapter 3 and feel panic that they can't afford all that. That said, however, there are reasons to prefer other patterns of food storage if you have more choices, or are willing to devote time and energy to it — you can get tastier and more nutritious food, you can give your limited dollars to people in your community, rather than multi-million dollar industrial corporations. I include multiple possible plans for food storage because it is so important that everyone, even those who struggle financially, who do not want to invest time or energy, or who simply can't handle the larger project have some kind of reserve. However, that does not make all of these plans equally good. The assumption here is that this is a bare minimum, stay alive, "I just need food but don't have time to source it," reserve. It is extremely valuable — but it should be the solution not of first resort, but last.

Five Dollars a Month Food Storage for Emergencies and/or Inflation for People Who Think They Cannot Afford Food Storage

I have to imagine that many of you reading this think that you could no more go out and buy 100 pounds of this and 50 pounds of that than you could fly. When you live close to the edge, having enough money to take advantage of bulk purchasing is a tough problem. Buying more stores on top of our already-skyrocketing grocery bills is a struggle for a lot of people who aren't on the edge of things. So how do you do this?

Well, I don't want to deny that this is a huge challenge. If you don't have a lot of money, you need to think about this as a gradual process. Instead of a one- or two-shot "buy it all and go from there" approach, you'll add a little more each time you shop.

While people in other countries *may* think that their government will come to their assistance quickly in a natural disaster, and Americans *used to* think this, we know from the bitter experience of New Orleans that this is no longer true. More recently, three entire years after Katrina, we know that many, many people in Houston received very inadequate help after Hurricane Ike.

Americans have also seen terrible increases in food costs for the past year. Foods costs across the US vary a lot by area, but I estimate that in our area the prices for foods have risen by 30 percent to 40 percent in the last year. These figures are, of course, not reflected in the official government-issued statistics on inflation; the government removed both food and energy costs from their inflation statistics a while ago.

Can you scrape together $5 extra each week for at most three months? You might need the extra $5 for less time than this. This can be in food stamps instead of actual money. If you can, I can suggest a food storage plan for you. If you cannot, then I cannot help you with storing food.

If you can get more money together, you can accomplish this plan faster. But if you can only get that little bit extra together—and not permanently, only for a while—you can do this plan. You cannot do it instantly, but you can do it.

In what follows, I'm assuming that you live alone. If you live with other people, you'll need to increase quantities.

The first step is to set a goal, make a plan, write it down. Write down what you need to do each week to accomplish your goal. The initial goal I suggest is this:

Initial Goal

- To have on hand, at all times, enough water to keep you alive for one month.
- To have on hand, at all times, enough natural and nutritious food—no junk food—to keep you alive and functioning for one month *without needing to cook anything.* This food must not require refrigeration and it must keep for a fairly long time.

To me, this seems like a very reasonable initial goal. When you have accomplished it, you can stop and re-assess the situation. You may want to stop there. You may want to increase the variety of food that you store. You may want to get some means of cooking in a power failure (assuming that your kitchen stove is electric, which is the worst case).

You will probably cook some of the foods that I suggest in normal times. But you can safely eat these foods without any cooking at all, if necessary.

If you need to evacuate the area and you have a car, or a friend or relative with a car, you can take some of this water and all of this food with you.

If you need to evacuate the area and you must get out by public transport, then you can only take what you can carry. Some things cannot be helped so there's no point in worrying about them. I try hard to be prepared for what I can be prepared for, and to let the rest go without fretting about it. I pretty much succeed at this now.

OK, so how are you going to accomplish this initial goal?

First, you must learn and follow the Basic Rule of Food Storage: use what you store, and store what you use. This means that you must *only* store what you will actually eat. You will *regularly eat all the items you store.*

People with more money can afford to buy other foods for storage. But people with very little money, like you and like me too, cannot afford that. We must *use what we store and store what we use.*

I am also assuming that you can only get to a regular, normal supermarket. So I'm going to suggest a plan that can be accomplished completely, totally at a normal supermarket.

The Five Dollar Plan: Part One

Here's what I suggest for Part One of your Plan. Part One may take you a week; it shouldn't take more.

1. A hand-operated can opener. If you only have an electric can opener, then please buy a hand-operated can opener the first week. It can be a cheap one. You can buy these in normal supermarkets, although perhaps a Dollar Store will have one cheaper.

2. If you have a gas stove, make sure that you have matches. We have a gas stove with electric ignition. But when the power is off, we can light the top burners (only) with a match. So far as I know, you can light the top burners of *all* gas stoves with a match. So buy a box of matches if you don't already have some.

3. Do you have a bottle of multi-vitamins on hand? If not, please buy a bottle of multi-vitamins. They don't need to be expensive ones, the cheapest ones available will do. Please get enough for at least 30 days, that's important.

4. Store enough water for a month. Water should definitely come before food: people can go without food an awful lot longer than they can go without water.

So far as I know, everyone who has running water in the USA and Canada can safely drink the water that comes out of their taps. You cannot afford to buy water. So you will store the water right as it comes from the tap. Enough water to keep you alive for a month is a minimum of one gallon per day. You're not going to drink a whole gallon of water any day, but you are going to wash your hands at least once per day and you can splash some water on your face (then catch it in a dishpan or pot and use it to wash your hands).

So you'll need 30 gallons for one person for one month. What can you keep it in?

You may already have this much water: if you have a hot water heater in your home or apartment, see if you can figure out how to drain it. You might need to slide a dishpan under the drain place, but you can probably do this. If you cannot figure it out, ask someone who knows how if you possibly can. I want you to know how to do it if you need to.

Large, empty, clean soda bottles with tops are great for storing water. Ask everyone you know if they can please give you their empty bottles. Empty clean juice bottles are equally good. Empty clean whiskey or wine bottles are also fine—again, ask everyone you know. (Some cheap wine comes in gallon or half-gallon glass jugs—these are perfect.) Milk jugs will become brittle and break eventually, but they should be OK for a month. Meanwhile you can work on getting better containers. Wash milk jugs very carefully and rinse, rinse, rinse. Then fill with water and keep them out of the sun.

You don't need to treat water in any way if you replace one third of it every month. Just count how many bottles of water you have stored, and dump out, rinse, and refill one third of them each month on the first of the month. Then none of the water will be more than three months old.

Where to put the water? Let's just say this: if you really want to do this, you'll find a place to put the water. You can store water under beds, in your freezer (if you have space, it will help your freezer run better), anywhere you have space. Remember, everything doesn't have to be in one place.

I will also make one more suggestion about water. For some natural disasters, people have considerable warning. Hurricanes do not sneak up on people; ice storms or blizzards generally don't either. We have warning.

I have always seen advice to fill your bathtub with water if you think the power may go off. It seems to me that this is terribly bad advice. I have always tested the bathtub in every one of the many, many places where I have lived and every single one of them has a slow leak through the drain. No bathtub that I ever lived with would store water overnight. In the morning, it's all gone.

What you can do is put any kind of large container(s) in your bathtub and then fill the container(s) with water. I'm thinking here specifically of the very common 18-gallon Rubbermaid or similar totes used for storage. Many people have these around. But *any* large container will do for this purpose. That way, if the container should spring a leak, OK, it's in the tub anyhow, no problem. If the container does not spring a leak, you'll have more water.

You can flush the toilet with this water or drink it (in an emergency only, since these are not food-safe containers) or wash with it, whatever. If you have warning, you can also fill any large pots and pans you have with water, and any five-gallon or cat litter buckets you have too.

Congratulations on a job well done! You've accomplished Part One. Now we'll move right along to Part Two.

The Five Dollar Plan: Part Two

Now we need to think about food. The initial food goal I suggest is this:

- To have on hand, at all times, enough natural and nutritious food—not junk food—to keep you alive for one month *without needing to cook anything.* This food must not require refrigeration and it must keep a long time.

How do you accomplish this initial goal and spend the minimum necessary amount?

Here is what I suggest. The quantities given are for one month for one person. If you have more than one person in your household, you will need to increase the quantities.

I have to caution you: you are going to be eating these foods *regularly* and *anyway.* If you are allergic to any of the foods I suggest or cannot eat them for some other reason, or you just cannot stand them, you need to find a substitute.

The first food that I suggest you buy is rolled oats: you can buy regular rolled oats or quick-cooking rolled oats in every supermarket that I have ever seen in the USA or Canada. (I hope you can eat oats; it is difficult to find a substitute because you can eat oats uncooked and that is not true of most grains. I know of two possible substitutes, but they cost considerably more—more on that later.)

Please don't buy instant oats which are generally jammed full of sugar and artificial flavor and are a rip-off. Regular or quick-cooking rolled oats are a very valuable food. You may call these "oatmeal" or (as in the UK) "porridge" or "porridge oats." They're the same thing.

You can eat these oats in one of three ways. Two of them do not require any cooking because oats are actually partially cooked before you buy them, as part of their processing. I eat them uncooked, regularly, in homemade muesli.

1. Cooked. Then you have hot oatmeal for some of your breakfasts. This is a very valuable and nutritious food. Add raisins or other fruit and, if you wish, serve with milk. My father didn't put milk on hot cereal (including oatmeal), he dotted it with butter or margarine, then sprinkled a little cinnamon and brown sugar on it. Hot oatmeal is nice that way too. You can cook oatmeal either on the stove top or in the microwave. If you cook it in the microwave, it wants to puff up and get all over the place. Use a *very* oversized glass cup or casserole dish to prevent this.

2. Uncooked, mixed with fruit and yogurt. This is called muesli. I eat it for breakfast most days—just the uncooked oats, fruit, plus yogurt. Add raisins and sunflower seeds if you wish. You can soften the oats by mixing them with yogurt or fruit juice ahead of time, or you can eat them right away.

3. As a cold cereal. In this case, you put the oats in a bowl, add raisins if you have them, perhaps a sliced banana if you have bananas. Then you pour milk over them and eat them as a cold cereal. If you have no milk, you could use fruit juice. If you have no fruit juice, you could use water.

Four ounces of rolled oats provides 434 calories and 18 grams of protein.

You could eat—*if you had very little other food available because of some emergency*—eight ounces of oats daily. That would give you 868 calories and 36 grams of protein. This is a *very* substantial part of a woman or man's calorie and protein requirements, although it wouldn't be very exciting.

I'm going to recommend that you wind up with 15 pounds of rolled oats *per person* for storage for one month. I do recommend that you eat oats for breakfast two or three times per week in normal times. It's a very substantial and good-tasting breakfast.

How much will this 15 pounds of rolled oats cost? At a little general store near where I live I can buy them for 71 cents a pound. Let's assume you pay as much as $1.00 per pound. The 15 pounds of oats will cost you about $15.

Once you have managed to save the 15 pounds, then you just keep replacing it; never let it go much lower than this. Or you can decide to buy more and keep 20 pounds on hand, if you prefer. Or 30 pounds or even 50 pounds.

Note that you are now buying the oats *as part of your normal breakfast regime.* So you don't need to set aside separate "food storage money" for oats anymore; you can use your normal food budget for this. This gives you more money for other food storage.

If you cannot eat oats for some reason, the only two substitutes that I can think of *that don't require cooking, do not require refrigeration, keep a long time and are very nutritious* are sunflower seeds and Scandinavian-style crispbread, such as Kavli and Wasa Brod, which are available even in supermarkets in low-income neighborhoods. The crisp breads are mainly whole grains, so they are nutritious. I don't know if sunflower seeds are available in every supermarket or not. If they are, you want to buy unroasted, unsalted sunflower seeds if at all possible. They won't keep as long as oats or crispbread, however.

Now what other foods do I recommend you start buying for the bare-bones, minimal, cheapest possible useful food storage?

I recommend that you also buy canned beans. Not baked beans, just plain canned beans. There are many kinds, they all have approximately the same food values, and they all cost about the same. If you live alone I suggest you buy 16-ounce cans. There are black beans, kidney beans, white beans, pinto beans, many, many varieties. You can buy one kind of beans only, or several. Beans are good food, and they are a very versatile food. They are also good for your health.

In normal times you can base many, many dinners on beans—tacos, chili, soups, frijoles refritos, salads, beans and rice, etc. You'll probably want to cook most of the beans, though you can use them in salads and cold plates too. But you don't *need* to cook them. I recommend that canned beans be rinsed very well with cold water before eating (in normal, non-emergency times) if you are concerned about sodium. Even if you aren't concerned about sodium, I think they taste better if you rinse them first.

You can find thousands of bean recipes on the Internet. Recipe Source.com is one of my favorite recipe sites; just put "beans" in the search box and you will be presented with 2008 recipes using beans! That's a lot of bean recipes.

I'm looking at a can of black beans; they are probably my favorite kind. The beans have 315 calories and 24.5 grams of protein. If you ate the whole can of beans, which I only recommend in case of emergency, plus 8 ounces of oatmeal, this would give you 1,183 calories. Together with two other foods I will recommend in a minute, this would be enough to keep going for quite a while in an emergency—indefinitely, in fact—unless you are already emaciated before the emergency. It would also give you 42 grams of protein. This is not the Recommended Daily Allowance (RDA) for protein, but it would certainly keep you going for well over a month. You wouldn't develop malnourishment in a month's time if you were eating this much protein each day together with the calories you would have. Many people throughout the world live their entire lives with lower daily protein figures.

What does a can of beans cost? We can get them (or we could, until very recently) for about fifty cents a can on sale. But let's even say that you need to pay a dollar a can. I don't think you will, but I don't know what food costs in other places.

If you plan to store 30 cans of beans (per person), then you would need to spend $30. *But* you can also start eating these beans regularly, as part of your normal food. I would recommend that. Then if you know that you have eaten two cans of beans in a week, and you are still increasing your supply of beans, you buy four or six cans—simple. When you get up to 30 cans of beans, then reassess your situation. You can maintain that inventory, or buy more beans. It's up to you.

Let's assume that you want to accumulate the 15 pounds of oats and the 30 cans of beans before you start eating them. You have now spent $45. If you can only spend $5 per week for food storage, this will have taken you nine weeks. If you can spend more, you can do it faster. But it's really not fair to consider all these costs as food storage costs; after all, you are going to put these foods into your regular diet. Some of this money can come out of your regular food budget.

Now what other food do I recommend you buy as part of your basic, bare-bones food storage?

I recommend that you buy cans of tomatoes too; they are very useful when cooking beans. You can buy stewed tomatoes, diced tomatoes or whole tomatoes—they are equally useful. Perhaps the diced tomatoes are a little more useful. You can eat them without cooking them. These will provide you some vitamins and some more calories (but not many). They will also make the beans much more palatable.

So for a month's storage for one person, I suggest you buy—as quickly as your money will allow—30 16-ounce cans of tomatoes. I recommend that you use them as part of your regular diet also. When you have 30 cans of tomatoes, you can either maintain that level, or increase it. Treat the tomatoes just as you are treating the beans: always replenish or increase your supply of them. Rotate them—eat the oldest cans first.

My last recommendation for a basic, bare-bones emergency food storage supply is to get cans or jars of fruit. Applesauce is very useful and nutritious, and most people like it. If you live alone, get the smaller jars. It will make the rolled oats more palatable. Many people normally eat applesauce; it can fit into your normal food regime nicely.

I also recommend that you get some other fruit in cans. Both my husband and I like canned pineapple packed in its own juice, so we keep a supply of that on hand. If you prefer peaches, then get peaches, or some of each, or some other fruit altogether.

I'd recommend building up to 30 cans or jars of fruit, just as you did with the beans and tomatoes. Treat the fruit just as you treat the rolled oats, beans, and tomatoes—replenish whatever you use.

At the end of this plan, you'll have the following on hand:
- 15 pounds of rolled oats
- 30 cans of beans
- 30 cans of tomatoes
- 30 cans or jars of fruit

Your supply of these will not diminish: you will always replenish them. Since all of these are now being eaten as part of your normal food regime, all the money to replace them should now come out of your normal food budget.

None of these foods is expensive. And you would have enough to live on for one entire month.

Now that you have one month's food supply safely on hand, congratulate yourself on a job well done! Then think about what you want to do next.

The foods I personally would add next would probably be raisins, some cooking oil and dry skim milk. All would add interest to the rolled oats. And you can use all of them in your normal food regime.

The next thing I would probably want to buy is a guaranteed method of cooking food: Sterno cans would do (don't forget that you need matches to light them). You can probably buy them in a regular supermarket or hardware store. You can build a little holder for it from bricks. Then you put your pot on the bricks, and the Sterno under the pot.

After that, I would probably want a few herbs and spices—maybe oregano, cumin and chili powder for the beans, and cinnamon for the oats. Some brown sugar would be nice on the oats as well. Maybe you already have these in your kitchen.

I cannot think of any food storage plan that would be cheaper, and yet have the following features:

1. The food is all nutritious.
2. It all keeps a long time without refrigeration.
3. You can eat it uncooked if necessary.
4. It all fits into a normal diet.

If you do this, I absolutely guarantee that you'll be glad, and that it will give you a very good feeling of security.

I hope you will never have an emergency, but even if you don't, you will always feel more secure with at least one month's food on hand. This is definitely worth the little bit of work and expense it requires.

More Ways to Build
Up Stores Inexpensively

The people who most need a food reserve are the people who struggle the most to get it. As food and energy costs inflate and the safety net for the poor begins to be strained, the lower your income, the more necessary it is that you have some reserve to tide you over in hard times. It's all the more urgent that you take advantage of economies of scale to buy food at lower prices. But that's incredibly tough if hard times are already here, as they are for so many of us.

And often, the people who have the least ability to take advantage of food storage and preservation are the ones who need them the most. Millions of really poor Americans are homeless, or effectively so, living in subsidized motels or other housing that have no cooking facilities. Millions of American working families combine two, three or four jobs and leave the cooking to younger children — or simply have no time to cook or shop at all. Millions of Americans have budgets that already don't reach the end of the month, and can no more put together an extra $50 to buy beans and rice in bulk or pay for a CSA share up front than they can fly to the moon. And these are precisely the people most likely to lose their job, have their kids go hungry and find that their barely-making-it budget is a no-longer-making it budget.

Now much of the time when I'm speaking of food, I advocate ethical practices. Because most of my readers — not all by any means — have some ability to pick and choose their foods, either because they are middle class or because they have carefully and consciously managed to make good food their priority. I want to be clear. For those with enough money, ethically produced food is of the first importance. The dollars we spend now are investments in future food systems, and these are the systems we will need to feed us in difficult times. We can't afford to throw that money away on systems that won't be there, if there's another choice.

But for those without a range of choices, just having some food stored is essential. At present, the safety nets are fraying. The food pantries are struggling, food stamps and other social welfare programs are heavily burdened, and a food stamp budget no longer enables people to make it to the end of the month. Those programs are likely to struggle further as energy and food prices rise. And because there are no large government stockpiles remaining, because costs are rising so rapidly and because jobs are so unstable, it is essential that lower income families have a reserve of food, no matter how they have to buy it.

So here are some suggestions on how to build food storage cheaply.

1. Emphasize foods that haven't had huge price rises — for example, potatoes, peanuts and peanut butter, and oats all have gone up, but not nearly as much as corn, wheat and soy. Consider a storage program that emphasizes these lower cost foods, but make sure you are focusing on items with high nutritional value. Low cost foods with high nutritional value include beans, peas, lentils, brown rice, whole grain flours, most root vegetables like carrots, beets and sweet potatoes, cabbage, kale and collards, rolled or steel cut oats and other whole foods.

   The more you can adapt your diet, the better off you will be. So do some research on what foods are reasonably priced and find recipes and practice with them if you can.

2. If you have minimal or no cooking facilities, or if the household cooking is being done by children, you need foods that can be heated up easily, using Sterno or hot plates. The best really cheap

ways to get a lot of instant and pre-processed foods are to dump-ster dive and frequent odd lots stores. Because stores discard cans with damaged labels, or anything dinged or damaged, processed foods are often discarded when they are still safe to eat. (Do not eat anything from a can that appears to be leaking or has odd bulges on it). Do this carefully. Wear gloves if possible and watch out for sharp objects. I will note that dumpster diving is on the rise, and you may find more competition than in the past. The other advan-tage of dumpster diving is that it may cut your food budget enough to allow you to make additional bulk purchases, even if you don't need pre-processed food. And don't forget drugstores for slightly-past-expiration vitamins to supplement your diet.

Odd lots stores buy stuff up that other stores can't sell. You get weird brands, sometimes cans with no labels, but often quite good prices. And sometimes you get good stuff cheap. The one near my mother offers tons of gluten-free foods from Bob's Red Mill at very low prices — tough things to find for low-income people who need special diets. It's not as cheap as dumpster diving, but I've seen canned goods listed at ten for a dollar there.

3. Minimize waste. Create a "soup jar" and make soup out of leftovers. Do a daily check of your fridge — what needs eating? Don't think that just because it isn't a meal's worth, you can't eat it. Fruits and vegetables are especially expensive on a low budget, so make full use of them. Peel and eat the broccoli stems, grate the orange zest and dry it for flavoring baked goods if you can. Make fried rice out of bits of leftovers and cold grains (you can make fried rice equiva-lents out of barley, bulgur, etc.).

4. Some food pantries have trouble getting rid of bulk foods like wheat berries, dried beans, etc. They receive these items, but com-paratively few people know how to use them. Ask if they ever have extras of these to give away, and explain that you are trying to build a food reserve. The worst anyone can say is no.

5. Give and ask for the gift of food. If someone wants to buy you a present, consider asking for a gift certificate to Wal-Mart or Sam's Club or Amazon or some other place that sells food and other

goods. That way you don't have to admit that you need the food badly, but you can use the certificate for what you need most.

6. Don't expect to do it all at once. All of us need to scale up gradually, unless we're Bill Gates. If your budget is tight and you are new to food storage, it will take time to build a reserve. An extra can here, a few pounds of beans there — it doesn't seem like much. Remember that it is. Small things add up. If you can find $10 in your budget to cut out of something — get rid of an appliance, turn down the power — it will count and it will build up. I know you may have already cut all the fat you've got to cut and it may be a struggle to find a little more. But this is worth it. This is a measure of hope and security for your family.

7. If you can cook at all, beans, rice, lentils and cabbage are probably your best friends in the world. They are cheap, bulky, nutritious and can be made to taste good. It is hard to get used to a limited diet of these foods; it is also worth noting that a limited diet is a norm in most of the world. It is not at all unusual for most people worldwide to eat beans and rice twice a day, or bread and lentils the same. Americans put enormous emphasis on diversity in their diet and our nutritional information convinces us that we must eat a wide range of foods each day. But all you need is a reasonable quantity of several fruits and vegetables and nutritious staple foods.

The cheapest places to buy these are from co-ops, buying clubs and warehouse stores, although you should check that the warehouse membership will pay for itself. Or maybe go along with a friend who has a membership or take advantage of free one-month trials. Buying in bulk can be tough, but if you can find the money anywhere, you'll pay so much less than you will at the store. Remember, if you can't afford many vegetables, most grains can be sprouted, and offer the benefits of fruits and vegetables this way.

If you are buying in bulk, you can use the $5 a week strategy as well. The same reasoning applies. Putting a little aside each week works fine, but you'll need the self-discipline to "hold over" your money for a few weeks or a month while you save the money to buy what you want. Bulk foods are often less expensive than you think. My local farmer sells 50 pounds of potatoes for $12 — an economy of scale you simply can't get buying them by the pound at $1.89 a pound. One mail order source I found, for example offers 50 pounds of 16-bean mix for just under $50, while my grocer sells a pound of kidney beans for $2.50. You'll save a great deal in the long term this way.

8. What else can you do if you don't have money? Well, growing your own is often a bargain. If you haven't got land, try a community garden or even asking if you can rent a vacant lot for a small (and I mean small) fee or if you can grow on a neighbor's lawn and split the produce with them. If you can't afford seeds, your county extension office can probably put you in touch with other gardeners who might be willing to share.

You can try gleaning. Gleaning is an ancient tradition in which people follow the harvest, picking the food left by harvesting equipment in the fields. You might be picking windfall apples or extra potatoes, harvesting citrus or olives from trees on a campus or a range of products from a CSA. If your local area has a gleaning program, you can often get food for yourself and food to donate by simply working farmers' fields after the commercial harvest. If there isn't such a program near you, you might consider starting one.

There is often a great deal of free food out there for the harvesting. Fruit trees have fruit that is allowed to fall, wild edibles go unharvested, even garden plots get started and then never fully harvested. If you are willing to do the work, sometimes there is a lot of food to be had. You also can forage for other foods — wild plants of all kinds are nutritious and delicious. You definitely need good books. Two of my favorites are Steve Brill's (who teaches foraging in Central Park — you don't have to be a country mouse to forage!) *Identifying and Harvesting Edible and Medicinal Plants in Wild (and Not So Wild) Places* and Samuel Thayer's *The Forager's Harvest*. Both are excellent books, and with a field guide to edible and poisonous plants and some practice, should help a lot.

9. If you visit your farmer's market at the end of the day, there are bound to be things the farmers don't want to take home. This is what you should can or root cellar or otherwise store. You'd be surprised at how much you can get, particularly if you are willing to do the work of cutting the bird peck out of the tomato or the earworms out of the corn. You can get some organic meats if you are willing to eat hard-to-sell parts of an animal. Make soup stock out of chicken bones or feet (sounds strange, but they actually make fabulous stock) or eat liver or organ meat. If you learn to can and preserve these, you'll have nutritious sources of protein for little money.

10. If there are places in your budget left to cut — cable TV, meals out, other luxuries — then perhaps it is time to cut them and put that money towards your food reserve. I don't claim that this is easy, but the closer to the edge you live, the more important it is that you have some kind of cushion because as food prices go up, your vulnerability rises too.

Getting the Tools for Storing and Preserving on the Cheap

Several people have told me recently that they are frustrated there are so many things to buy when you are preserving food. They are experiencing what many of us probably will sooner or later — they have no money. So while some people are using what they have while they have it to get good equipment, others cannot afford to, and it is hard for them.

So let's go over the lowest cost ways to store food, and the best strategies for getting equipment cheaply.

The cheapest technique is definitely root cellaring, and the cooler you keep your house (a characteristic of low-income folks) the more things you can keep just sitting around on a counter, or at worst in a cooler on the porch..

Squash and pumpkins like cool house temperatures, and garlic and onions do pretty well at those temperatures too. Most other storable crops, including roots and apples, require colder temperatures. If it's naturally cold where you live, you can probably put together a root cellar on the cheap. See Chapter 8 for more advice.

The next cheapest method is lactofermentation. All you need is salt, water and vegetables. This is a great way to use wild greens that you harvest from your yard or a public park (just make sure they don't spray). Dandelion, plantain, lambs quarters can all be fermented and flavored with a few pennies' worth of hot pepper or caraway or other spices. If you want to keep them a long time but don't have a cold cellar or a fridge, bury them in the ground.

If you have a garden, season extension probably comes in next in terms of cheapness. South of the Mason-Dixon line or in the Pacific Northwest, you can probably overwinter most of your greens and roots with just mulch and the right crops. In more extreme climates you might need to scavenge some old windows to put on top of a few bales of hay or straw over your crops (for this you can get the ones that were rained on in the field, or ones that have started to rot, or last year's dusty ones — you might be able to get them free). Plastic sheeting will work too.

Root crops can often be heavily mulched and survive — parsnips, carrots and leeks, for example, will survive the winter in upstate New York. In Alaska, that might not be an option, while in North Carolina you can probably keep lettuce going all winter without a cover.

The next cheapest option is dehydration. If you live in a dry climate, you can lay things out on a hot day in the sun, or hang apple rings and green beans under the eaves of your attic. If you live in a humid climate and have a car or can get your hands on a junker, try drying food in the car. If you heat with wood, hanging things behind or near the wood stove will work. If you have a pilot light oven you should be able to dry in that. Dehydrators are commonly for sale cheap, but it might take a while to find one at your price. Consider posting a request on Craigslist.

Preservation in salt requires an awful lot of salt. This is not yet expensive, but can't usually be scavenged and does require an initial purchase. The major issue is that comparatively few foods are tasty and healthy this way.

Preservation in alcohol is kind of pricey, unless you can make your own wine and preserve fruit or cheese in it. Most of the equipment for winemaking can be scavenged.

Canning can be cheap or expensive. If you can find free or very cheap canning jars (and they are common where I am), already have a big pot (for water bath canning) and something to put on the bottom of it (cake rack, canning jar rings laid flat, anything that makes a rack that will elevate the jars), the only cost is the heating energy and the jar lid. Pressure canning requires a pressure canner that is reliable and in good condition —poisoning your family with improperly canned food is never a good option. Make sure you have the correct equipment.

Freezing is the most expensive method, and one we won't talk about much here, because I think for most of us the rising price of electricity will make it inefficient. On the other hand, this gets me into one thing that I do want to talk about — sharing. While I think that for many people, a large home freezer may not be financially doable, there are a lot of those freezers out there, and people could reasonably rent or barter space in them and share them.

Which brings me to the second point — what's the best strategy if you can't afford a piece of equipment? Find someone to share it with. Maybe get to know a local home canner and ask if you can borrow their pressure canner in exchange for cutting some wood or watching their daughter. Talk to the guy with the dehydrator about whether you could trade something for a few hours of dehydration a year. Now this is tough stuff in our culture. We tend to be extremely autonomous. But it is time, and past time to start. If we don't learn to share, we're not going to get very far in a lower energy future.

I've written before that I don't think there should be any conflict between the people who can afford to buy stuff and those who can't. The odds are good that we're going to need each other — even if it is just someone willing to help cut out a few zillion strawberry hulls in exchange for a chance to use the dehydrator next. The person who owns enough food preservation equipment to feed India is going to have a labor shortage in many cases. The person who has no money often has some time they can share.

Someone I once knew referred to this as "building the village before the villagers are ready." The truth is that if you've got money, spending it on useful tools is a good thing. If you haven't, get knowledge, a little practice, and share what you can, because you are bringing something absolutely essential to your village — time, energy and ability. All of us are participating in this project of creating an independent and sustainable food culture. Whatever we come with, we're part of the community.

Recipes

There are a lot of recipes out there that call for pre-made ingredients. The problem with these is that they tend to be expensive for what you get. In the end, that bottle of pancake syrup is really just corn syrup and maple flavoring. The can of cream-of-whatever soup is really just a white sauce with a little bit of vegetable flavoring. Knowing how to make these is essential — and the homemade versions are tastier too.

Pancake Syrup

This is a modified version of the one offered at "The Hillbilly Housewife" — hillbillyhousewife.com — a great site that focuses on low-cost cooking. I've modified it to make it a little less sweet, since that's how we like it. This makes enough for several batches of pancakes.

- 2 cups warm water
- 1 tbsp maple syrup or 1½ tsp of maple flavoring
- 3 cups light brown sugar
- 3 tbsp molasses

In a large pot (because it foams up) combine the water, sugar and molasses. Put the pan on the stove over medium heat. Stir every now and then until the syrup comes to a rolling boil and starts to foam a little. When the syrup boils, cover the pot and turn down the heat and simmer it for ten minutes over a low flame. Do not stir. Remove the pan from the heat and let it cool until very warm but not hot. Stir in the maple flavoring or maple syrup. Let cool further and store in a clean quart jar.

Pumpkin Pancakes

These are extremely nutritious, really tasty, cheap and filling. My kids adore them, and so do the adults. The pumpkin and whole wheat flour mean that these are very good for you.

- 1 cup pumpkin, squash or sweet potato puree
- 3 tbsp honey or sugar
- 2½ cups whole wheat flour
- 1 egg plus 1 tbsp soy flour (or 2 eggs)
- 1 tsp salt
- 1 cup milk, buttermilk, soymilk or water

Mix together egg, orange vegetable puree, honey and liquid. Mix dry ingredients. Whisk together and fry in a pan with a little oil over medium heat. Eat with jam, applesauce, honey, maple syrup or pancake syrup.

Homemade Cream of Mushroom Soup Base

This is much tastier and less salty than the canned version. It can be diluted to make a good soup, but is even more perfect in the recipe below. It might be cheaper than store-bought or it might not be, depending on whether you've got broth on hand and whether you can get some mushrooms. You can substitute almost any vegetable for the mushrooms, making, say, cream of celery or cream of garlic. So use whatever is on hand.

- 4 tbsp butter or oil
- ¾ cup broth or wine
- 2 tbsp flour

- 1 cup sliced mushrooms (fresh or rehydrated dried, wild are good if you know what you are foraging), or chopped celery, chopped onion and garlic or any other vegetable you have on hand
- 1 cup sour cream (you can purchase sour cream starter online and make your own from your stored powdered milk or fresh milk, or you can buy sour cream powder if you want to include this in your food stores). Or, you can use yogurt, for a slightly tarter taste.

Sauté mushrooms or other vegetables in 2 tbsp oil until golden and softened. Remove from heat and reserve. Melt or heat remaining 2 tbsp butter or oil and whisk in flour. Cook for one minute over medium heat until the flour starts to change color. Whisk in sour cream and broth or wine, and add mushrooms. To make into soup, dilute with water or milk.

Creamy Greens Casserole

This is super cheap, absolutely delicious and really easy. Even people who hate greens will eat this happily and ask for the recipe. Serves 4.

- 3 lbs of greens—all one kind or a mix of anything you can find, including dandelions (just make sure they come from a place that hasn't be sprayed). The original recipe called for turnip greens, but really, almost anything is good this way.
- 1 ½ cups cream of mushroom (or other flavoring) soup mix, above.
- 2 eggs   • 1 small onion, diced
- 2 tbsp oil

Sauté the onion until golden in the oil. Add chopped, washed greens to the oil and cook until they are wilted and ¼ in volume. Lay greens in a baking dish, cover with onion bits. Mix mushroom soup and eggs, beat well, and pour over greens. Bake at 350° for 30 minutes, until golden. You can add breadcrumbs if you like as a topper.

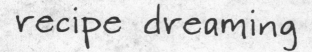

recipe dreaming

Is there anything more enticing than a cookbook? Ideally, they are lavishly illustrated with pictures of food that you want to devour right now, or perhaps full of words that draw pictures of delicious food in your mind. Even more ideally, they inspire us to go cook — they push us into the kitchen saying, "I want to make that."

The problem, of course, is that a lot of cookbooks, and the cooking and lifestyle shows that have supplemented them, show us a kind of food that is fundamentally alien to real home cooking. How many of us pan sear tuna in a wasabi-pecan crust on a regular basis? In fact, when you think of it, why on earth would anyone want cookbooks that emphasize that sort of recipe, assuming they are not professional chefs, and also assuming that they are normal, busy people who don't want to show off but to produce three meals a day at a cost that doesn't require a second mortgage?

Laurie Colwin, whose wonderful books carefully drew the distinction between home and restaurant cooking, spent a lot of time talking about what it was like to produce real food for real people. She wrote about what cookbooks are supposed to do for us:

> Cookbooks hit you where you live. You want comfort; you want security; you want food; and you want to not be hungry; and not only do you want these basic things fixed, you want it done in a really nice, gentle way that makes you feel loved. That's the big desire, and cookbooks say to the person reading them, "if you read me, you will be able to do this for yourself and for others. You will make everybody feel better."

Colwin gets what we're really looking for. And when we start cooking out of our pantries, rather than from the supermarket, we particularly need that kindness and that sense of support. After all, our culture teaches us that food comes from the fridge, and the average American doesn't cook much anyway. Even our collections of cookbooks are likely to trouble us. How do we get from where we are to where we need to be?

The answer, as always, is a step at a time. We add one pantry meal a week. We take a first stab at baking bread, making yogurt, canning venison, making ketchup. We experiment a little, and we laugh if the experiments go wrong. We find some cookbooks we can trust, some mentors to guide us gently into the new way of eating. We enlist our family members and share what we learn with our neighbors and with people far away engaged in the same projects. Most of all, we do it because we realize how important this is — that being able to keep everyone fed is the ultimate expression of our care for one another.

5

Eating From Food Storage—Every Day

You will never get out of pot or pan anything fundamentally better than what went into it. Cooking is not alchemy; there is no magic in the pot.

— Martha McCulloch-Williams —

THE QUOTE ABOVE encapsulates the reality of cooking—what you get out of it can never be greater than the sum of its parts. That's not to say it isn't possible to transform food, but the best food begins with good ingredients. The good news is that pantry eating means that you will have among the best ingredients—if you've never tasted freshly ground cornmeal, you will be stunned at the difference in your cornbread. If you have only ever eaten canned beans, with their high salt content and metallic taste, the reality of cooked heirloom beans will stun you. Home-ground, really fresh spices, home-preserved ingredients—what you get out of your pot will almost certainly be better than what any industrial production can put into it.

We've already talked about eating out of our food storage regularly, and the links between our food storage and preservation and a local diet. But saying "store what you eat and eat what you store" doesn't always tell us how to navigate a fundamental dietary shift from eating out of our fridge and the supermarket to relying on our own home-preserved and home-stored foods. How do we get, as they say where I'm from in Massachusetts, "from heah to theah?"

The first question that needs answering is perhaps the most complicated one. If I grow my own food and/or supplement with basic storable staples, what will I be eating? The answer is complicated by all sorts of factors, including regional adaptations, climate and your personal tastes and ethnic origins. A person who is already eating a grain- and legume-based diet and a lot of fresh leafy vegetables may have very little trouble, while a family that normally shops daily and emphasizes meats may have more trouble. So how do we come to terms with the idea of a staple diet, and integrate that into our goals of increasingly eating locally?

It is deeply important that we do so, because an abrupt dietary shift can lead to something called appetite fatigue. We tend to assume that when people get hungry enough, they will eat what is in front of them, and in normal circumstances, and for healthy adults, this is true. But during World War II the phenomenon of appetite fatigue was discovered—people confronted with a diet of unfamiliar or unpalatable food, particularly when under stress, simply stopped eating. In many cases, they simply lost interest in food. Now for healthy adults this is mostly self-regulating, but for the elderly, the medically fragile and children, this can result in a period of malnutrition and extended health problems. It can even contribute to premature death. So it is absolutely crucial that we get comfortable with eating from our pantries, have good and accessible ways to do this, and get our whole family adjusted to a pantry diet.

And, of course, if you are trying to eat what grows well in your climate and region, that may mean shifting your staple foods. There was a time when southerners mostly ate corn and beans, while prairie folk ate a lot of wheat, but modernity and industrial society have homogenized our diets. Few of us really live on a staple food diet based on what grows well and locally in our regions. But if we are trying to build local food systems and local food security, we may want to try shifting our focus towards the foods that grow well in our region, learning to eat more tortillas and less rice, or more potatoes and less corn. That doesn't mean we will all shift to a boring, repetitive diet, but that we will start developing truly local cuisines again.

You run up against a host of prejudices against eating this way, and very little cultural support. In our book *A Nation of Farmers,* Aaron Newton and I write about the fact that the diets common in the rich world *appear* to be very diverse, and that diversity and the idea of constant "choice" are something we emphasize a lot. Eating out of food storage and eating cheaply both seem to constrict our choices dramatically — so we may feel deprived. If we feel like we're eating beans and rice and rice and beans over and over again, we may be unhappy.

Now the truth is that as Michael Pollan showed so clearly in *The Omnivore's Dilemma* the classic American diet isn't diverse at all — it is almost all corn based. Corn is as central to our diet as it was to any Native population. The difference is that our corn is processed into corn syrup, confinement meat and a whole lot of other things that aren't good for us. We really haven't changed anything. We're eating corn three times a day, just like our ancestors, but we're eating the worst possible form of corn for us and the planet. It would not be a loss of diversity to go back to eating whole corn or some other staple grain more often — and it would be a gain for the planet.

But that doesn't change the fact that we're used to the idea of eating a "varied" diet, and eating a lot of staple foods doesn't necessarily line up with our mental image of what we or our families should be eating. In fact, it is pretty much precisely what we should be eating — we've seen this several times. There's the Western diet paradox, in which immigrants from cultures with staple-style diets made up of fresh fruits and vegetables, whole grains and legumes and small amounts of meat become less healthy and have shortened lifespans when they move to the US and start eating a typical American diet. The same point is made by research from World War II, which showed that the British got healthier during periods of restriction in which they were eating more grains and fewer meats, fats and sweets.

But the stigma of "poor people's food" of reduced "choice" (which often isn't any kind of meaningful choice) is huge, and we've got to overcome it. That means making the staple diet a badge of honor, talking about it, enjoying it and integrating it into the culture as a source of pleasure. The thing is, food trends are fairly easy to start and move — and they can be really powerful. All of us have the potential to change the culture's relationship with inexpensive, basic staple foods, simply by cooking them well, eating them enthusiastically, serving them to guests. The words you want to hear are "I never knew lentil soup/beans and rice/whatever could be so delicious."

And that means learning to cook inexpensive foods well, and to create a varied diet using basic ingredients. Which means you need recipes and ideas, other people who are doing this, and a supportive, truly seasonal food culture.

How To Get the Actual People In Your House To Eat the Food

In a perfect world, of course, our partners, roommates, children and other assorted people in our lives would say, "Oh, I'm so thrilled you are growing a garden and storing food — now I can get rid of the honey-barbecue chips and the fast food, and start really appreciating rutabagas like I've always wanted to." In our perfect world, when Daddy unveils his laboriously created six-vegetable risotto with an enthusiastic "Voila!" the kids would say, "Wow, Dad, is there really, truly bok choy in it? And we can have seconds? Yay!" instead of, "What's 'wallah'? It looks gross. And ewww, what's that green stuff?"

I would say the odds are good that most of us live in a somewhat imperfect world. If we've been lucky enough to have started our kids on this stuff from birth, we may avoid the latter (mostly), but since most of our lives also involve some adults we didn't get a hand in raising, and who we love despite their weird habits, we're stuck with them and the painful reality that shifts in diet run up against people's weird habits pretty hard.

The thing is, changing someone's food habits is a big thing. We can do this for ourselves — all of a sudden we see the light and begin eating a new way. But making others do it? That's a challenge. In many ways, we define ourselves by what and how we eat, so attacks on diets look like attacks on people, and often are fended off with the ferocity of warfare. Nor does moralizing work very well. We all know the truth — the Western diet causes obesity, heart disease and other illnesses that result in debility and death in many cases. The dying often cling to it with a passion that proves firmly that you can't make most people change by simply telling them how bad their choices are.

As far as I can tell, with rational adults, and extremely rational teenagers there are a few ways of at least getting them on board for the broader project of changing diets.

1. You enlist them in the name of self-improvement and being better people. You can do this straight out, or manipulatively. (And yes, I know, in a perfect world you'd never manipulate people at all, but I've never met a family in which there was no manipulation at all, if you include the sort of blatant, half-humorous stuff.) The straight way is simply to say, "I think we all ought to be eating better — do you agree? Here's what I want us to do." This works in some families and with some people — and it doesn't with others, even if we wish it would. Don't forget to mention the chance to be self-righteous if they like that sort of thing — "I can't believe those people who eat all those processed chips and snacks."

    If you do need or want to be sneaky and manipulative about this, it helps if you start the discussion from the assumption that you both care very much about these things and want the same things. That is, some people can be confused a little by simply starting with, "Of course we both care desperately that everyone have enough food in the future, so I know you will agree with me." Some people will assume that if you are assuming they care about this seemingly good thing then they must, and that gets you part of the way. Or perhaps you could enlist their help against a larger obstacle. "Katie our two-year-old is so terribly picky, and I'm so terribly concerned that she be able to eat things…perhaps you can help me make it easier for her…" Or if you think that it will work (and if they are a person you'd say this sort of thing to) you can tell them it turns you on when they eat lentils or greens. Heck, you've got weirder kinks than a taste for seeing your girlfriend devour kale, right?

2. You use a different motivator than the one that moves you. If you know the person you are thinking of is, say, cheap, you talk about how much money you'd save eating this way. If the person is into cool gadgets, talk about the neat tools you can buy to preserve food. With small children, a great strategy is to convince them that you don't really want to share your asparagus, or to describe the food in disgusting terms. You aren't just offering them healthy food, you are offering them roadkill stew with sweet potatoes, and if they eat it, they can tell their friends that they ate week-old raccoon. It is important to remember that most people in our lives don't always have the same reasons for doing things that we do, and really helping them change involves understanding what matters to them.

3. You sneak the food into their diets gradually. This is often the case when the motivated person is the primary cook, and has some control over what goes into food. Suddenly, the noodles are whole wheat or brown rice flour. Secretly, the meatballs are half textured vegetable protein or ground zucchini. The yogurt is in the old containers, but it comes from home and has homemade strawberry jam mixed in. You don't talk about it, unless someone says something nice. The word "fritter" shows up in your meal, and the fritters are suspiciously green. The cookies get browner and a little denser. When asked about these things, you tell people they must be imagining things.

4. You are a total hardass. This works only if you are the sole cook for someone without much power to get food elsewhere — young kids, teenagers too young to drive or too poor to buy food, spouses so accustomed to eating the partner's cooking (or sufficiently well disciplined) that they won't dissent too much. It starts out once a week — there's this meal, and no snacks unless you eat it. Then it goes up to two or three meals a week — dal instead of burgers and the beer is now homemade. Don't like it? Tough patooties. Guess who is holding the car keys? The problem here is the danger of mutiny, or that someone else might actually learn to cook.

5. You compromise — a little of this, a little of that — and the truth is that while you have to eat more out of your storage, and you find

some meals that everyone will like, you never quite get to the point where everyone is really eating this way all the time. There's still some frozen stuff and take out in your life. And that's OK — just as long as you have a range of things people will do with the 75 pounds of dried chickpeas that don't involve sculpture.

Here are some practical ideas:

1. I've had great luck (as have other people I know) getting kids to eat raw cabbage dipped in ketchup, even if they won't eat it cooked.

2. Root vegetables roasted in a pan are the basis for tons of meals. They can go inside enchiladas or wrap sandwiches, act as a starchy side dish and are great at room temperature or cold.

3. Fritters. You can dip them in anything, and make them from just about anything. Dumplings are also a good way to conceal vegetables — chopped up fine enough, who can tell what's in them?

4. Sweet potato pie (or less-sweet pumpkin) can be breakfast, lunch and dinner (although maybe not in the same day).

5. For people who like strong flavors and mixed-up foods, foods like jambalaya, gumbo and casseroley things are your friend, because it is hard to tell exactly what's in it — particularly if you chop the mustard greens finely.

6. For people who like everything to be separate with nice clean lines, the potato is your friend. Meat and potato people can get used to an ever-increasing amount of potato and a gradually decreasing amount of meat.

7. Vegetarian cookbooks are your friends, even if you aren't vegetarian. They often have recipes that you'll be able to put together from only your pantry and garden.

8. Teenagers like power. Get them cooking — and give them the power, within certain parameters, to choose some of the meals.

9. It really helps to let go on some things. If you reassure your honey you aren't trying to take away everything she loves, that you will still love him if he stops at the convenience store, your kids that candy is still allowed now and again, this will help the transition. In fact, it helps if you instigate. Let them have ice cream sundaes

for dinner once a year, and they put it on the schedule! Work with them, at the same time you are working "against" them.

10. Sometimes using a fat/salt/sugar-laden technique is what is needed to get started with a new food — make rutabaga chips fried in oil with salt — and once they admit they like rutabagas, then you can work on mashing them.

The Joys of Food Storage and Preservation

It is never enough to simply make food acceptable to people. That's not what food is for — it is supposed to be for pleasure and for joy. So when we talk about how to get people to eat what you are serving, the best and most important step is to make it clear that the process of making and serving, preserving and eating food is a pleasure and a gift.

Now let's be reasonable here. All of us have our days when all we can do is get dinner on the table — expecting us to be happy about it, or treat it as a pleasure is far too much. And yet, there are joys to be had here. The joys of feeding yourself and others. The joys of knowing that you have a measure of personal security. The joys of good dinners, cooked with other people and eaten with them.

Much of our talk about how to get others to eat the food comes down to the fact that we live in a society where food is seen mostly as fuel, rather than a blessing and pleasure. Regaining the idea that food and its management — including storage and preservation — are the basic, ordinary work of human beings, and that there is honor and grace in that work, is perhaps the first project in making our food palatable. Gratitude for what you have is, perhaps, the first key to loving your food.

But it isn't the only key. Perhaps the next most important is the ability to see what we are doing as good work — not always an unadulterated pleasure, but a work as good as any other we do and better than some. Work that has honor and a sense of satisfaction attached to it. That can be hard in a world where we are constantly told that our efforts at preserving and cooking and storing are unnecessary, that if we just sit back and let the industrial food system take care of it for us, we will be free to do other things. But we need to recognize that what they offer is not freedom, nor are the results equivalent to the good work of our hands.

But whose work? This, of course, is always the question. How many women, reading this are thinking, "OK, perhaps she makes sense, but is all the work of this going to fall on me, while my children and spouse complain that dinner isn't familiar anymore?" And that is a real question — perhaps the real question. And the only answer I can offer is that the benefits this way of eating gives us — freedom from the industrial food system, food security, better food, more justice, less waste — are things that we all need to participate in. None of us can do this work alone, and the hope of enjoying it, of understanding what it gets us and finding pleasure in it, depends on enlisting the people we love — not just to share the good work, but to share the pleasure of planning and cooking, preserving and eating.

 Recipes

Hearty Hearth Corn Muffins

These are filling, delicious, great with chili and terrific with butter or jam for breakfast. Makes 6–8 muffins.

- 1½ cups freshly ground or purchased cornmeal
- ¾ cup whole wheat flour
- 1 tsp baking soda
- ¼ cup packed brown sugar
- ¾ cup butter or oil

- 1 cup buttermilk, sour milk or milk with 1 tbsp yogurt
- ¼ cup sugar
- ½ tsp salt
- 1 egg or 1 tbsp soy flour

In a bowl, stir together corn meal, flour, sugar, baking soda, salt and brown sugar.

In a second bowl, whisk egg with buttermilk (or sour milk) and oil.

Add liquid ingredients to dry ingredients all at once, stirring until just blended.

Spoon into well greased muffin pans, filling them about ¾ full.
Bake at 425° for 20 minutes or until a golden brown.

Potatoes, Peas and Onions with Tomatoes and Mustard Seeds

My husband lived with mostly East Indian roommates through most of his years at MIT, and picked up a whole bunch of bits of the culture (including the ability to mimic accents so well that a friend's wife couldn't tell him from her husband), and this wonderful recipe, which is a whole meal served over rice. Serves 4 with leftovers.

- 4 medium or 6 small potatoes (this is good with new potatoes or old ones, just cut them up if they are older)
- 3 tbsp brown mustard seeds
- 1 tsp whole fennel seeds
- 2 tbsp minced garlic
- 5 tsp ground coriander
- 1 cup cooked dry split peas, fava beans or limas
- 1 tsp black pepper
- 2 cups of chopped tomatoes, fresh or canned
- 10 curry leaves or 2 bay leaves (we keep a curry plant on our windowsill for this)
- ½ cup water
- A couple of sliced onions
- A bit of oil
- 1 tsp salt
- 2 tsp red pepper (cayenne or Indian—omit if you want no heat)
- 3 tsp ground turmeric
- 1 can of unsweetened coconut milk
- 4 dried red peppers (more or less as you like)

Cook the potatoes (cut up into quarters if large, halved or whole if not) in water, coconut milk and fennel seeds, simmer on medium until potatoes are cooked and liquid is somewhat thickened. If the peas/beans need more cooking to be tender, toss them in too, otherwise reserve peas/beans/whatever to the very end. Sauté the onion in some oil until slightly browned on the edges, add the garlic and brown. Add all the spices except the mustard seeds to onion and garlic mixture, fry for 30 seconds, add tomatoes and cook until tomatoes are soft and thick—about 5 minutes. Dump in with the potatoes. Add a little bit of oil to a skillet, and put in the mustard seeds. Cook on high until the mustard seeds begin to pop (you'll know, trust me). Toss in and simmer together for 15 minutes. Serve over rice.

Smoky Black Bean Stew

This is a slightly modified version of the wonderful recipe for Black Beans in Chipotle Adobo Sauce in the equally fabulous cookbook *Veganomicon*. The cookbook is a terrific book for pantry folk—many of its recipes are pantry-friendly and all of them are delicious. Serves 4.

- 2 cups of dried black beans, soaked and cooked or 2 cans of black beans

• 1 bay leaf	• 3 cups water
• 1 large onion	• 4 cloves garlic
• Salt and pepper to taste	

Chipotle sauce:

• 1 large onion	• 4 cloves garlic
• 3 tbsp oil	• 2 chipotle peppers
• 2 tbsp adobo sauce from the chipotles	• 2 tbsp lime juice or cider vinegar

Combine all ingredients and simmer until the beans are tender and the water is cut in half. Meanwhile, make the sauce—cook the onion and garlic until soft, add the chipotles and cook for 1 minute, then remove from heat and puree (it will be good even if you don't have something to puree with and chop it finely). Add lime juice or vinegar and serve over beans, ideally with corn muffins.

PART TWO

Food Storage and
Preservation How-To

Pleasures

I confess, before I became aware of the energy implications of my actions, I was one of those people who liked to think in the shower. When you have children, a shower has magic powers. It makes a cone of silence around you. It warms you when you are cold. It cools you when you are hot. And until I started paying attention to my water usage, I showered a lot — it was a self-indulgent pleasure.

The funny thing is that when I began to cut back to shorter and cooler and less frequent showers, I didn't mind it that much. The only time I missed long hot showers was on the first day of my cycles, when I could remember how much pleasure I got from hot water against my back, easing my cramps. And for a while, I grumped around for a bit over the fact that I no longer took morning showers, or long hot showers at all.

And then it occurred to me that I could have my first-day-of-the-cycle shower if I wanted — I just had to shorten the other ones. So I did that. I skipped one extra shower a week, and shortened my other ones slightly. Once again, I stood in the water in the morning, blissfully contemplating how good that hot water felt on my back.

But it didn't just feel good. It felt *great* — all day long I felt wonderful. And it struck me that this is the payback for all the scrimping and conserving we do — the transformation of ordinary comforts into delights.

We get this too with our small percentage of non-local food. We buy a very few non-local fruits and vegetables each week. And each week, my husband and the children choose carefully — what shall we have? One week it was mangos, and none of us have ever tasted anything so delicious as those juicy, dripping yellow fruits. This week it was avocados, and every molecule of our bowl of guacamole was scraped out and enjoyed with homemade tortilla chips. My sons discuss what special fruit they will choose next week at the co-op, and what we should do with it.

If these pleasures are so acute, why deny yourself at all? Why not get mangos every week if we love them so? But when I ate all the tropical fruits I wanted, I never enjoyed a mango like I do now. Would my children take so much pleasure in their selection? Would I, if we had them all the time? Experience suggests to me that we would not. The funny thing is that most of the denial isn't a hardship — that is, the intensity of the two experiences doesn't run in parallel. Having fewer showers isn't awful at all, merely a mild inconvenience. But having an extra one is terrific! Occasionally limits do feel awful, and then we have to rethink. "Is there a way to make this better?" Usually there is and often we can get the hardest things down to nothing more than a minor inconvenience — and one, shortly, we become used to and don't notice at all.

Not all pleasures are diminished by frequency, but as we get accustomed to things, they no longer delight us. Thus, we must find new sources of stimulation, new delights — usually by raising the bar higher and seeking out more and more of what we crave. And "more and more" gets us into trouble pretty quickly — not only because we consume more and more but because there isn't always more to be had and so we feel dissatisfied.

I know someone, who, for their child's fifth birthday, took him and two of his friends to Disney World for the week, including a party with a favorite cartoon character. They spent thousands of dollars, and reported to me how much the child had enjoyed himself. I have no doubt that is true. My son, for his fifth birthday, had a group of children, lunch, a homemade cake, and enough balloons for each child to have one. And he too had a glorious birthday. It is possible that the child who went to Disney World had exponentially more pleasure, perhaps thousands of times more pleasure, but I doubt it. At the end of the day, Simon told me, "That was a great birthday."

What would he have said if we'd taken him to Disney World "That was a super-duper great birthday?" How big is the difference, if it never even occurred to you that Disney was an option? (I'm not totally clear that my kids know Disney World exists, which is fine with me.)

I am by nature no ascetic. I like my pleasures: I like to eat, have sex, giggle with my family, be warm, be comfortable. My children are like all children. They love treats, sweets and anything special or new. If there is a difference between us and other people it is this: we try as hard as we can (with varying degrees of success) to keep the bar for happiness low. In fact, we consciously try to move it lower as often as possible — not because we like to sacrifice, but because we enjoy the sheer intensity of the pleasures that come with this life. We're not ascetics, we're sensualists — and the most sensual pleasures are available to you when you work to avoid becoming jaded.

When I was a child, my mother was into healthy eating. We ate carob brownies (to this day I can't bear the stuff) and macrobiotic stuffed peppers instead of chocolate brownies and hamburger helper. I remember acutely how stricken I felt when my mother informed me that I would be the only one of my peers who never got to have a marshmallow fluff and peanut butter sandwich for a school lunch. But once a year, every year, my mother would tell us, "Today we're not having dinner — we're having ice cream sundaes." We would go out to a local restaurant that was an early leader in the "sundae bar" phenomenon, and make the most elaborate ice cream sundaes imaginable. My mother would never mention the green vegetables we didn't eat and would enjoy her own dessert with ours. I remember every single one of those moments, and remember thinking that I had the best mother in the whole world.

It was only later that I realized how much our delight in those moments depended on my mother and step-mother providing a healthy dinner with vegetables 364 days of the year, how a life where ice cream was a norm (and of course I had ice cream more than once a year) would have taken the shine out of that glorious, glorious experience.

We did it for the first time this year. One day over winter break, when it was cold and snowy, the children were told "Today." They were encouraged to spend the whole day in their pajamas. No one had to go anywhere or do any chores and the boys kept asking us, "Are we really going to have ice cream for dinner?" Yes, we really were. And we did. Dinner was all the ice cream sundae with all the toppings you could possibly want. And it was great.

6

The Mechanics
of Food Storage

Buckets

WHAT ARE THE buckets for, you ask? Well, when you start buying 50-pound sacks of food, that food can't stay in its bag forever. If it does, you will get bugs, and the food will get damp from humidity, and you will be sorry. Ask me how I know this.

So when you buy bulk food, you should decant it. If you have a ton of mason jars, you can just put it into that, but that takes a lot of jars, and most of us don't have that much shelf space. So we call on the magical powers of the five-gallon food-grade plastic bucket.

Personally, I don't think it is possible to have too many of these if you are growing, preserving and storing food. And the great thing is that for most people you can get them completely free from any restaurant or store that has a deli or bakery. When you have all you want to store your food, you can use them to haul zucchini in from the garden, to bring feed out to your chickens, to ferment pickles, as a drum for subway busking — you name it!

The only problem with storing things in them is getting the lids on and off. That stinks if you have to do it often. It takes a lot of work, since the lids have to be hammered on to be airtight, but it can be made easier with a lid lifter tool (cheap). If you can afford it, it is worth acquiring Gamma Seals for the buckets you use most often. Gamma

Seals are much easier to open and close than conventional food storage buckets. They consist of a ring that goes over the edge of a bucket and an airtight lid that spins into place. They cost about $7 apiece, so aren't inexpensive, but you don't need them for every bucket, only the ones you open regularly. That is, let's say you keep oatmeal in a jar on your counter. You refill the jar from one bucket, but maybe you have two or three other buckets of oatmeal — the only one that you have to open regularly is the one you might want to have a Gamma Seal for. Again, you don't have to have them, and shouldn't worry about it if money is an issue. It is perfectly possible to use the lids that come with your buckets, merely a pain if you are doing it often. Gamma Seals are available at a number of sources listed on my website.

The other issue is the air inside the buckets. If there's air, your food won't last as long. There are a couple of ways of dealing with this. One would be to buy oxygen absorbers (available through Emergency Essentials, listed on my website), another is to buy dry ice and pack a small piece in each bucket (use gloves and handle very carefully). You can also use a tea light (carefully) and put the lid on — when the candle burns out, the oxygen is gone. I have not tried this technique, so be cautious.

To prevent insects, the ideal solution is to freeze all grains for a few days. This can be done outside if the weather permits, or in your freezer if you have space. If not, mix in a little human-grade diatomaceous earth, also available in the resource section of my website. Some people add a few bay leaves as well as a bug repellent — it can't hurt.

Grain Basics

Most human beings rely primarily on wheat, corn and rice for their calories, and these will often be the staple grains of any food storage program. That said, however, a lot of people have sensitivities to wheat or corn, so those people simply can't follow food storage advice that emphasizes these common grains. Other people may not be aware that they cannot tolerate large quantities of wheat or corn until they try. I know at least two people with a great deal of stored wheat who have discovered they can't eat it. Moreover, families with young children should not rely on wheat as a primary staple. If they rely on corn, it must be nixtamalized — that is, treated so that its niacin becomes accessible (there's more on this in the section on corn). So generally speaking, a wider mix of grains is important.

It behooves all of us to have some familiarity with, and perhaps some storage of, a range of grains beyond these big three. Moreover, minor grains often haven't had the major price rises of the major ones. As far as I know, as yet, no one is making ethanol with amaranth (I'm sure someone is or will be, though).

Generally speaking, whole grains store for quite a while. Bleached white grains, with all their nutritional goodness taken off also store a long while but are bad for you. What stores very badly are any cracked, crushed, ground or processed grains with the germ attached. Whole grain flours, cracked grains or brown rice (more on this below) have a storage life measured in months, not years. This is no problem if you don't buy more than you eat in six months, and you rotate well. But just in case you might not be as careful as you should be on this one, generally speaking you want to store whole grains.

The other issue that applies is whether a grain has a hard outer coating or a soft one. Grains with a hard coating store longer than the softer ones. The hard grains (which include "soft" wheat — a designation that refers to its baking qualities, not its structure) generally store for at least a decade, often 20 years or more. Depending on which reference you look at, given a cool, oxygen-free environment, soft grains will store for six to nine years.

Many people who are storing whole grains will want a grain grinder, and I discuss my recommendations for this in the chapter on tools. A grain grinder is very nice, particularly if you would like to eat foods in familiar forms — for example, bread or pastry-like things. But you can get along without one. For much of human history, grains were pounded or ground by hand or eaten whole. You could just not eat breads or other ground foods and mostly eat bulgur, hominy and whole rice, quinoa, amaranth, etc. A grain grinder is a nicety — a very, very useful nicety — but not necessary to life, and you can store grains without one.

Wheat is a great storage food, but most of us probably shouldn't eat just wheat. Any food storage should include a balance of grains. Especially if you have young kids, no more than 50 percent of your food storage should be wheat based unless your family comes universally from genetic populations that ate wheat as their primary staple and you still eat huge quantities of wheat every day. It should be noted that wheat is a wonderful food and for those who can tolerate it, a great base for a diet, particularly if you are "from" bread. Just don't make it the only thing you eat. The good thing about wheat is that, properly packed into buckets with oxygen absorbers, dry ice, etc. it will keep for decades. Kept at below 70 degrees, it stays good for 20–30 years. I am not recommending that you keep it that long—better to eat and enjoy it. But it will last.

Corn is also a good food, although also allergenic. For corn, the major issue is that it lacks protein unless it is nixtamelized—that is, unless an alkaline substance is added to it. The native peoples of the Americas routinely added wood ashes to their food, which resolved the issue. European colonists in the new world adopted corn, but not the technique of making its full nutritional value accessible, and thus suffered from pellagra. Nixtamelization is not necessary if you are only eating corn occasionally or as part of a wide range of grains, but because corn grows so well and so widely, I suspect some of us may come to rely on it more than we do now.

If corn is one of your primary staple foods, you should learn to make hominy, which is hulled (nixtamelized) corn. Or you can simply grind or cook corn and add two tablespoons of culinary ash (clean hardwood ash that you haven't burned anything else with) to each cup of your corn.

To make hominy, take three cups of dried corn and ten cups of water. Soak the corn overnight in a bowl of the water. The next day, put the corn and water in a pot. Cover and bring to a rapid boil. When the corn comes to a boil, add either one cup of the culinary ash or two tablespoons of baking soda. Use an enameled or ceramic pot if using the ash—unenameled metal will react with the ash. You'll see a dramatic color change in the kernels—they will get brighter looking.

Lower the heat and cover. Simmer over low for 5½ hours (the corn can be brought to a boil on the stove and then simmered in a sun oven) until the hulls start to come loose and the corn changes back to its original color. Stir occasionally, and add water if necessary. When all the corn is softened, put it under cold water, and rub to remove the hulls. Discard the hulls (compost it, give it to chickens), and drain the hulled corn. You can serve the hominy with butter, or with straight milk, or you can dry it in the sun or a dehydrator (to check if it is dry enough, use a fingernail to break open a kernel — if there's any moisture, keep drying). It will keep one to two years in dry form.

Dried hominy can be reconstituted, and is delicious in posole, a stew of dried chiles, meat (usually pork) and dried hominy.

Or you can make masa, which is ground hulled corn. For dry masa meal, you can dry the hominy and grind it, but traditional masa is ground in a metate (a ground stone mortar) from freshly hulled corn. It is delicious, but a good bit of work, since most grinders can't easily handle something that wet. We've pulled off a rough parallel with a stick blender, though.

In *Little House in the Big Woods* Laura Ingalls Wilder describes her mother making hominy with lye but this is rough on the skin. I think baking soda or wood ash is much safer to deal with and will give you similar results. The instructions there are pretty clear, though, if you really want to try it. Be *careful* if you do — lye is very caustic. Laura talks about eating hulled corn fried in pork fat with maple syrup, or like cereal in milk.

If you want to store whole grains but can't convince family or friends you will eat this stuff, you might try storing lots of popcorn. Now popcorn has the same issues as un-nixtamelized dry corn, and can also be ground into meal. Popcorn's greatest virtue is that it is such an accessible food that occasionally even food storage opponents will be OK with a 25-pound bucket of popcorn and the mental image of endless movie nights that it suggests.

OK, on to **rice**. Here we come to one of the most common confusions in food storage. Most of the foods we recommend storing are whole grains, which generally store better than grains that have been hulled or ground. Brown rice looks, to most people, like a whole grain. The problem is that it isn't. Rice actually has a hull on it, and once the hull is removed, the oils in rice go rancid very, very quickly. Many people cannot taste rancid grains or tell if the oils have spoiled, and rancid grains are not good for you. You shouldn't eat them. Rancid grains have been associated with the risk of stomach cancer and can also cause short-term digestive upsets. Rancid oils also contain free radicals that are a cancer risk.

Brown rice oxidizes and spoils very quickly. The maximum storage life for brown rice out of a freezer is 6–12 months, and that's a maximum. I've had it spoil faster. Which is why most storage programs recommend white rice. Generally speaking, don't buy more brown rice than you will use in 6–12 months, and less if you can't taste (or aren't sure if you can taste) rancid grains.

Now 80 percent of the world's population mostly eats these three grains. This can be an advantage if you prefer to buy from smaller producers. But there are a lot of other great grains out there.

Most of us know **rye** best from bread. The big advantage of rye is that it will tolerate colder climates than wheat, and added to wheat flour, it makes delicious bread. Rye grains, sprouted, also make a delicious porridge. Rye is a soft grain and keeps, properly stored, for five to six years.

Amaranth is wonderful. It is also tremendously easy to grow in many climates, including mine. It can be popped like popcorn and has a terrific flavor. We love it, and it is one of the most beautiful and useful plants I grow. It is great in flatbreads or granola. I've seen several reliable sources with wildly differing estimates of how long amaranth keeps — from three years to ten years and beyond. To be safe, I'd keep it for less than five years in its whole form.

Quinoa is hugely popular among people who can't eat wheat, people keeping kosher for Passover (it isn't a true grain so we can eat it) and a host of new converts. It is often used like rice or couscous, with food served over it. It is a soft grain and keeps six to nine years. Quinoa has a coating that contains saponins, that are very bitter and soapy. You must rinse it until the water stops soaping before eating it. The rinse water can supposedly be used to do laundry, believe it or not. Meanwhile, don't let that put you off quinoa, which is a terrific food, incredibly rich in protein and nutrients, and truly delicious.

Barley is one of the oldest grains. One of the best things about it is its sweetness when sprouted. Malted or sprouted barley adds a light, sweet flavor to breads. Pearled barley is essentially the white rice of barley, and keeps forever. Whole barley also keeps forever, but has hulls which are not the sort of thing you want to eat. Whole barley at the home level, without some way to hull it, is mostly good for making beer. There are hulless barleys, but there's no clear answer on how long they store — at a minimum, I would recommend treating them as a soft grain. Hulled barley keeps five to seven years.

Buckwheat is essential at our house in pancakes, in soba noodles and as kasha. Easily grown, easily ground, it makes a crop quite quickly in late summer. The greens are nutritious (as are amaranth's) and a good salad green in hot climates where lettuce bolts, or anywhere you are using it as a cover crop. It is a hard grain, and lasts for decades.

Millet is a hard grain as well. Most of us know it as birdseed, but it is a common food grain in India and much of Northern Asia, and has a delicate taste. It is quite delicious. We use it like rice or couscous. It is also very digestible. It stores for decades.

Spelt, kamut and emmer I'll deal with together, because they are all forms of wheat with special qualities. All keep like wheat — more or less forever. Emmer is a very old form of wheat that some people with wheat sensitivities can tolerate (although it is not good for those with celiac disease). It has a heavy hull. It is also a good variety for those growing wheat on extremely poor soils. Kamut is a commercial variety that some people with wheat allergies seem to be able to tolerate. Those who produce it claim it is a very old variety, but there's limited evidence on this. The same is true of spelt, which is either a wheat or a close relative, depending on how you interpret the genetic evidence. Again, it is not suitable for people with celiac disease. All keep very well, all are lower gluten than conventional wheat and make a heavier bread, but all taste good.

Not a true grain (neither are amaranth or quinoa), **flaxseed** in its whole form also keeps for a decade or more. Given the importance of omega-3 fatty acids and the pleasant taste of flaxseed, this is an excellent thing to keep in storage. We love it.

All of these are worth eating, experimenting with, and storing. But please don't just store them — eat them.

Storing Water

I know that to some people, the idea that you have to store water seems a little nuts. But think about what happened in just the year 2008. In much of the Midwest, heavy flooding left millions with contaminated water and no power. In coastal Texas more than three million people had contaminated water, no power, and no ability to run out to buy bottled water. And at the end of the year, 1.2 million Northeasterners lost power, and many lost water as well, either due to contamination from the heavy rains that followed the ice storm or because their well pumps relied on electricity.

Remember the mantra — failure is normal. It isn't that uncommon to end up in a crisis with no water. And while an unprepared life without electricity is usually merely inconvenient and uncomfortable, life without adequate water is very dangerous. A large percentage of the deaths during Hurricane Katrina, for example, were due to dehydration — people were surrounded by toxic, undrinkable water. Because water is bulky and hard to store, finding a place to put a fair bit of water seems difficult. It is easier just to say that it will never come to that — but it often does, and the lives of your family may depend on your water reserves.

Right now you may be thinking, OK, she's probably right, but she's *insane* if she thinks I have any way to store 56 gallons of water. And this is true — it probably won't be convenient or easy to find a spot. But if you recognize the need, you will find space, just as you do for other things you need.

The traditional recommendation is that you store one gallon per day per person, plus half a gallon for each dog and one quarter of a gallon for each cat. This will get most people through a day, with maybe a moist washcloth to wipe off with and enough to drink. The problem is that this isn't enough to let you work hard in hot weather (you can require a quart an hour for that), and it isn't enough to allow you to cook, or wash your hands regularly.

I think two gallons per person per day for two weeks is better, although this means finding space for a lot of water. Thirty gallons of water, stacked in square five-gallon containers to save space will take up only a few square feet, but if you have to store it in individual jugs, or have a large family and need much more water than this, you'll need more space. If you can't find that much space, you really should store some alcohol-based hand sanitizer, to keep from passing around illness. And if you live in a hot place, storing more water is better. Don't forget your pets and livestock.

There are a couple of ways to handle water. The first is to make sure you have a reliable way of getting it out of the ground if you need to — a hand pump, a bucket for your well, a spring. This works fairly well in the country, where there aren't sewer overflows to contaminate water supplies, but urban and large town water supplies are likely to be contaminated in a crisis, so it won't help you there. Still, if you live in a rural or exurban area, you might consider, instead of storing water, putting a manual pump on your well or some other mechanism of getting water such as solar direct water pumping. If your water table is less than 20 feet down, you can use a cheap manual water pump, available at any hardware store, to get water from the ground. Between 20 and 200 feet, you can use a manual well pump, but it will be much more expensive (more than $1,000 installed), or you can make one yourself from plans available from Jim Juczak (woodhenge.org). Much more than 200 feet, and you will need powered pumping to get water out of the ground.

So what do you do if you have to store water? Well, first of all, it is generally better not to store it in the plastic jugs you get at the supermarket if you are storing for the long term. These last only a matter of months, and have a tendency to decompensate in storage (that is, burst all over the place). If you want to rotate your supply, purchase water every six months, use it up, and buy new ones.

If you don't want to spend money on water (and there are good reasons not to — bottled is not safer and it causes a lot of environmental damage), use heavier duty, food-grade plastic (never store your water in anything but food-grade plastic unless there's no choice) — soda bottles, juice jugs. Don't buy them, take them out of your neighbor's recycling or ask someone to save theirs for you. One place you can put them is in your freezer, if you have space. Since freezers run best when full, keeping water in there will both preserve it and help you reduce your energy usage. Just don't fill the bottles all the way — leave room for the water to expand when it freezes.

FEMA's recommendations are to add one teaspoon of bleach to a quart of water. This will prevent algae growth, and allow you to keep the water up to a year. Unfortunately, this is also a lot of bleach, more than any of us want to ingest. Other agencies suggest one teaspoon bleach to one gallon of water, which I think is more appropriate. Mark the date on the container, so that you will know when you filled it. If you don't add bleach, keep the water in a cool place, and rotate every month.

You can purchase five- or seven-gallon heavy duty water jugs on the Internet. They are not cheap, but you can reuse them forever. Seven gallons is as much as most people will want to lift (and if you are elderly or disabled or have carpal tunnel syndrome, you might want to lift much less). The containers are square, so can be stacked to save space. Fifty gallons of water can be stacked in a comparatively small space or slid under a bed. If you have a garage, you can get 50-gallon barrels, fill them with your hose and keep them there.

If you have a hot water heater, you can drain it and drink that water. Count that into your water storage.

If you have some kind of rainwater catchment, you can drink that water, as long as you *filter* it. In fact, a filter is a really good idea no matter where your water is coming from. Even if it keeps coming out of the tap, municipal water can be contaminated by flooding, sewer leaks, chemical leaks, etc. And stored water has to be stored with bleach, which you might also want to filter out. Plus if an emergency goes on for a long time, you may find yourself drinking groundwater or melting snow, and you would want to rid yourself of contaminants (for that matter, you may want to remove contaminants in your town water).

Infants, children and pregnant women should be especially careful not to drink contaminated water.

I use a British Berkefeld water filter; its manufacturer claims you can pour raw sewage in the top and drink what comes out the bottom. I have not experimented with this feature, and don't plan to. It is not cheap, but I do love mine, and it is cheaper than regularly buying bottled water. PUR Scout and Katadyn Combi portable filters are also good, and much cheaper. It is worth having a camping filter or a heavy gravity-fed one in your house. The camping filter is probably sufficient if you don't expect to use it often, but the gravity-fed ones will deal with water issues now, if you have any questions about your water supply. Another choice to ensure safe water supply would be to distill your water — solar distiller plans are out there.

Capturing Water from the Sky or Ground

We can store some water for short-term emergencies, but if we anticipate long economic or other disruptions in our energy supplies, we need to also think about how we would get water day to day in an extended situation where we were too poor to pay the water bill, or were without power.

The very first step on this is to begin to research your local watershed. Where does your water come from? What are the long-term planning issues facing your region or community in regards to water? What impact does climate change seem to be having? What projected impact might it have? What issues are there with contamination? How safe is surface water? Do you have problems with acid rain? Pesticide runoff? PCB contamination? Mercury? What about your well? What about the local reservoirs? What are the legal issues of your water use? Can you collect rain? Can you make use of surface water? These are things you need to know.

Basically, you have three choices — you can get water from under the ground, on top of the ground or the sky. It is worth understanding fully where your water comes from and where you might get it. This section is necessarily an overview, rather than a complete resource. If you are concerned about water, I recommend *The Home Water Supply:*

How to Find, Filter, Store and Conserve It by Stu Campbell as the most complete resource I've seen on this subject.

Most of us can get some water from the sky but how much varies a lot. Some cities do prohibit rainwater capture, and in those places it is worth working on the legal issues. More and more cities are recognizing that home capture that can help keep heavy storm rains from causing problems is a benefit, and that home irrigation from rain barrels is wiser than using city water. More and more areas are seeing strong movements towards permitting rainwater collection.

Rain barrels can be made or purchased. Or you can put in either an above ground water tank or a cistern to catch larger quantities of rain. A cistern can be a large, pre-made tank, or you can build it yourself if you are handy enough, or have someone put a water tank in with a backhoe. If you can put your rainwater capture close enough to the house, you may even be able to bring water into the house from the cistern or tank for doing dishes and laundry. An above ground tank located on a hill above the house, or held up by posts can provide gravity-fed water, or a manual shallow well pump can be put on a cistern, rain barrel or tank.

Whether you will be able to get water from under the ground depends on where you live. Generally water tables are higher in the east than the west. You need to know how deep your well is if you are pumping directly from underground.

If you have a well, and the power goes out, you have several choices. The first is to put a manual pump on your well. This is only feasible if you water table is less than 200 feet down, and it isn't cheap — usually above $1,000. One option would be for communities to get together and share the cost of these well pumps, putting a manual pump in public places like parks, libraries and schools so that members of the community will be able to get water if they need it.

If your water table is high enough, you may be able to hand dig a well. The difficulty is that most surface water often isn't that clean. But if you have a good filtration system, you might find this useful, particularly if you already have a source of drinking water and primarily need irrigation, laundry and livestock water. Remember, most of the water we use does not need to be drinking quality. Use drinking quality water only for drinking, rather than flushing, washing, etc. Conservation is your first tool here, as it almost always is.

For that matter, while conserving, you can also use gray water (water used for laundry, washing hands and dishes) for flushing your toilet and irrigating your garden. It is possible to re-route your pipes and set up complex systems for this, but you can also open a pipe and put a bucket underneath, then carry it to where you want it. Do not use blackwater, from toileting or bathing for this purpose.

If you have a deep well, and are concerned about losing power to it, solar or windmill pumping is probably your best bet, but this is not cheap. If you are permitted to capture water from the sky and have sufficient rainfall, you might find the cistern option much less expensive. Or you might not, depending on what you can put together.

If you are lucky enough to have a spring, you can tap it. Many springs can be usefully developed, either for home use, irrigation or grazing.

Getting water from surface sources is pretty simple — you go there with some buckets. If you have to carry a lot of water a long distance, you may want tanks that strap on your bicycle, or at a minimum a yoke and bucket set up, which allows you to put the weight of the water on your shoulders instead of in your hands. In the winter, if you have it, you can melt snow, but it takes a lot more snow than you think to make much water.

I hope everyone will at least give some serious thought to water sources in the longer term. The truth is that adequate water can make not just the difference between life and death, but between a life of misery and one of comparative comfort.

Recipes

Posole Verde

This is a delicious soup. I'm told (we're kosher) that a little bacon in with the greens makes it even better, but we like it this way just fine. Serves 4.

- ½ cup hulled, raw pumpkin seeds, toasted
- ¼ lb dandelion leaves or other greens (chard is good), rinsed, stemmed
- 2 tbsp oil
- 4 cups chicken or vegetable broth
- salt to taste

- 1 cup salsa verde (tomatillo salsa — recipe in the canning chapter)
- 2 serrano chile peppers, seeded, quartered or 1 tbsp hot sauce
- 3½ cups cooked hominy
- fresh epazote if available

Grind the pumpkin seeds in a food processor or metate (a Mexican mortar and pestle) until they are powdery; set aside. Meanwhile, sauté chile peppers and dandelion greens in oil. When wilted and soft, add salsa verde. Stir in the ground seeds and cook 10 minutes longer. Add the hominy, broth, and epazote. Simmer for 15 minutes, then season with salt.

Creamy Quinoa and Butternut Squash

Yum. Ok, I'm supposed to say more, but…yum. That about sums it up. Serves 4.

- 1 2-lb butternut squash, peeled, seeded and diced (keep the seeds, they are delicious baked and spiced)
- 1 cup organic quinoa
- 1 tsp salt
- 4 cloves garlic, minced

- 2 cups water
- 2 tbsp olive oil, divided
- 2 tbsp shallots

- 2 eggs
- 1 tsp sugar
- 1 cup yogurt
- shredded cheese if desired

Steam the squash until just tender — you can microwave it or steam it over the stove. Place the quinoa in a colander and rinse it thoroughly (about 5 minutes) until water runs clear. This is very important, as quinoa has a bitter protective coating — save the rinse water if you like for washing things.

Mix squash and quinoa together. Add water and salt to pot and bring to a boil, then reduce heat to low and allow to simmer for 15 minutes or until liquid is absorbed and the quinoa blooms into little spirals. Remove from heat and let rest.

Meanwhile, heat 1 tbsp olive oil over medium heat in a small frying pan. Add shallots and cook 3 minutes. Add garlic and cook a minute or two longer, being careful not to let garlic burn. Pour over the quinoa and squash mixture, mixing thoroughly. Add eggs, yogurt, salt and pepper and top with cheese if desired. Bake at 400° until golden brown.

Golden Coconut Rice

This is the perfect enhancement of rice — rich, very slightly sweet, and absolutely delicious with curries, with pickles, with everything. Serves 4.

- 1½ cups jasmine rice, white or brown
- ½ cup coconut cream or coconut oil
- 2 cups water
- 1 tsp ground turmeric
- ½ cup shredded unsweetened coconut
- 2 small hot chiles, or 1 tsp hot sauce or to taste
- 1½ tsp salt
- chopped basil or cilantro

Put all ingredients except basil or cilantro together in a covered pot and bring to a rapid boil over high heat. Reduce the heat to very low and without lifting the lid, cook for 7–12 minutes (longer for brown rice, shorter for white). Uncover, and stir, leaving on heat until all liquid is absorbed. Cover and let sit 5 more minutes. Then stir in herbs and serve.

Tex-Mex Millet

Another recipe borrowed (OK, stolen) from *Veganomicon,* this frankly kicks ass. It tastes like Spanish rice, but better. I've changed it to be a bit more of a pantry thing, but the original is pretty terrific too. Maybe they won't sue me if you run out and buy their cookbook. Serves 4.

- 2 tbsp butter or oil
- 1 cup millet
- 2 pickled jalapenos, diced, or to taste (I like a lot more, but then I'm a chile head)
- 5 tbsp tomato paste
- 1 tsp ground cumin
- 2 cloves garlic
- 1 onion
- 2 cups vegetable or chicken broth
- ½ tsp salt
- ½ tsp ground coriander

Sauté the onion, garlic and jalapeno in the oil until golden and soft, about 7 minutes. Add the millet, stir and sauté another 5 minutes, until the millet looks golden and toasted. Pour in the broth and add tomato paste, salt, cumin and coriander. Bring the mixture to a boil, lower heat, cover and cook on the lowest setting for ½ hour, or until all the liquid is absorbed. Fluff up and eat.

Oops

Did I mention that this is a little different than most books about food preservation and storage? Besides talking about what you should be doing, I thought it might be productive to shift our focus to my personal failings and discuss what you should *not* do when storing and preserving food. I would feel remiss if I did not offer you this useful advice. Of course, being a food storage goddess, I've never actually done any of these things, but a very dear friend did them once.

1. When you store many heavy jars of home-canned food on metal shop shelves, do not glance into the storage area and notice that the shelves are bowing and have an odd tilt to them, and then think, "That's interesting," because you have another urgent project in your head, and close the door and not do anything about it. Not that I would know, but if you do so, you may experience a giant crashing noise, tiny pieces of pickle-scented glass in everything, a godawful mess and an extended period of cussing.

2. When you make daikon kimchi, do not put the jar lids on very tightly and then forget that you have it fermenting, unless you enjoy a kimchi-scented kitchen and the sight of bright red Korean pepper liquid dying your ceiling.

3. Do not ever convince yourself that you will get around to labelling the buckets…eventually. Do it now, or accept that you will never figure out what's in them without unpacking them.

4. Do not leave the lid off the oatmeal bucket and your two-year-old unattended while you talk on the phone. Do get used to picking little things out of the oatmeal bucket before you eat any for a while afterwards. Do not think too hard about what the things are.

5. Unless you are sure your family is the kind that eats pickled figs, do not pickle figs. You've got better uses for your time.

6. Do not lose the little magnet thingie that allows you take the metal jar lids out of the boiling water without a big hassle when you are canning. When you do lose it, make sure the tongs you are using to get the lids (with giant hassle) are long enough that you don't dip your fingers in the boiling water while chasing the lids around. Keep band-aids in the kitchen.

7. Do not pick the tomatoes with no clear plan about when you are going to get to them. Do not convince yourself that during a spate of 95 degree weather, a bucket of tomatoes will keep on the counter for just one more day. Do not think the fruit flies will go away easily.

8. Do not expect your spouse or partner to believe you when they ask where all the dried sweet peppers and blueberries went to and you shrug and blame the children. Do not even try to look innocent.

9. Do not expect to hang up herbs to dry like in the pretty pictures without tiny bits of dried herb ending up all over the place.

10. Do not think that the children will buy the "black currant is just as good as strawberry" argument.

11. When reading the recipe for ginger-pear chutney, do not think, "That doesn't sound like enough ginger — I'll just triple it and see how it goes." Do expect to be the only one eating ginger-pear chutney for a decade or so.

12. Do not think you are done preserving just because you've had a hard frost. You forgot about the green tomatoes, greens, cabbages and roots.

13. Do not think that just because you did something right last year, you can't screw it up this year. Hubris is always punished.

14. Do not accept, "Well, maybe this is how it is supposed to smell/look," as an answer. Throw it out!

15. Do not think that anyone will ever let you get away with buying commercial pickles or jams or store bread again. Once you start, you are stuck for life.

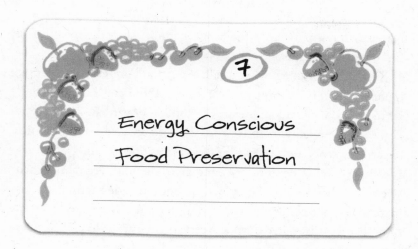

7

Energy Conscious Food Preservation

S O YOU'VE GROWN the garden, or visited the farmstand and the quantities of tomatoes and zucchini are getting really embarrassing. How do you preserve it, using the fewest possible fossil fuel inputs?

A lot of what I'm talking about here applies best to people with space for decent-sized gardens or even small farms, but even the smallest lot dwellers can forage for herbs and greens to eat and preserve. In many cities it is possible to keep rabbits or chickens for meat and eggs that you can preserve, and many cities have fruit trees on private or public property whose fruit goes unharvested. Simply asking may get you abundant citrus or peaches or apples. And, of course, everyone can go to local farms and farmers' markets, buy large quantities of food and put it up. If money is an issue, the best time of day to go is late in the afternoon, when farmers have a strong incentive not to haul everything home. Buy what they have in abundance when it is cheap, and enjoy it all winter.

The odds are good that unless you are adding a major energy hog appliance (that is, you are going out and buying a big freezer), you will be reducing your fossil fuel dependence in total when you put up food, no matter how you do it. The food you grow or buy locally to put up has already used vastly less fossil fuels to produce it, and when you preserve things, you are saving yourself trips to the grocery store, which many of us do by car. So whatever choice you make will probably be better than not putting up food. But it still makes sense to cut fossil fuel use whenever possible.

Generally speaking, when I talk about food preservation, people immediately think canning and freezing. Those are the most familiar methods of extending the life of food in our garden. But they are also the most energy-intensive choices. Both are also water intensive (electricity generation takes a lot of water, as does canning), canning is comparatively time intensive, and generally both are more expensive than other options. So while I do both, my long-term planning increasingly deemphasizes canning and freezing. There are other options. Food can be salted down, preserved in sugar or alcohol, lactofermented, root cellared, dried or dehydrated or preserved by keeping it alive in the garden or barnyard through season extension or "keeping it on the hoof." I'll describe all of these methods in more detail in the following chapters.

Freezing is probably the most common way we preserve food, and is generally the most energy intensive. In *Eating Fossil Fuels,* Dale Pfeiffer notes that if food is kept more than four months, freezing is usually more energy intensive than canning. But of course, this information is based on an average person, canning on an average gas stove, compared to an average chest freezer. There are any number of factors that might change this equation some. If you are using an electric stove, which is generally very inefficient, and have a small efficient freezer, it might make more sense to freeze than to can. Or, for example, you might do much of your canning on a wood stove you'd be using anyway to heat your house. But generally speaking, freezing is the most energy- and emissions-intensive methodology. And freezers have the added disadvantage of putting more freon into the world.

On the other hand, if you have a freezer and are going to run it anyway, the most efficient way to run it is to keep it full all the time (I'm assuming you are using a newer chest freezer, which is vastly more efficient than an upright or much older model). All of which is an argument for freezing if you are already using a freezer. For example, our family has a freezer, but that enables us to do without a refrigerator — during the winter we enjoy natural refrigeration on our porch, and during the summer we rotate reusable ice packs from the freezer into our old fridge, now permanently turned off. The ice packs keep our milk and vegetables plenty cool, with approximately half the energy usage of a fridge and a freezer. So for us, for now, a freezer makes sense.

The things that I think are best kept frozen are: raw meats, apple cider, milk, butter, blanched brassica vegetables (broccoli especially), okra, pesto, zucchini, some leftovers and peas. That really isn't a very long list, but given that we generally have our poultry for the year butchered all at once, the turkeys and chickens keep our freezer full. Even though brassicas other than broccoli freeze well, we don't bother with them much because they almost all keep well by other methods. So at the end of the year, the freezer generally has some broccoli, some peas, some okra, our meats and a bunch of gallons of apple cider that we stick in to have over the course of the winter. Honestly, the more I look at this list, the more I wonder whether we really do need the freezer — and of course, that's one of the advantages of asking the question.

At this stage, we don't freeze much milk or butter. But it is worth noting that they are produced by feeding human food — grain — to cows. That's not evil, but if the goal is to make as much food available to human beings as possible, seasonal milk from grass-fed goats, sheep and cows might make more sense. This is the historical way of doing this. Animals were allowed to dry up during the winter. Grass-fed dairy could be produced here for seven months of the year, more or less, and the rest of the time we'd be eating preserved (frozen or salted and kept cool) butter and cheese. If we were running a freezer, we might keep some milk frozen too.

Other people freeze other vegetables, but generally speaking, I find that most of the typically frozen veggies do as well or better in other means of storage, or my family simply doesn't like them frozen that well, so we eat them only in season. Chief in this latter category is green beans. I love green beans — fresh. I'll eat a few as dilly beans. But generally speaking, both canned and frozen are distinctly inferior to my mind. Which means that we enjoy green beans from July to October, and then just stop worrying about it, and eat other things. We feel asparagus is another such vegetable.

In fact, seasonal eating is helpful in putting all of this in perspective. If you insist on eating the exact same things all year around, you can expect to find food preservation time and energy intensive. But if you are content to enjoy things in their season, you can concentrate on giving yourself a small, luxurious taste of summer in winter. We eat our fair share of bread with blueberry jam in the winter, but it is helpful to recognize that things have their time, and that winter is apple, not blueberry, season. That means I don't have to worry about a year's worth of blueberries — just enough for our regular jam fixes and a few dehydrated for winter pancakes.

Canning is the next most energy-intensive method, in part because it requires extended periods of boiling, and also because each canning requires new canning jar lids. Canning is also time intensive. Some of that time you don't have to be paying attention — for example, with practice I've found I can pressure can and do chores at the same time, as long as I stay in the kitchen. But much of the time you spend canning food, you have to be keeping an eye on it. The good thing is that much of one's canning can be done either in intensive batches or casually, a little each evening. One way to cut back on difficulty is to do some of your canning later in the season. Applesauce, for example, can be put up in the fall after you get the apples, or in the winter, as you sort through the stored apples and sauce the ones that are getting wrinkled. I often wait to do pickles until things have cooled down and the stove is welcome.

If you are replacing a fridge or freezer with canning, or doing it when the heat is wanted anyway, canning is generally a good method for longer term storage. It is less energy intensive than freezing, and while in the short term there's some loss of nutrients, by the time frozen food is six months old, it has lost more nutrients than canned. Canning is by far the best method of putting up jams and jellies, some pickled things, and is, I think, a good way to store cooked meat items, like chicken broth and stew. Such food is convenient and tastes good.

I make jams (strawberry, blueberry, black currant, raspberry), apple butter, pumpkin butter, and other sweets. I usually put up some grape juice and can some pickles. And, of course, tomatoes as sauce, salsa and canned tomatoes. Later in the cold weather, after we butcher, while the stoves are running anyway, I'll put up turkey and chicken. But everything but the water-bathed jams, pickles and tomatoes could be preserved in other ways as well. For all that we tend to think that canning and freezing are essential to get through the winter, they really aren't. If they were, humanity wouldn't have survived for the last few thousand years before they were invented.

Root cellaring is the easiest and the lowest-energy method for us. I don't actually put my food down in a cellar — our cellar is gross, damp and floods occasionally. Instead, I store food in a closet on our enclosed front porch and in our attached garage. This does require a cold period, but if you have one, it is well worth a one-time investment creating a secure space for cool food storage. Attics will often work, so will existing basements — you can build a small separate area which is insulated with foam board insulation and vented. If you do it yourself, it might not cost more than a few hundred dollars, and could provide you with thousands of dollars of food storage every year. Heck, a closet on an outside wall could be lined with board insulation and an outside air source added — instant root cellar!

We store more food this way than any other. We store potatoes, carrots, beets, turnips, parsnips, celeriac, apples, pears, quinces, cabbages, persimmons, salsify and more, and there are plenty of things you can store that we don't. These are the basis of our winter eating. It does take up space, but surprisingly little if kept well organized. A bushel of apples, say, will be about 50 medium apples and can fit in a space about the size of a television.

We also store some food in our house. Some foods — like sweet potatoes, pumpkins, squash, onions and garlic — tolerate or prefer cool home temperatures. They like the temperatures that conserving people have in their homes in cool weather — in the 50s to low 60s. So it is simple to store squash under the bed, stick the sweet potatoes in a spare closet, and hang the garlic up in your kitchen. These vegetables can and should keep us company.

Then there is **dehydration**. We have an electric dehydrator, and we dry some things in the sun outside. My husband is presently building a solar dehydrator so that we can dehydrate more of our food without using energy at all. Electric dehydrators are commonly available at yard sales and generally speaking use the equivalent of a 40-watt bulb's worth of energy. Mine takes about a day to dehydrate most items. So depending on how much you use it, this could be a big energy expenditure or a small one. If you can buy green electricity, electric dehydrators have a moderate impact, but the sun is always preferable.

For those who live in dry climates, particularly in the west, it should be possible to simply lay the food outside on a screen, with a layer of cheesecloth covering it. For us in humid places, a solar dehydrator is a little more complicated. But there are many plans on the internet, and they work beautifully. I've also used my car as a dehydrator, and while there are some concerns about outgassing, I tend to think if you *sit* in your car, you have more to worry about than eating food dehydrated in a car with the windows left partly open. It works very well, although the entire vehicle smells like strawberries if you do those. Your gas oven with a pilot light on will work quite well, as will a rack hung at a reasonable distance from a wood stove.

Dehydrated food keeps less of its essential nutrients by piece, but more by weight. That is, while a dehydrated apricot has fewer nutrients than a single canned apricot, a serving of dried apricots is more nutritious than a serving of fresh apricots. Generally speaking, the most nutrients are retained when food is dried away from direct sunlight, at comparatively low temperatures, the lower the better. Thus, the best way to dry many quick-drying things is simply to hang them up in a well ventilated, airy place away from direct light. This works very well for herbs, greens, hot peppers, and even apple slices and green beans (called "leather britches" when they are dried this way). Take a needle and lace a string through the peppers, or just bunch the herbs and hang them. Once things are dry, no matter how pretty they look, store them in glass jars (a great use for those old rubber ring canning jars and the jars with nicks)or other bug-proof containers. I regularly find metal tins from flavored popcorn at yard sales. These work well.

We dry herbs, greens, tomatoes, sweet peppers (if you like sun-dried tomatoes, dried sweet red peppers are even better), sweet corn (delicious!), almost all fruits, pumpkin and fruit "leather," garlic and hot peppers. We've also made dried meats before, like jerky, but since poultry doesn't work, local fish is mostly contaminated and we don't eat much red meat, it isn't a big thing for us.

We also dry some foods on the plant. In dry climates, I'm told you can pull up the entire plant of "Principe Borghese" tomatoes and hang it over a fence and the tomatoes will dry on their own. That doesn't work here. But beans, peas, limas, favas, corn and grains will dry on the plant. I find that popcorn often needs a little more time drying inside, but generally speaking with peas and beans, all you have to do is leave some on the plant and harvest when the pods are dry and rattling.

I tend to think that dried foods are among the tastiest, and dehydrating, like freezing, is quite quick — just cut up the food and ignore it until it is at the stage of dryness you want. Using solar energy, ambient air circulation or heat that you'd be creating anyway, it requires no additional fossil fuels. After root cellaring, drying food is a favorite.

But not quite as favorite as **season extension/keeping animals on the hoof**. After all, in most of these cases what we're seeking is to get as close as we can to the flavor of fresh growing things. There are exceptions, of course — jams or sun-dried tomatoes, flavors we enjoy in their own right. But generally speaking, we don't freeze peppers to get the terrific flavor of frozen pepper. We're trying to get as close to fresh as possible. So the best strategy of all is to extend your garden season as much as possible so that you can have fresh, really local things when you want them.

We find that with very basic season extension techniques — no greenhouse, artificial heat or anything like it — we can have fresh greens and salads as well as a few extras from the end of March to the end of December. But as Eliot Coleman's *Four Season Harvest* demonstrates, the possibilities are much, much greater. You can have food 12 months of a year with minimal inputs in many climates.

Everyone, for example, can sprout seeds all winter long. Most of us can keep some fresh herbs alive. And if you have no garden, you might consider talking to local farmers or your CSA farmers, and telling them that you'd be glad to pay for local greens all winter long. Perhaps someone will start the project.

I don't freeze most cabbage family vegetables because we can have them all year. Kale will overwinter in the garden with minimal protection — it often isn't easily available to us because of deep snow, but it is there all year round. The same is true of leeks and greens like miner's lettuce and arugula. Brussels sprouts and cabbage will generally hold out until December here, and the Brussels sprouts will last another month in cold storage if the plants are pulled up whole. Cabbage will last many months — often through the whole winter. Lettuces can be grown in a sunny window all winter long to provide some salads. So there's really no reason for the inferior taste of frozen cabbage or Brussels sprouts.

Turnips and beets will sprout greens in cold storage, and these can be cut several times. I've never done it, but endives can be forced in winter. Leeks will overwinter here pretty reliably, as will parsnips and salsify. So if you are reasonably content to eat turnip greens, beet greens, kale, lettuce, spinach, arugula, Asian greens, cabbage, sprouts, fresh herbs, Brussels sprouts, and supplement these greens with root-cellared vegetables, dried ones, and other methods I'll talk about, there's really no reason, even in cold snowy places like upstate New York, to *need* freezing or canning. You may want them, and that's fine. But they really aren't necessary for a delicious and diverse winter diet.

For those who choose to eat meat, keeping meat animals alive may or may not be a more efficient way of preserving their meat than canning or freezing. Generally speaking, if you can produce an animal's winter food without too much in the way of fossil inputs, either with scraps, garden leftovers or feed you grow yourself, it may make more sense to simply care for the animal until you are ready to butcher it. The meat will be fresher, have greater nutritional value and will taste better. And no, this need not apply only to farmers. For example, a suburbanite or even many urbanites can easily keep several hutches of rabbits which could be fed mostly on food scraps, very small quantities of grain and "hay" made from dried weeds from your yard cuttings (before you do this you'll want to do some research into the nutritional needs of the animals you are raising). This technique is particularly useful if you eat meat mostly for festivals, and share with neighbors and community members. For example, in many cultures, extended families will come together on holidays to butcher a sheep or goat and share it.

If you are feeding purchased, grain-based feed to get an animal through winter, you probably would be better off butchering and preserving some other way, rather than wasting food, especially grain, on an animal whose destiny is to be dinner. And generally speaking, this requires you be willing to do your own butchering, rather than sending animals away to be processed.. There's no better way, I think, to sort out your relationship to the meat you eat (if you do) than to be responsible for the animal's life and death. This isn't feasible for everyone, but more people could and perhaps should do it than do right now. I realize that meat eating and butchering are controversial subjects — but if we are going to eat meat, doing so humanely and honestly is important.

The other food preservation method I recommend as extremely low impact is **lactofermentation**. The two forms of lactofermentation most Americans are familiar with are sauerkraut and barrel pickles. If you've ever bought a pickle from a barrel or a refrigerator case, or *fresh* (not canned) sauerkraut, you've had a lactofermented food. But there are many other kinds, chief among them kimchi, the Korean national food to which I'm entirely addicted.

Lactofermented foods use a salt brine to encourage natural bacterial fermentation, which makes them very good for you. Unlike any other method of food preservation, some vegetables stored through lactofermentation are actually more nutritious than the original vegetable, because the fermentation makes additional nutrients available. For example, kimchi has levels of B vitamins that are twice as high as the Chinese cabbage alone. The acid preserves the foods naturally, and they will last for many months kept in a cool place. You can can them, but I don't recommend it, because the hot water will kill all the bacteria and reduce the nutritional levels. Sauerkraut (which really tastes in-

finitely better homemade than anything you've ever eaten from a store)
is high enough in vitamin C to prevent scurvy over long winters.

You need only pots and salt to do this, so it is very cheap, very low
energy, very low effort and very tasty. You can make many complicated
and delicious flavors — for example, my great-grandmother made
sauerkraut with sour cherries in it. When most people think of kimchi,
they think fiery, but in fact there are hundreds of kimchis, some sweet,
some spicy, some very sour. All the ones I have ever had are delicious.
The average Korean eats 200 *pounds* of kimchi a year.

Another advantage of lactofermented foods is that some of them
produce natural narrow-spectrum antibiotics that are specific against
E. coli, listerian and clostridium bacteria. That is, they protect you
against food poisoning. With all the food contamination scares we've
had recently, this is not a trivial benefit. Fermented foods like yogurt
and miso all tend to have these natural antibiotics, but sauerkraut,
brined pickles and kimchi have especially high levels.

If you have a spot cool enough to keep potatoes, you can keep lactofermented foods. They will very gradually get sourer over time, but this
isn't necessarily a bad thing.

So what's the best way to preserve food? Well, the lowest energy
techniques are generally root cellaring, season extension (especially in
climates that require little or no protection), solar/ambient dehydrating and lactofermentation. The fastest ways are generally root cellaring
(the overall winner), season extension, solar dehydrating and freezing.
The most nutritious methods are generally lactofermentation, season
extension and root cellaring, followed by freezing for short periods.
Canning and freezing are generally speaking not best at much, and I'm
personally working on reducing them in my life.

The best tasting way? Depends on the food. For each one below
I've listed the methods in order of my personal preference, but you'll
have to experiment and see what you like.

Happy Preserving!

Apples: root cellaring, dehydrating, canned as applesauce or butter
Apricots: dry, canned as sauce
Asian greens: season extension, lactofermentation

Asparagus: fresh

Bananas: dried, frozen

Basil: frozen as pesto

Beans, dry: dried

Beans, green: eaten fresh, pickled/lactofermented

Beets: root cellared, pickled

Blueberries: jammed, dried

Brussels sprouts: season extension

Carrots: root cellared, season extension

Cabbage: root cellar, lactofermentation

Corn, sweet: dehydrated, canned, frozen

Corn, pop: dry

Corn, flour: dry

Citrus: root cellared, salted (preserved lemons), sugared and
    dehydrated (orange slices), liqueurs, dried (peel), canned (juice)

Cranberries: jammed, sauce, frozen, dried

Eggs: root cellared, on the hoof

Figs: dry

Garlic: root cellared, dried

Greens: season extension, lactofermentation

Grains: dry

Herbs: most dried, some salted

Lettuce: season extension

Meats: on the hoof, canned, frozen, dried

Milk: fermented as cheese and yogurt, frozen, preserved as salted
    butter

Onions: root cellared

Pears: root cellared, canned, dried

Peas, snap and snow: frozen

Peas, shell; dry, frozen

Peaches: dry, canned

Peppers, sweet: dried, frozen

Peppers, hot: dried, frozen

Plums: jam, dried

Potatoes: root cellared

Pumpkin: root cellared, dry, seeds dried (the USDA recommends
    against canning pumpkin or squash at home)
Raspberries: sauce, jam
Squash: root cellared, dried, seeds roasted and dried
Strawberries: dried (fabulous), jam
Summer squash: frozen
Tomatoes: Season extension, root cellared, dry, canned
Zucchini: dry, frozen, pickled

The Food Preserver's Year

Now let's look at the organizational aspects of putting up your own
food—something that I have never managed to get perfect, by the
way. If you haven't done it before, thinking about food preservation
can be overwhelming. Or if you have done it in the past, but did it in a
couple of very intensive bursts, it can seem impossible to find the time
to devote whole days to food preservation multiple times a year. Being
able to plan your harvest or your visits to the farmers' market, to know
when things will be coming ready, is a large part of managing your time
and saving energy and money when you're preserving food. Knowing
when the farmers have peaches to spare, or when you'll find wild raspberries locally, is the key to making sure you get your food cheaply, at
low energy cost and in season.

My own strategy is to take Carla Emery's idea of planting something every day that one can plant and putting up something every day
that there's something to harvest as my ideal, and a model. So instead
of trying to do all the strawberries in one swell foop (so to speak), I try
to stick some in the dehydrator one evening, and make six pints of jam
the next. A little here, a little there—sooner or later it all adds up to
real food.

Now some things still are big projects and there are times when you
want to take advantage of doing it all at once. But once you have a little
practice, you know when that is coming, and can reserve some time for
it. I know that once a year I'm going to buy sweet corn from an Amish
farmer who sells it at peak at 100 ears for $10, and put up 200 or 300
ears of corn cut off the cob. Corn chowder wouldn't taste the same

without it, and we don't want to do without that essence-of-summer-in-winter. But because I know that I'm going to do that in late August every year, I simply put on some loud rock and roll, accept my fate and get to work. I build the time into my life.

To do this, it helps to have a sense of how much food you are going to need for the year. This is one of those things that takes some practice — actually, I'm still practicing. I somehow forget that my four sons get bigger each year and eat more. I also would note that when eating homemade, quantities tend to multiply. Home produced is *so* much better than most commercial foods that you may find that jam or pickles or dried peppers go way faster than you thought they would. My own rule of thumb these days is when starting out, take what I'd expect us to use and multiply by two. That's probably not as useful a metric for a family with fewer growing kids, though.

One of the best reasons to eat home preserved food is the nutritional content — particularly if (like me) you are trying to eat less. Agricultural research has shown that conventional industrial agriculture has cut heavily into nutritional and trace mineral levels in food so much that we often are deficient in minerals even if we eat quite a bit. Food you produce on your own good soil or buy from farmers who care about soil, not just yield, and food you put up right after picking will provide not just filler, but nutrients.

Technically our food preservation season starts with dandelions, but while I dry a few for herb teas later on (they are great for your heart and a natural diuretic), I don't usually preserve anything until the rhubarb comes along. We usually put up a compote of rhubarb cooked in a bit of water (enough to just barely cover), with sugar to taste and about 1 teaspoon of almond extract and lemon juice per quart of rhubarb. Water bath can for 15 minutes for quarts, 10 minutes for pints, and you are in good shape.

We also sometimes mix rhubarb with the last of the stored apples, cook both down to sauce, add sweetener to taste, puree them and spread it out in the dehydrator to make fruit leathers.

Once the greens start in earnest, some of them get lactofermented for various kimchis. Any green is good this way — cover them with water, add a teaspoon of salt, and soak overnight. Then fill clean quart mason jars with the greens, half a teaspoon of salt, and a bit (or a lot if you like it hot) of Korean pepper or cayenne. We use wild greens a lot this way.

As the summer goes on, we get busier with preserving and we preserve right into the winter season — sometimes, if things can wait, it is nice to wait until it cools off. For example, I've started planting a late crop of cucumbers that produce heavily in September here, and am pushing back some of my pickling to the cooler weather. The reality is that there is no rule that says you have to do things one way or another — you can experiment. If you never have time in June because that's the rush time at your job, plant everbearing strawberries and put up your jam gradually, over the course of the summer. If you don't like pickles, don't pickle. The world is full of other good things to eat.

The information I'm giving you will be most useful for people living in approximately the same climate I do. If you live in the Southern Hemisphere, or much south or north of me, you'll have to get to know your local food sources, and find out what time of year things come at. And our family eats somewhat differently than most other families. We put up a huge amount of foods that most people wouldn't need nearly as much of, and there are foods we don't bother to preserve, because we are content to eat them fresh. But I think the process of making up a food-year calendar for yourself can be a great exercise, and I'd encourage all of you to do it.

How do you do it? Well, you take a good look at what is available in your garden, at local farmers' markets and elsewhere. How do you like the foods preserved? (Here you may need to do some experimentation to see what you and your family like to eat.) What recipes do you use them in?

I do want to emphasize that while you can go crazy trying to can or dry every single thing you've ever liked to eat so you can have it every day of the year, honestly, I think that in many ways, that's just as nuts as eating the pasty supermarket strawberries in January. That's not to say that I'm not just as addicted to salsa in the winter as you are, just that the more you can get used to eating the foods that are actually in season, either fresh (think season extension) or stored fresh in a root cellar or equivalent, the easier on you all this preserving will be, and the easier it will be to find the time to do it. Prioritize, prioritize, prioritize.

On the other hand, sometimes a little hard work really does save us time. Yes, it can be a pain to chop up all those tomatoes for pasta sauce, but it is so convenient to be able to dump the whole wheat pasta into the pot and pour it over not gloppy, super sweet, supermarket sauce, but your own roasted tomato and vegetable sauce. You are investing time now for freedom later.

So here's my food preservation year. It sounds more impressive than it is, since often I don't get it all done. I'm going to start my preservation year when things first start get going, in May. Some of you will be able to start it much earlier, others later.

May

- Can rhubarb sauce — a favorite dessert, and quickie breakfast dumped over raw rolled oats. It tastes much better than it sounds.
- Freeze eggs for baking and scrambling.
- Sell any extra eggs.
- Bake eggshells, pound them up and store in a coffee can to be added to home-produced chicken feed and to the watering can.
- Lactoferment dandelion green kimchi, although this isn't really a "storage" item since it always gets eaten almost immediately.
- Freeze and can up any squash or sweet potatoes we haven't used up.

I'll also coat some eggs with shortening and store them at room temperature, but because I won't want them until fall, that will be later in the season. They keep about six months, so I do this more with late eggs.

June

- Pickle garlic scapes.
- Dehydrate strawberries.
- Can strawberry jam, strawberry sauce and strawberry-rhubarb pie filling.
- Freeze snap peas.

- Dehydrate sweet shelling peas.
- Dehydrate greens (this is especially good for greens on the verge of bolting late in the month — they can be ground up and added as a filler to flours and soups).
- Can mint syrup for adding to water in the winter.
- Dry onions.

I should also pickle some early baby beets, but somehow I never get to it.

July

Preserving Boom Begins!

- Can blueberry jam, blueberry sauce, currant jam, currant juice, peach sauce, peach jam, apricot sauce, apricot jam, raspberry sauce, raspberry jam, peach chutney.
- Dehydrate blueberries, apricots, peaches, black currants, red currants.
- Can beets.
- Make kimchi out of various greens and roots.
- Freeze grated zucchini to use as a meat extender for ground beef.
- Dehydrate zucchini.
- Pickle green beans. (I don't bother to preserve green beans any other way. We don't like them frozen, dried or canned, so they, like asparagus, are one of those things we enjoy when we've got them.)
- Dry and braid garlic.

For us, tomatoes, corn and peppers do start this month, but they are too new to bother preserving — I wait for the glut later in the season. I manipulate my cucumber harvest so that most of them come in around September, when it is cooler.

This is also when I seriously start my root cellaring garden. Some things, like parsnips, potatoes, sweet potatoes, winter squash and Brussels sprouts have already gone in, but most of the carrots, beets, cabbage, celeriac, and other root crops are planted in July, as is some more kale and collards.

August

- Can tomatoes for salsa, tomato sauce, diced tomatoes.
- Dehydrate tomatoes.
- Dehydrate sweet peppers.
- Freeze watermelon.
- Can watermelon juice (surprisingly good).
- Dehydrate watermelon (really good!).
- Make watermelon rind pickles.
- Freeze sweet peppers.
- Pickle, dehydrate and freeze hot peppers (this depends on the variety: cayenne, kimchi, aleppo and poblanos get dried; jalapenos, fish peppers and bananas get pickled; serranos get frozen).
- Freeze and dehydrate sweet corn.

I might make some cucumber or zucchini pickles too, if it isn't too hot. Or I might not.

August is also when the last crops of greens, peas and favas go in, except spinach and arugula, which can keep going until September. Oh, and when I make raspberry vodka.

September

More of all of the above, plus cucumber pickles and beets. I also usually pickle some onions. By late September I may be harvesting dried-on-the-plant foods like dry corn, popcorn, amaranth and dried beans as well, or I might wait until October, depending on how things look.

We also start canning applesauce and dehydrating apples. Most of the early apples don't keep that well, so they are better eaten fresh, sauced and dried. Since September tends to be the last month I can reliably solar dehydrate, I try to do the dried apples then, but if I don't get it done, they can be hung up behind the wood stove.

October

- Harvest all the stuff we dried on the plant.
- Can more applesauce, pear sauce, green tomato pickles.
- Preserve late fruit (raspberries, apples, quinces, pears) in liquor.

- Make apple butter.
- Make cider syrup for pancakes.
- Make late fruit leathers.

It is also when we start butchering chickens and turkeys, and if I'm really ambitious, I'll can some of them — the meat and the broth — since I'm trying to minimize my freezer usage. Usually they get frozen, though.

I make more late tomato sauce until the last harvest comes in. Also my own V8 juice.

We also start filling the root cellar — digging the potatoes, beets, turnips, harvesting the cabbages, etc. But the balance is hard. Because our root cellar is actually an unheated porch, we have to wait to put things in until it is consistently cold, but if we wait too long we get the fun of pulling beets out of frozen ground. So there's always a race.

November

Most years, the race goes into November. We're still preserving food, although the focus has moved away from canning and dehydrating. In November it's cold enough to do large-scale lactofermentation. Until now, we've been making kimchi and sauerkraut in small quantities, to be eaten right away. Now we move towards big bucketfuls, because the process of fermentation slows down and we can keep it for months. So…

- Ferment daikon, cabbage, carrots, napa, bok choy and other greens.
- Dig potatoes and see if we have to buy more.
- Put the carrots in buckets of sand.
- Hang the onions.
- Add in fall butchering and late canning.
- Put up the coldframes and mulch things to overwinter.
- Gather the nuts — if we can beat the other nut-eaters.

December

This is the time to make presents and make cute little baskets of things. And to rest on our laurels a little. It's usually a quiet time in the food preserver's year. Most of the root-cellared stuff is new enough that there's no need to preserve it another way, and there's little new coming in, maybe just a few greens from the garden.

January–April

Now comes the project of management in earnest.

You have to track the stores. When onions show signs of shriveling, we put them in the dehydrator. When the apples start to go soft, I start canning applesauce. A squash develops a spot? Great, cut it up and freeze it, or can it. It isn't intense, the way summer preserving is, but it is constant, a little here, a little there, it all adds up.

And that's pretty much the way it will be until May, when the cycle starts again.

Recipes

Pickled Jalapenos (or Other Hot Peppers)

Ok, I like food hot. I mean really hot. And so I grow a lot of hot peppers. I love these in everything from spicy Spanish-style rice to macaroni and cheese (yup, really), or stuffed with good stuff and baked with a cornmeal coating (leave peppers whole if you are going to eat them that way), and, of course, they are great on enchiladas. Never enough pickled jalapenos! Makes 8 pints.

• 1 quart cider vinegar	• 1 cup honey
• 1 cup water	• 3 lbs jalapenos or other hot peppers

Slice jalapenos if you want them sliced (you get more in a jar this way, but then you do have to slice them — wear gloves, and don't touch your eyes!). Meanwhile, bring vinegar, water and honey to a boil. Dump jalapenos in and cook 1 minute. Then use a funnel to transfer jalapenos and enough liquid to cover into pint jars with ½-inch headspace, and process for 15 minutes in a boiling water bath.

Happy Tummy Tea

OK, we've all eaten something we shouldn't now and again. This really does make a good stab at fixing it, and even the kids love the taste. It is also very relaxing—the catnip will help you sleep if you need it. Oh, and the cat will happily lick the used tea bag, although maybe I shouldn't mention that part.

Put a smile on your face with this soothing and yummy tea.

• 1 part catnip	• 1 part peppermint
• 1 part lemon balm	• 1 part skullcap
• 1 part rosemary	• 1 part fennel seeds

Place all herbs in a tea ball or bag, put in your nicest, most favorite cup or mug, and cover with boiling water. Steep for 8 minutes. Remove tea ball or bag, and add milk or sweetener if that's to your taste.

Pumpkin Leather

• 2 cups canned pumpkin or 2 cups fresh pumpkin, cooked and puréed	
• ½ cup honey	• ¼ tsp cinnamon
• ⅛ tsp nutmeg	• ⅛ tsp powdered cloves

Blend ingredients well. Spread on a dehydrator fruit leather sheet or a cookie sheet lined with wax paper. Dry at about 140° until chewy and bendable. Coat lightly with cinnamon to keep from sticking and store away from heat. Eat as a delicious snack. Makes 8 servings.

Homemade Yogurt

Once you've made your own yogurt, and realize how cheap and delicious and easy it is, you'll never spend money on little containers again. The stuff is simple—and fabulous. This recipe comes from Kathy Harrison's wonderful book *Just In Case: How to Be Self-Sufficient When the Unexpected Happens*. Makes 1 quart.

- 1 quart milk, any kind—whole, skim, powdered (obviously, you have to add water), goat, cow, sheep...
- ¼ cup powdered milk (to thicken)
- 2 tbsp plain yogurt with a culture (i.e., any kind you buy at the store that says it has live culture in it)

Warm the milk over medium heat until bubbles form around the edge of the pan. Stir in the powdered milk, remove and let cool until the milk is lukewarm. You should be able to hold a finger in the milk for ten seconds.

Add the yogurt and stir until well combined. Pour the mixture into a wide-mouthed jar. Place the jar in a warm spot and let it sit for 4 to 6 hours. Don't disturb it or you risk breaking the yogurt's structure and it won't set. That's all there is to it.

I find a thermos useful in keeping it warm, if you don't have a warm spot in your kitchen. Eat it straight, or stir in a little jam to make fruit yogurt.

Once you have homemade yogurt, you can make:

Beets with Tahini Sauce

OK, I know you hate beets, or think you do, but this is the platonic beet recipe. There is something about this amazing combination that just transforms the beets. Try it—really. I've adapted the recipe from May Bsisu's spectacular book *The Arab Table*. Serves 4.

- 5 large or 10 small beets, peeled and diced
- 2 tbsp oil
- 2 tbsp tahini
- ½ tsp cumin
- 3 tbsp yogurt
- ½ tsp cinnamon
- Salt and pepper to taste

Coat the diced beets with oil and roast in a 425° oven until tender. Mean-while, mix all other ingredients. When the beets are tender, toss with the tahini-yogurt sauce. This can be served warm, cool or at room temperature and is absolutely, amazingly good.

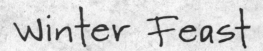

Winter Feast

The kids and I ate about half a raw cabbage this afternoon. We had four heads left in the garden, marginally protected, and we're going out of town this weekend, so we decided to harvest. The kids always want to eat what we pick, so off we went to get a knife, and nibble at slices of cabbage. And since we've gone through some heavy cold temperatures, the cabbage's starches were all converted to sugars. I knew it happened, of course, but I rarely have cabbages in the garden so late, so I'd never tasted one quite this good. So we ate and ate until we were full of raw cabbage and happiness, partly from the sheer surprise of it.

I don't think a lot of people write paeans to cabbage, or imagine watching their children devour nearly an entire head. But that's because they don't quite realize that the taste of home-grown, home-preserved food cannot be acquired any other way. This is food that even the richest people cannot buy at the store — the store never sells a cabbage that grew in rich soil and sat through the late frosts until it is perfectly ripe and as sweet as candy. And no store could sell the mix of wood smoke and winter air that perfectly accompanied the meal.

We still have turnips and beets, parsnips, carrots and daikon mulched in the ground, and kale, mustard and spinach as well. It has been a mild year, but even in the coldest winters here, with minimal effort I have been able to overwinter leeks and kale.

I've heard people say, "I love to garden so much I have to garden all year round, so I could never live where you do." Well, I do garden all year round. By the time most of the garden is finished, in mid-December, I'm picking out seeds. Leeks and the earliest container tomatoes, some greens and pansies will be started in January. When the first thaw comes in February (it is a fake, of course, but we'll take it), we dig parsnips, transformed by frost into confections, and check the cold frames for signs of life. The first protected greens are ready by the third week of March, by which time my house is exploding with seedlings, and at the beginning of April, the potatoes and onions go out, along with various greens and roots.

Global warming may have extended our season some (a pleasure not worth its price, of course), but even without it, gardening — and local eating — goes on forever and ever, each food in its time.

8

Root Cellaring and
Season Extension

Season Extension

My favorite way to eat most foods is fresh, just picked. That means my absolute favorite way to store food is to extend my garden's season so I don't have to do any real work to preserve the tastes. And this is so easy. Fall gardening is fun, there are no pests, and the food generally tastes better after a frost or two — the difference is huge. Kale eaten after a hard freeze is tender, with a deep sweetness. Kale before a freeze isn't bad, but it can't compare to the way it tastes in cold weather. Carrots that have undergone some cold weather are sugary, cabbage is sweet and crisp, winter lettuces aren't just background for salad but something transcendent.

Even in chilly upstate New York, without a greenhouse or a hoophouse (I'm hoping to have one someday) and with wintertime lows at −30° F, I can keep stuff going through December and into January. The last few years, I've occasionally managed to overwinter spinach, kale and leeks completely unprotected. Throw a foot or two of leaves or old hay on top of them, and no problem.

The book to get on this subject of cold climate season extension is Eliot Coleman's *Four Season Harvest* and I really recommend it. Obviously, the degree to which you can do this or need to do this will depend on where you live. In the coldest places, you can't leave anything out at all. In warm ones, season extension might be throwing a

161

blanket over the watermelon and lemon trees during the occasional frost. In hot climates, season extension may be all about using water-conserving crops, shade cloth and extremely heat tolerant varieties to get some food coming in during the hottest and driest period.

There are two kinds of season extension, to my mind. The first is the protection of crops so that you can harvest during cold or dry, hot seasons, the second is the planting of crops that will grow or regrow at the end of those unproductive seasons, to tide you over when nothing else is growing. Both are good. Kale, winter lettuce and carrots are crops we protect over the winter so that we can go out and harvest a bunch or dig a carrot on a warm day all winter. Overwintered spinach, on the other hand, isn't always that appetizing in January, when it is half frozen, but perks up beautifully come late March or early April before the plants we have started from seed are ready.

For the former, here in upstate New York, most of the growth generally has to be done by mid-September, which means planting in July or August. Down in North Carolina, where my friend Aaron lives, July and August are too hot for good germination, and the warmer winters mean that fall crops can be planted in September or later. Peas are started in peat pots inside, roots are planted or transplanted to be harvested in October or later. Quick growing greens like mizuna, arugula and spinach can be planted as late as early September even where I live.

Then the question is how much protection do they need and do I want to give them? Cold frames are great — you can build them or make them out of straw bales and old windows. Floating row covers will offer some protection, as will mulch. Even blankets thrown on at night and taken off in the morning will extend your season a week or two in many cases. You can cut the bottoms off old milk jugs and soda bottles and put them over plants you want to preserve. Don't forget to bring in containers and keep them growing on a windowsill — that's season extension too!

The amount of effort you put in will depend on what you are trying to accomplish. To keep a full crop of vegetables in place all winter will probably involve, at a minimum, a hoophouse and floating row covers, and maybe supplemental heat in a cold spot. To extend your season an extra month or so might be easily done with some plastic and some leaves.

Once, when people depended on their stores, early spring was called "the starving time." All of the fall's harvest was running out, and nothing new was growing. After enduring "the long winter" of near starvation, for example, Laura Ingalls Wilder's family saw the winter end and the world turn green again, but there was still no food to eat while they awaited the train bearing supplies after a winter with no deliveries.

> April went slowly by. There was no food in the town except the little wheat left from the sixty bushels that young Mr. Wilder and Cap had brought in the last week of February. Every day Ma made a smaller loaf, and still the train did not come…
>
> "I've thought of greens," Ma said. "But I can't find any weeds in the yard that are big enough to pick yet."
>
> "Could we eat grass?" Carrie asked.

Although most of us can hope never to endure that sort of hunger, the story reminds us that in some ways it was not winter, but early spring that was to be feared, when stores ran out and nothing was ready.

This is where the second kind of season extension makes such a difference — those crops designed to be enjoyed in early spring, because they got a head start in the fall. Parsnips, spinach, and greens are common examples. Salsify and scorzonera work this way too. Kale, leeks, collards, roots, winter lettuces, mache and other very cold-hardy things can also be overwintered with mulch. They will die back during the winter, but regrow vigorously long before you can get down into the soil.

Making this work will take some practice, and will depend on your region. The exact timing of planting and protecting is something that you'll need to work on by experimenting. But having some fresh things from the garden can soften our workload and increase our pleasure.

Making the Most
Out of Your Garden Mistakes

Ok, you are a terrible person and you are totally doomed. You see, you meant to plant a garden this year (or a bigger garden, or a better garden or something), you really did. But you were sick in May and then there was a work crisis, and the tiller didn't work, and the guy who was going to bring the horse manure never came and somehow, here it is, the last week of June, and your garden isn't even started, or is only half the size you intended, or three of the beds aren't planted. Or maybe you did plant your garden, and the drought or the floods or the locusts or the herds of armadillos destroyed it completely, or weeds the size of Godzilla have sprung up and you are fairly sure there were some carrots in there once, but you can't find them. And here it is, the end of June, and you have no garden, or only half of one, or nothing like what you'd thought you'd have.

And you are thinking, "I'm doomed. My family is going to be eating bugs, and not the good kind of bugs, which will all have been harvested by Sharon and her family who are so far ahead of us. No, we're going to be eating the bugs no one even has recipes for." You are thinking, "If I can't even get one stupid little garden planted, or plant it and can't protect it from disaster, my whole family is going to starve to death and it will be all my fault. I am bad. I am worthless."

Ok, stop. Guess what. You aren't doomed, and my family is pretty much like yours. You see, there were these sheep, that escaped the fencing and ended up in my garden. That took care of the strawberries and the early tomatoes. Then there was this book. And then there were a host of reasons, some real and some stupid, why half my garden is in cover crops or something else. I could claim it was because of my deep commitment to the soil, but that wouldn't explain why I was crawling around on my knees sticking random unplanted onions in between things. Do you know when you are supposed to plant onions here? The middle of April. And I was planting them on June 26. Nor would it explain why there are sad-looking hot pepper plants looking at me and crying, "Plant me...for the love of god...plant me...I could fruit still before frost if you'd just get me the hell out of my flat, where I've been since March!" And here I am ignoring them.

Am I panicked? Nope. Guilty? Nope. But only because I've been here so often that I've gotten pretty comfortable with the reality. All the perfect gardens live in my head, and the truth is, every year's garden is totally messed up. The thing is, I end up eating a lot of food from that messed up garden, and it does get better every year. Or at least every year without sheep in the front yard.

Heck, this sort of thing happens to everyone — and I do mean *everyone*. There are thousands of farmers in the Midwest who endured flooding in the summer of 2008 who had absolutely no choice but to say, "OK, no corn this year…hmmm…soybeans or do I wait for winter wheat?" That's not to suggest this isn't hard or scary or painful, or that the consequences of having a bad garden couldn't get a lot tougher than they are. They certainly are for those farmers, and I'm not trying to mock the sheer pain of seeing something you've worked on washed away. But now that we've mourned our follies or nature or whatever, it is time to move on. And for most of us it is never too late to produce a good bit of food, while loftily implying that you meant things to come out this way. (Gardeners are like cats — everything we do is intentional, even when it isn't.) The trick is knowing how.

One option for most of us is to just say, "The heck with the summer garden, I'm going to have a super-amazing *fall* garden. For us northerners, that means starting in mid-summer. I finish my summer planting on June 30, and then I begin my fall planting on July 1. Sounds crazy, but that's when I need to start cabbages and other late crops by (OK, actually it's usually more like July 7, but it sounds better this way). The thing is, most fall crops need time to mature while days are still long. Some things, like spinach and mustard greens, can be planted as late as September here, but this far north, most of the fall garden gets planted in July and August. And fall gardens are the best — no bugs, things don't require as much attention since the weeds grow slower, etc.

You can also plant most short season summer crops as late as mid-July in my climate. Near me it is by no means too late to plant cucumbers, basil, zucchini, green beans and lettuce. Other than a few beets and carrots for summer enjoyment, I don't even really bother to plant my main crop of most root vegetables until early July. We are so busy in high summer eating tomatoes and eggplant that I don't really want turnips, cabbage or the main crop of carrots until late September, so why rush about madly trying to get them planted when everything else is going in? And some crops, like lettuce, broccoli and rapini do better in the cooler temperatures of fall anyway. Don't worry about the broccoli going to seed at all — just enjoy having a good fall crop.

The other things I plant late are canning vegetables. I used to plant my cukes in late May, when everyone else did. Then I realized something — I don't really love standing over a hot canning kettle in July. Now I do it for the blueberries — that's their time, and there's no good way around it. But the cucumbers keep coming until October, so why is it I was melting here in July? Oh, because I have a giant glut of pickling cucumbers, and I don't want to waste them. But if I make the glut come when I want it, I can can when I want to. So now I start my cucumbers in mid- (or sometimes late) June and the glut comes in early September when it is cooler, and I don't mind canning as much.

By the end of June it probably is too late for tomatoes and peppers and eggplant, at least from seed. But what if you have seedlings or your local nursery is trying to get rid of its stuff so it can start the chrysanthemums, and you want to try it? Well, my suggestion is to go for it. Pull off any blossoms, plant them deep, and take a shot at it. Or even better, stick them in a nice big pot. Because then, if frost hits before the tomatoes fruit, you can drag the pot into the lobby of your building or into your garage for those first few frosty nights, and stretch the tomatoes out a bit. The peppers and eggplants are true perennials, and you might even be able to overwinter them, if you've got the right conditions, and then brag to everyone about how smart you are and that you've got hot peppers in June.

The other possibility is that you can put in cover crops. Now this is especially good because true, serious gardeners know that soil is everything. In fact, serious gardeners believe that their vegetables are mere by-products of good soil. You pretty much just plant the chard to keep the earthworms happy. So if you tell everyone, "Oh, I put 80 percent of my garden into vetch and oats for green manure this year, I really felt the soil needed it," other gardeners will nod wisely and feel sad and selfish because they don't love their soil enough to forgo pumpkins and parsnips. It helps the effect if you look sad at their selfishness too.

Some of these cover crops actually produce food, too. For example, buckwheat is a delicious salad green, and if you are lazy about cutting it down (which I often am) produces tasty and nutritious seed. It isn't quite as good for your soil after going to seed, but it isn't terrible either. Red clover makes a nutritional tea if you harvest the blossoms. Daikon radishes break up soil, and I promise not to tell if you accidentally harvest one or ten and make kimchi or Japanese pickles with them.

You could even experiment. I have some seed potatoes I have not planted this year — I ran out of space in the potato patch, and I thought I'd allocated all the rest of my garden to other things. But I found a spot and I'm curious as to what kind of yield I'll get from potatoes planted at the end of June. For those in warmer places, fall is a good time to plant potatoes. And since my potatoes keep best if they are harvested when it is quite cool, this might actually work out well. It's worth a shot, anyway.

"Experiment" explains anything. Just point to your flooded-out plot and look wise and say, "This is a test garden, planted to compare how well hybrid corn does in marginal conditions vs. open pollinated." Imply there's a comparative plot "over there somewhere" and that it is all supposed to look that way.

Most of all, remember that you are not doomed. Your next garden will be better, because you will have learned from experience. Next year you will do remarkable things. You will probably make a whole new set of mistakes next year, and come up with a new, creative range of personal excuses. See, you've learned something!

And you needn't worry that my family will get all the good bugs. We'll be right there along with you, trying out recipes for the rejects while some other family, who always does it right, eats the locust croquettes with their correctly succession-planted arugula that never bolts before another crop gets put in place. I already hate them, don't you?

Root Cellaring

The term "root cellaring" is something of a misnomer. You see, most of us probably don't have a root cellar attached to our house. At best we have a basement. If you are like me, and live in an old house with a basement that floods once in a while, your basement isn't a very appealing place to think of sticking your food. So you may dismiss the idea of root cellaring out of hand.

That would be a shame because a surprisingly large number of people have some space where they can store food in its natural state. And that's all that root cellaring actually is. Root cellaring is finding a way to mimic the natural conditions that some foods store well in. You may end up keeping your food in a basement, but you shouldn't limit yourself to that.

So what conditions do food require? Well, it depends on the food. The basics of root cellaring involve taking a hard-shelled or very dense fruit or vegetable that naturally has a good storage life, and keeping it very cool. For most foods (there are a couple of important exceptions) the closer you can get to just above freezing the better. More realistically, most root cellars will vary by 10 or 15 degrees over the course of the year. For example, our "root cellar" is actually an unheated porch that doesn't freeze. By November it is usually cool enough to keep most root cellared vegetables. We store them in bins, bags and boxes out on that porch. On really cold nights, we add blankets for extra insulation, and they do fine. We do not, however, achieve the perfect root cellar temperatures, so it helps that we choose good storage varieties.

Pumpkins, squash and sweet potatoes actually like warmer temperatures in the high 50s to low 60s, that is, the temperatures all of us conserving people keep our houses at anyway. So pumpkins, squash and sweet potatoes can go right in the house with you — in the cupboard, under the guest bed or in a convenient closet. Just don't forget they are there. Even apartment dwellers can preserve these foods — you just find a spot and put them there. What kind of preservation could be easier?

Onions and garlic like conditions quite dry but cool. Your attic in the winter is probably too dry for good storage of apples and potatoes, but it might be just perfect for your onions and garlic. Just watch out for those unseasonable warm spells.

Where else might you find space? Well, what about outside? In cold climates many crops can be pulled up and left in trenches or holes in the ground, and then covered with a thick (several feet in my climate) layer of hay, straw or leaves. Straw bales laid over the trenches are perfect. You may get mice or other critters occasionally, but often things survive fairly well.

You can dig a hole and bury a wood or metal barrel, an old cooler, an old fridge or freezer in the ground and then cover the top with straw or leaves or hay to insulate it. Voila — instant root cellar. The only problem, of course, is that in places like mine where you often get deep, heavy, extended snow cover, you may not really want to dig three feet of snow off the root cellar. But that is the price of simplicity.

Or you could dig a traditional root cellar. Mike and Nancy Bubel, who wrote *Root Cellaring,* the definitive book on this subject, have dug a number of such cellars and offer plans that look feasible even to construction dummies like me. The idea of making a hobbit hole in the ground may appeal to more people than just me.

Regardless, no one should dismiss root cellaring. I know a woman who keeps her root cellared crops in a Manhattan apartment in the spare bedroom, with a window cracked to keep it cool. Writer and nutritionist Joan Dye Gussow built a closet into her home, with a vent coming up from the basement so that she could have an easily accessible root cellar. Other people I know have insulated a portion of their garage or even a garden shed to create a space for natural cold storage. It mostly takes imagination.

Choosing Varieties for Root Cellar Storage

If you are going to use natural cool storage to keep vegetables and fruits in a root cellar, it matters a great deal which varieties you grow or purchase from farmers. Some varieties simply will not keep, others will last nearly forever. For example, a Yellow Transparent apple from one of my trees will turn to mush in a matter of a few weeks, while a Stayman Winesap or Northern Spy apple will be crisp and sweet well into April. So as you are planning, make sure that if you intend to root cellar, you are choosing seed varieties or making purchases from farmers with keeping qualities in mind. Again, I highly recommend that you refer to the Bubel's book on the subject, which has a much more extensive list of varieties than I could hope to include here.

Here are varieties I have experience with storing.

Apples: We store *tons* of these, and the best keeping varieties we've found are: Roxbury Russet, Northern Spy, Winesap, Lady, Winter Keeper, Smokehouse, Winter Banana, Mutsu, Sheepnose, Cortland.

Beets: Lutz Longkeeper is by far the most famous storage variety. Detroit Dark Red does reasonably well, but our favorite storage variety is Rote Kugel, huge and dense and delicious.

Cabbage: January King and Glory of Enkuizen are my best keepers. Mammoth Red Rock, a red cabbage, stores almost as well. I've had great luck with older heirlooms, and have not bothered with hybrids here. We usually eat cabbage into March or April.

Carrots: I've found that most large carrots store fairly well in buckets of moist sand. Oxheart stores very well for us, but any thick variety will do well. We use playground sand and five-gallon buckets.

Garlic: I haven't noticed a lot of problems with keeping garlic. If it seems to be drying up, we just dehydrate it for garlic powder.

Potatoes: The big issue with potatoes is that you want to store late-crop potatoes, for the most part, because they haven't been sitting around. Katahdin, Green Mountain, Carola, Yukon Gold, German Butterball, Purple Peruvian all store well for us.

Pears: Bosc, Anjou, Bartlett and Kieffer will all store for a couple of months.

Quince: I've only grown one variety; it seems to keep several months.

Rutabagas: Laurentian keeps very well.

Turnips: Purple Top White does the very best keeping for us, but Golden Ball is a close second and tastier.

Onions: New York Early does very well for me. Stuttgarter, the common set hybrid also does very well. For sweet onions, Candy will keep for a month or two.

Sweet potatoes: The only two varieties I've tried are northern-adapted versions, Georgia Jet and Porto Rico. With care, they'll often last until the next summer.

Daikons: They all seem to keep for a couple of months.

Squash: These vary a great deal. There are lots of excellent keepers out there, but some of our favorites are: Marina de Chioggia, Butternut, Green Hubbard (the big ones keep much better than the little Hubbards), Waltham Butternut, Pink Banana, Futsu, Hopi Orange and Thelma Sanders. At times, we've eaten last year's squash in August just to make room for the next crop.

Eating From the Root Cellar

In *A Nation of Farmers* Aaron Newton and I wrote about "vegeculture," which is a reliance on root crops over grains. Among the staple vegetables that people have relied on are the familiar potatoes, sweet potatoes and turnips, and the less familiar (to those of us in temperate climates) taro, manioc, mangel and cassava. It is hard to overestimate the degree to which root culture has shaped our society. Some anthropologists date the European Renaissance to the widespread cultivation of turnips and mangels, which allowed populations to keep more of their animals over the winter. New evidence has shown that the Maya relied more heavily on roots than was ever expected in the growth of their civilization.

We might even suggest that emphasizing "root culture" over "seed culture" (most grains and legumes are seeds) might provide a fundamental shift in our society as a whole. Most root crops are flexible in ways that seed crops are not. They can provide heavier yields and more calories per acre. Moreover many roots can tolerate being left in the ground in quite cold climates, so they can often be harvested more flexibly. Root crops tend to be tough crops. They might survive where seed crops fail.

And yet most of us are fairly unfamiliar with, or even hostile to, root-cellared vegetables. We "know" that we hate turnips and beets. We eat our potatoes frozen, as tater tots and fries, so we think of them as bland. We have forgotten that potatoes taste radically different depending on variety and season. Most of us have no idea what to do with a kohlrabi or a daikon. So now that we know how to keep these foods, more importantly, how do we come to eat them?

Like any shift in our diet, as we've discussed, this begins gradually. None of these foods are essentially off-putting. Russia has perfected beet cuisine, and the British love parsnips so much they import out-of-season ones from Australia so they can treat parsnips like we do tomatoes. Knowing what to do with them is part of the food storage project.

My family eats roots more or less constantly in the winter. A common dinner here is roasted vegetable enchiladas, in which a mix of roots, roasted with oil, garlic and spices, are layered under a warm pepper sauce. Or it might be roasted potatoes with greens and a chipotle-garlic cheese sauce. We might eat potato-salmon cakes, or latkes with applesauce, a delicious curried stew of sweet potatoes, onions and peanuts in coconut curry sauce, or a delicious bowl of borscht, rich with beef and beans among the beets.

Shifting to a root-based winter diet is not really that hard. There are cookbook suggestions on my website. We simply have to get over our prejudice against these foods, and begin to really integrate them gradually into our lives.

Recipes

Stuffed Cabbage with Dried Fruits, Mushrooms and Wild Rice

This is adapted from Georgeanne Brenna's lovely book *France: The Vegetarian Table* and has become my favorite way to eat stuffed cabbage. Serves 4.

- 1 large cabbage (Savoy is the easiest to separate)
- 2 tbsp salt
- 1 large onion, diced
- ¼ cup golden or regular raisins
- 2 tsp white pepper
- 4 tbsp butter or good oil
- 10 dried prunes, chopped
- 4 dried apricots, chopped
- 1 tsp ground cumin

- ¾ cup fresh or dried and reconstituted wild mushrooms, the more flavorful the better
- 1 tbsp chopped rosemary
- vegetable or chicken broth
- 2 cups wild rice cooked until tender in meat or vegetable broth or apple cider
- ⅓ cup heavy cream

Peel off the dry outer leaves of the cabbage, if any. Put the whole cabbage in a pot, cover with water, add salt and boil for 15 minutes. Remove cabbage from pot and drain in a colander until cool. Unwrap and remove leaves from the outside in, setting them aside. When it becomes impossible to keep removing leaves, cut the stem out of the center, and chop the center cabbage — you should have 6 cups of chopped cabbage. Melt the butter in a large skillet, sauté cabbage and onions until translucent. Add dried fruit and mushrooms and cook for 5–7 minutes, until tender. Add pepper, cumin and salt to taste. Remove from heat and mix with cream and rice.

Wrap a small amount of filling in each cabbage leaf, fold until closed and place in a baking dish. Pour enough vegetable broth over to come about halfway up on the cabbage, cover baking dish and bake 35 minutes at 375° until tender.

Mashed Potatoes with Garlic and Olive Oil

These are rich, delicious and addictive. We like them at Thanksgiving and, really, anytime. Serves 4.

- 3 lbs Russet or Gold Potatoes
- 1 cup vegetable or chicken broth
- 12 large cloves of garlic, unpeeled
- ½ cup high quality olive oil

Place potatoes and garlic in a steamer, and steam until both are tender. Squeeze garlic from the skins when cool enough, and mash the potatoes, adding the broth and oil until fluffy and tender. Season with salt and pepper and serve at once.

Balsamic Glazed Onions

When I started keeping kosher, I found that I could substitute for almost every item on the family holiday menu except the creamed onions. But fortunately, these are so good that no one misses the creamy stuff. Serves 4.

- 12 medium onions
- ¼ cup balsamic vinegar
- 4 tbsp oil

Peel onions, but leave whole. Place in a lightly oiled baking dish. Drizzle a bit more oil over them, and pour balsamic vinegar over. Bake at 425°, turning over once, until the balsamic vinegar is thick and the onions are golden.

Root Vegetables Massaman Curry

This is one of my favorite Thai curries. We keep tinned curry paste (which isn't as good as fresh, but will do) in our pantry. Root vegetables have an affinity for curry, I find. Serves 4.

- 1 lb peeled carrots, cut into 1 inch chunks
- 1 cup coconut milk
- 1½ lb red potatoes, quartered
- ½ cup whole, roasted peanuts
- ½ cup pineapple juice
- 3 tbsp rice wine vinegar
- 2 bay leaves
- ⅓ cup massaman curry paste
- 1 lb onions, sliced
- 1 cup canned pineapple chunks
- ¼ cup soy sauce
- 1 tbsp brown sugar
- 1 cinnamon stick

Cook the curry paste in a bit of the coconut cream from the top of the canned milk for 3 minutes, until fragrant. Stir in the rest of the ingredients and bring to a boil. Reduce heat and simmer for 25 minutes, or until all vegetables are tender. Serve with steamed rice.

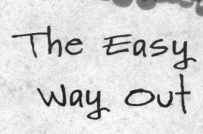

The Easy
Way Out

I've never liked the hot weather. Other people sweat but I wilt (oh, and I sweat plenty too). That's why I understand why people who think of food preservation as standing over a hot canning kettle all summer think, "I could never do that." I'm right there with you.

Today, however, when it is 92 degrees in the shade, I am preserving food, and, well, I'm no hotter than I would be if I were napping on the couch. I've got zucchini ready to go — you know about zucchini and its tendency to take over the garden, right? Well, I have several ways of taming them. I grate some zucchini and freeze it to be mixed with ground meat. It extends the meat and improves the textures. I pick off the squash blossoms and stuff them with cheese and fry them for a treat. My kids think eating flowers is the coolest thing ever. And best of all, we make zucchini chips.

I slice the squash into small, bite-sized bits, dust them with oil, garlic powder, salt and other spices, and then set them outside on the solar food dehydrator to dry. When they are finished, they are crunchy, spicy and tasty. My kids eat them as though they are fried.

But best of all, the sun does the work, transforming the blazing heat into something other than an annoyance. Meanwhile, I have nothing to do but sit in the shade and slice zucchini in slow rhythm, as the sun beats down and cooks my winter's treats for me.

So much of this is really about working smarter, as they say, not harder. With a little practice you begin to see ways to integrate food preservation into your life. Instead of it owning you, you are using it to make time for yourself in the coming winter months, when one day you will be too busy to cook and need a little essence of summer to cheer you.

9

Dehydration

DEHYDRATION IS PROBABLY the oldest food preservation strategy known to man, and almost certainly the most frequently used over the course of history. It isn't difficult — the idea is that you remove enough of the water in foods to make them unattractive to bacteria. Once you do so, the food should keep a long time. Dehydration is one of the least energy intensive ways to store food, and while you can use electricity to do it, you don't have to, so it is also attractive from a sustainability perspective.

You eat dried foods all the time. Grains, beans and peas are left to dry on the vine or stem, and are used only dry. You've almost certainly enjoyed dried fruit and fruit leathers. If you've ever eaten a package of instant soup, or made soup from a mix, you've probably eaten dried vegetables. Things like sun-dried tomatoes and dried apricots are quite costly when purchased, but inexpensive (and wonderful) when you make them at home.

The other good news about drying is that you don't need a lot of space for your dried foods. A bushel of tomatoes, when dried, will fill up a few quart jars on a shelf. If you are a city dweller, drying food is probably the most efficient way to make use of the bounty from your farmers' market, and even apartment dwellers can make space for quite a bit of dried food.

Nutritionally, according to the Rodale Institute, most dehydrated food is roughly equivalent to frozen food. Most of the nutritional loss comes if you blanch things — the steam or boiling water takes away a lot of nutrients. Sometimes this is useful, though, because it preserves flavor, color and texture. Because dried foods are concentrated, pound for pound they are much more nutritious than fresh foods. They are also more nutritious than canned foods, which lose nutritional value through high heat. That said, however, you do want to dehydrate at the lowest temperature possible and store dried food in a cool, dry, airtight place if you are concerned with nutrition. Greens and herbs especially require care in that regard. I usually dehydrate both of these by hanging in a cool, dark spot, rather than with any heat at all.

The Basics

Generally speaking, you want your food to be quite dry. Fruits (including tomatoes) can be 80 percent moisture free, because their acidity helps inhibit spoilage. Low-acid vegetables require 90 percent moisture removal. In practice, this means that fruits can often be stored at the flexible, chewy stage, while most vegetables need to get to the crisp dry stage.

The bigger and thicker the piece of food, the longer it takes to dry. Which means that generally speaking, you'll want to cut things up. Cherry tomatoes, green beans and smaller strawberries are about the only thing I dry whole. Everything else gets sliced up.

Blanching is one of those things that the experts vary on. Blanching softens foods, and makes them hold color and texture better. The best way to do it is to steam things a minute or two, rather than put them in boiling water, which dissolves the nutrients. My feeling is that blanching should be used only when it really improves the flavor of things, so while one home preserving book I own actually recommends blanching grapes, I think that's totally nuts. The only foods we blanch are tough-skinned vegetables that seem to need it — green beans, sweet corn and zucchini. The Rodale Institute also recommends blanching greens, but I dry them without blanching all the time. I've done it both ways, and the color is definitely nicer if you blanch, but greens work fine either way. Really hard things like potatoes, carrots and pumpkin do need to be softened up a bit as well. If you do blanch, do it for the minimum amount of time and plunge the food into cold water to stop the cooking immediately afterwards.

The range of opinions on dehydrating is huge. Someone in one of my food storage classes reported that one book said that dried strawberries were bland. I think they might be the food of actual divinities — bland is not the word. Some books recommend lots of blanching. Some recommend almost none. Some recommend microwave drying of herbs and greens. Others say that the food gets cooked and the nutritional value destroyed (I think this latter opinion is actually right). The truth is that you'll probably have to experiment. I think the most even-handed treatment of drying is in Carla Emery's *The Encyclopedia of Country Living,* which has been newly released in its 10th edition. She really offers a range of perspectives on pre-treatments. The only pre-treatment other than blanching I've ever used is ascorbic acid. I crush a vitamin C tablet into some water and dip fruit into it to keep the color. If you don't do it, it just won't be quite as pretty, but it won't hurt anything. I do this with apples and if I think about it, apricots. The rest I don't worry about.

The really definitive book on the subject, and well worth owning if you think you might do a lot of drying, is *Dry It — You'll Like It* By Gen MacManiman. It is a nice book, and not too expensive. She also has a great website, with recipes and lots of information and her own line of dehydrators: dryit.com.

Some people sulfur their fruit so they'll look pretty — I don't, and I don't recommend it. Breathing sulfur isn't good for you and the chemicals can cause severe allergic reactions in those sensitive to sulfites. I'm not going to tell you how, since I don't think it is a good idea, but if you really want sulfured fruit, *The Encyclopedia of Country Living* does discuss it.

One traditional way to dry some foods is to hang them on thread in a warm, dry spot, perhaps behind a wood stove or by a radiator. Apples and green beans (which are called "leather britches") were the traditional foods done this way. The apples are cored, peeled and cut into rings, the green beans are strung on a thread with a needle and hung up in an airy place to dry. This is a nice, easy way to experiment with drying. Greens and herbs, as mentioned above, can just be hung in a cool, dry, airy place until they are crumbly dry, and then transferred into jars.

Or, if you live in a warm, dry climate, you could just lay out some food on a mesh screen in the sun with a bit of cheesecloth over it — just don't dry meat this way! This is how many indigenous people dried their winter's food.

If you want to get started but aren't sure if you want to invest in any form of dehydrator, and can't do either of the above, as mentioned in the chapter on low energy preservation, a car can operate as a dehydrator.

Once you've decided what you want to dry, cut it into small, thin pieces, lay it out in the dehydrator set up of your choice and then check on it from time to time. If you want to use the sun, one way is to staple cheesecloth to light wooden frames and use tight strings across the back to support the weight of the food. Don't forget to cover the food with cheesecloth to keep insects off it. You'll want most veggies either crumbly or crisp. You'll want fruits quite stiff and chewy. If the fruits are sticky, you can toss them with something to separate them — some cinnamon is nice.

Once your food is dry, if you are worried about insect eggs, you can freeze it for a couple of days or heat it up in your dehydrator or oven to 175° for 15 minutes. But usually just sticking it in an airtight jar is enough. If you see any signs of condensation inside, your food is not dry enough and should be dried more — and fast before it molds. One option is to leave it out for a couple of days after it dries to further dry, stirring it every day. You could leave it out in a bowl, covered with a bit of cheesecloth, unless you live in a very humid climate. This will dry the food a bit further, without having to use high temperatures. Just keep an eye on it. Then store it in a cool, dark place in an airtight jar. You can also determine if dry food is dry enough by weighing it. If you had a ten-ounce cup of strawberries before, it should weigh one to two ounces when appropriately dry.

Dry foods keep a long time, but they do lose nutritional value and flavor in storage. Ideally you'll eat most of them within two years, but greens and herbs should probably be used within one year, at the longest.

How do we eat dried foods? We eat a lot of ours straight — dried veggie chips, dried sweet peppers and tomatoes, dried fruits, etc. are all great eaten out of hand, as are fruit leathers, which are made with purees. We also rehydrate some dried items. We might make a fruit compote, where a little water and wine is added to mixed, dried fruit which is then stewed. We sometimes rehydrate dried peppers or tomatoes in oil, adding a rich flavor, and making the oil great for salads. If you are making soups or stews, just throw the dried vegetables into the pot. Carrots and other dense things can go in early, while greens and herbs are added at the last moment.

We also use dried veggies to add flavor — dry them to crispness, run through a blender or heavy-duty spice grinder and then add them as a seasoning. The obvious choice here is onion or garlic powder, and can I just say how amazing homegrown garlic is powdered, compared to anything available at a store? The same is true of home-produced chili powder. But you can get fancier than that. We use dehydrated tomatoes, onions and garlic together with some herbs to make a soup flavoring that can't be beat. Orange peel and dehydrated sweet peppers blended to powder are delicious together and brighten up just about any cooked dish.

My kids love fruit leathers. Just make a puree of fruit, a little lemon juice and maybe a little honey, if the fruit is tart. If you use over-ripe fruit, you won't need the honey, and this is a great use for fruit a little past its prime. You do need a special leather tray, or some waxed paper, though. It can be done in the sun or a dehydrator. Don't overlook the possibilities of chocolate-dipped dried fruits or other treats as gifts!

Dehydrating Meat

Meats can be dehydrated as well, and this is a classic method of preserving them. Jerkies are one of those things you either like or don't — we like them, but some people don't. The dryer you use for drying meats *must* be kept between 140 and 150 degrees at all times. That means either using a solar dehydrator system that gets *hot,* that you check often (both because it has to stay hot and because if it gets too hot, it will cook the meat), and that you are very careful with, or an electric or wood-fired dehydrator, period. Don't mess with food poisoning.

Only beef from non-factory farmed, grass-fed sources, venison, moose and fish from safe waters should be dehydrated from a raw state. All other meats must be completely cooked before drying. The USDA recommends that all game meats should be frozen for at least two months before using, to kill all microorganisms. Use only extremely lean meats—less than 10 percent fat is recommended, since the fats can turn rancid and ruin the taste of the jerky. All jerky meats need to be marinated in a salty or soy sauce marinade before drying. The salt breaks down tissues, kills insects and helps preserve the meat.

For one pound of meat you need one and a half cups of salt dissolved in one gallon of water or half a cup of soy sauce (soy tastes better). Fish needs one cup of salt to the same quantity of water, and both should marinate for 24 hours. Cut off every bit of fat or gristle, cut the meat or fish into thin strips and dehydrate until leathery and tough. Store in a cool dark place for up to two months, checking for signs of rancidity, or freeze it for up to a year. White-fleshed fish and salmon dry best; oily fish like mackerel or bluefish don't do as well.

Dehydrating With—or Without—the Sun

If you live in a humid climate, you'll probably find that food will mold faster than you can dry it most of the time. Blue and furry food is not desirable, so you need something that will work better. Our homemade solar dehydrator works very well (there are links to plans on my website). We use black polyester fabric, and I use plastic mesh polypropylene screens from my electric dehydrator, since polypropylene does not contain bisphenol-a. Ours is way too small, and we're planning a much bigger one soon.

But what if you feel like you need a dehydrator that uses an energy source? Maybe you live in an apartment and don't get any sun. Or maybe your climate is cool and rainy and there aren't enough sunny days to dehydrate the food you need.

You might try building a wood fired dehydrator, if you've got a sustainable source of wood. Wood dehydrators can use very small twigs and scrap wood, and produce very small amounts of emissions. There are instructions for building these on the Internet and more information at the link vault on my website.

You can also dehydrate with a heat source that's already going. Some people dehydrate in their gas ovens with their pilot light on — I think the success of this depends a lot on how humid your climate is. I've heard of people doing it successfully and of people having problems. If you use a wood stove, you can dehydrate on screens placed near the stove (not too near — you don't want to cook the food), and if you have an earth oven, you can use it to dehydrate when it gets to the lower end of the temperature range.

It is worth stopping for a minute here to talk about temperature — as mentioned, most foods are most nutritious if they are dehydrated at the lowest possible temperatures. Herbs and greens can lose most of their value if they are dehydrated much above air temperature. You generally don't want them too warm. And with every food, you want to use the lowest acceptable temperature, because dehydrating already causes a fair loss of nutritional value. So you do want to be careful with oven drying of any sort. Yes, you can do it, but it can be hard to keep temperatures low enough for the food to be nutritious as well as good tasting. The same issue occurs with solar dehydrating in your car. If it gets up to 200 degrees in there, that's fine for beef jerky and it may not be much of an issue for tomatoes, but you do not want to put medicinal herbs, greens or berries like blueberries, elderberries or cranberries in there, since so much of their value is located in vitamins lost at high temperatures and with long cooking. Maybe do the berries on an overcast day.

Finally, there is electric dehydration. This is useful for people like me who have crops coming in during periods when solar dehydration isn't possible. Basically, an electric dehydrator is a set of stacked trays with a heating element and (sometimes) a fan. If you live in a dry, warm place, you probably don't need one at all — you might as well take advantage of the sun. In a cooler place, if you are content to be done dehydrating in September and October, you'd also be fine without one. On the other hand, electric dehydrators are convenient, and they are the sort of thing that shows up on Craigslist and freecycle and at garage sales.

If you buy one used, you probably will end up with a low-end plastic model. You'll definitely be putting your food in contact with polycarbonate, which means bisphenol-a. This is something to think about, but may or may not be a major concern for you. I've had two of these, both from yard sales — one American Harvest and one Ronco — and they both work fine. The Ronco gets the best reviews of the low-end models, but I've met people who like almost all of them. They use more electricity than the upper end ones, sometimes overheat things, and can take a while, but they aren't bad tools. For five dollars at a yard sale, there's only so much complaining you can do. If you have a choice, you do want one with a fan, not just a heating element, because you'll get much more even dehydration and fewer hot spots.

Most of these retail for between 35 to 60 dollars. I would tend to bet that most of you could find a used one, though. If you do buy used, make a quick check of the produce recall lists for the brand you buy. One older American Harvest model was recalled because the heating unit caused a fire. They are generally perfectly safe to use unattended, though.

There are a few more expensive, higher-end models, usually made by the same people (not always — Vita Mix has one). I have not tried any of these. When I do reviews, I generally try to test a range of things, and go around borrowing. In this case, I very pointedly didn't bother. And the reason I didn't is this — every single review I've read and everyone I've talked to says that if you are going to spend a good chunk of money on a dehydrator — for example, if you have a bunch of fruit trees or a large garden and dehydrate a lot — buy an Excalibur. And I'm going to go with that.

That is, the lower-end electric models are adequate to their purpose — particularly if you are getting them for $5 — but even at $35, they aren't bad tools. But if you are going to spend over $100 on a dehydrator, get an Excalibur. I simply don't think there's enough evidence that any of the mid-range options are good enough to bother with. Spend the money making a good solar one instead.

Eric gave me an Excalibur for my birthday last year, and it is a really good tool. It has multiple heat settings (and it actually keeps in that range, unlike any of the cheapies), it dries food quickly, it uses less electricity than less expensive electric dryers, has a huge amount of internal drying space and the drying screens are polypropylene, so they don't leach bisphenol-a. I know people who have had them for more than a decade with no problems. One source is the Lehmans catalog (lehmans.com).

But please understand me — my suggestion is not that you should break your budget on an expensive dehydrator. If money is an issue, you can get along very well with a solar dehydrator, your car, the sun alone, or those plus a cheapie from a garage sale. But if you have a lot of dehydrating to do, and a budget that can stretch that far, and if you live in a climate with a very short season for solar dehydrating, then I'd recommend the Excalibur wholeheartedly.

Dehydrated Foods — Our Favorites

What are our favorite dehydrated foods? We use drying for a wide range of food. For vegetables, we dry carrots, some potatoes (better than any instant variety), onions, garlic, sweet peppers (these are absolutely delicious when dried at the red-ripe stage, and we often nibble these as a snack straight out of the jar), tomatoes, of course (when you grow your own or get them at the farmers' market, there is an amazing range of flavors — for example, we dry Sungold tomatoes that taste like a combination of tomato and dried apricot, another variety that tastes remarkably like dried peaches and dried beefsteak tomatoes have a rich, almost meaty flavor to them). We also dry greens whenever we have extras. Some greens, like kale and chard, can be added to soup to rehydrate, while lighter greens like spinach can be ground up and added to flour for added nutrition in breads and pasta, or mixed with garlic and herbs to make a delicious, healthy flavoring for popcorn or homemade crackers. Two of our favorite dried vegetables are sweet peas, picked at their flavor peak, and sweet corn. When reconstituted, dried sweet corn tastes like the essence of summer, particularly if mixed with sun-dried tomatoes. The peas are better than any frozen peas I have ever had. Zucchini and summer squash are great peeled with a vegetable peeler into long noodles, and then treated as a substitute for pasta, or they make good dried "chips" with garlic powder, salt and chipotle peppers sprinkled on them.

We dry nearly all the fruits we can get our hands on — we've never had a dried fruit we didn't like. Apples, peaches, cherries, pears, grapes, berries of all sorts (strawberries and blueberries are fabulous dried), plums (dried prune-variety plums are "prunes" while other dried plums are "dried plums" by definition — helpful, isn't it), citrus zest (lovely to have and if you are peeling an orange or lemon anyway…) and every-thing else that grows here. We also treat some vegetables as fruit, most notably the sweetest cherry tomatoes, which rival any dried fruit, and pumpkin and the sweetest winter squashes, which, pureed, and fla-vored with cinnamon we put on fruit leather trays and eat as pumpkin leather — yum! We also use overripe fruit to make fruit leathers.

And, of course, we dry many, many herbs — our cooking just wouldn't be the same without a plentiful supply of homegrown dried herbs. There are a few that don't dry well — basil and cilantro, for ex-ample, as well as some more exotic herbs. But most of our culinary and medicinal herbs dry beautifully. We dry rosemary, thymes (regular, or-ange, lemon, wild), mints, catnip (a good, relaxing tea, and, of course, great for kitties), winter savory, lavender, chives, garlic chives, sage, zaatar and a host of others.

One wonderful and very simple use for our dehydrators is reducing waste. Almost every little bit of leftover food can be dehydrated and saved, including scraps of cooked meat and fish, even vegetable peels, which can then be added to stock. On the "Dry It!" website, Barb Moody writes:

> Instead of throwing away little bits of leftover food or vegetable trimmings, start drying them. You'll be amazed at the amount of useable food you can salvage. We often use the top tray of our dryer for little tidbits saved here and there.

Leftover pieces of cooked meat, fish or poultry can be dried and saved. Be sure to strip any excess fat before drying or dry fattier meats such as pork or bacon on a paper towel. Dried meats should be refrigerated or stored in a very cool place. Add dried meats to casseroles, soups, stews, or just use for snacking.

Dry leftover cooked or raw vegetables. Start a soup jar. A spoonful of peas, a few pieces of carrots, a couple of uneaten beans...all can be saved and dried, storing them in one jar. The next time you make a soup or stew, add your dried tidbits.

Vegetable trimmings can be dried and used to flavor soup broths. Even corn silk can be dried and saved. Not only does it make a tasty tea beneficial to kidney function, but it adds a wonderful flavor to soups. To use dried trimmings, tie them in a piece of nylon organdy, a cooking bag, or a laundered panty hose foot. Simmer in water. The broth will make a great basis for soups or stews.

Even bread scraps can be saved in your dehydrator. We use our solar dehydrator to make croutons or breadcrumbs for stuffings. There truly is almost no limit to the value of dehydration. It is simple, easy and accessible, inexpensive, often low energy and ties us back to our history.

Recipes

Peanut Butter-Banana Balls

These are one of my kids' favorite snacks—and I like them too! Serves 4.

- 4 tbsp peanut butter
- 3 ripe bananas.
- ¼ cup coconut

Melt peanut butter until liquid. Slice bananas into chunks and dunk in peanut butter and then roll in coconut. Dehydrate at medium setting until chewy and dry.

Salmon Jerky

My father lives in Washington state, and has access to wonderful, amazing salmon. I am hoping to bring some back from my next visit and try out this recipe. A friend of mine in the Pacific Northwest swears by it.

- 2 lbs salmon fillets, sliced against the grain into ½-inch thick strips
- 1 cup pickling salt
- 2½ cups brown sugar
- 1 cup soy sauce
- 1 gallon of water
- ⅓ cup white vinegar
- 4 tbsp cayenne pepper or to taste

Bring water, salt and sugar to boil and stir until sugar is dissolved. Add soy sauce and vinegar, and let cool to room temperature. Place salmon in brine and marinate 8–12 hours. Drain, pat salmon dry, and set in dehydrator on oiled sheets at 140° for 8 hours. Can be stored 2 weeks at room temperature or frozen for 1 year.

Dehydrated Sweet Corn

This is my favorite dried vegetable. Picked at the peak of flavor, dried sweet corn reconstitutes as essence of summer. It is a standard ingredient in soups and stews, essential in chili and succotash, and just fabulous all around. It is some work to cut it off the cob, but I put on loud rock and roll and just do it, because the results are worth it! Makes a bunch.

- 20 ears of sweet fresh corn

Steam corn until just barely tender, 5 minutes. Slice off the cob (there are various gadgets for doing this—none of them work very well, and I end up just using a knife). Dehydrate until hard.

Soybean Succotash

This is roughly based on Laurie Colwin's succotash recipe from *More Home Cooking*—the single best cookbook on the planet. That said, however, I think her succotash can be improved on, and this recipe does. Serves 4.

- 12 oz dried sweet corn, soaked in hot water until softened (you can also use fresh or frozen corn)
- 12 oz dried edamame (green soybeans), lima beans, fava beans, leather britches or black soybeans, depending on your taste. I like the dried green soybeans, cooked until just barely tender. You can also use frozen edamame, or even frozen green beans. This is a flexible dish.

- 3 tbsp olive oil
- 2 large onions, diced
- 1 carrot, diced
- 4 cloves of garlic, minced
- 1 tbsp ginger
- 1 tbsp good quality chile powder
- 1 tsp lemon juice, sumac or cider vinegar
- 1 12 oz jar of canned tomatoes plus juice or homemade salsa
- ½ cup of heavy cream or sour cream (this is optional, but very nice)

Sauté onion and garlic until translucent, add spices, and sauté for 1 minute. Add corn, beans and tomatoes and simmer under cover until tender, about 10 minutes, and add sour stuff.

Devour—this is a great meal or side dish. The recipe is also good if you use some rehydrated sweet peppers in it, or fresh if they are lying around. I like it with cilantro on top as well.

Dehydrator Apple Granola Bars

My kids love granola bars, and I love that I don't have to actually bake these. These are very tasty and have absolutely no fat in them, other than what's naturally in the oats.

- 3 tart apples
- 2 cups rolled oats
- ½ cup slivered almonds
- 2 tbsp brown sugar

- 1 tbsp honey in ¼ cup water   • 1 tsp salt
- ½ tsp cinnamon

Peel and grate apples. Place in a bowl with the other ingredients and toss lightly until thoroughly mixed. Place mixture on a dehydrator sheet and dry for 2 to 3 hours, or until crunchy. Cut into bars and store in an airtight container.

Canning

WHEN MOST PEOPLE think about preserving food, they think about canning. A pantry full of jams and pickles is perhaps the ubiquitous image of home food preservation, and there's just something about the way those filled jars make you feel. It is a tie to our grandmothers and a hedge against disaster — a magical way of preserving the essence of summer in winter.

That said, however, canning is time and energy intensive, and can be expensive if you can't get equipment used. And there are risks to canning that don't apply to most other methods of food preservation. I know many people who put up food who never pressure can. I mention this not to be discouraging, but so because even though our memories of grandmother mean that many of us think that canning is the most important food storage technique, it is just one of many, and one that didn't even exist two hundred years ago. For millennia, people relied on other forms of food preservation and did just fine. That said, however, there are lots of tastes that you can only get by canning, and it is a skill well worth having in your repertoire.

There are two kinds of canning, both of which use high temperatures to create a vacuum seal that prevents air and bacteria from forming on food. First, there's canning in a water bath, which is done by immersing sterile jars filled with high-acid food (more on this in a minute) in enough boiling water to cover them and boiling for the required amount of time. The second, used for foods that aren't acidic, is pressure canning. That involves a special piece of equipment, a pressure canner (not a pressure cooker) designed to achieve higher temperatures than boiling water can. This is for food that isn't acidic enough to prevent the growth of a particular toxin, botulism, which can kill you.

So given that last bit of information, the very first thing I'm going to say is that I don't want you to be scared, and I don't want you not to try this, but I do want you to swear up and down before you do any canning that you *will* pay attention, read instructions carefully and follow the rules. Because, even if your Mom always did it a different way, you really can die from not being careful with canning. It probably won't happen, but why mess with it? Properly done, canning is easy and safe — just do it properly.

Water Bath Canning

Water bath canning is the appropriate method for canning *only* high-acid foods. Such foods include pickles, jams, jellies and juices made from common, high-acid fruits, rhubarb (which is technically a vegetable but so acidic it can be water bath canned) and all tomato products. Everything else must be pressure canned. The reason for this is that the bacteria that causes botulism, *clostridium botulinum,* is endemic in soil. In most cases it is all over your vegetables and fruits. That's not a problem in an aerobic environment (one where there's plenty of air). Your body can handle it just fine (although babies under one year sometimes have trouble with it — this is why babies aren't supposed to have honey until they are over a year). But in a warm, anaerobic environment like a canning jar, the botulism bacteria goes crazy. And as I said, botulism will kill you and your family. It is not something to mess with.

Now any food with a ph lower than 4.4 is acidic and provides an environment inhospitable to botulism — which is why high-acid foods can be safely water bath canned. But the thing is, most of us don't have the chemist's equipment to confirm acidity. For example, tomatoes can have an acidity level as low as 4.0, or as high as 4.7, if they are overripe or a low-acid hybrid. And there have been a couple of cases of botulism found in tomato products. This is why following the instructions of a *recent* canning book is essential. Any cookbook written before 1994 is not safe to use. You can use the recipes, but you must follow current guidelines for the canning.

Generally speaking, if your ingredients include anything but fruit, sugar and spices, or don't have a vinegar base, as in pickles, you must follow the instructions for the ingredient in the food that requires the longest and most intense processing. That is, if you are making salsa with tomatoes and hot peppers, unless you know the recipe is safe (that is, you have gotten it from a USDA-approved, recent book or website that specifically says that it is a combination food that is safe to water bath can, *and* you have followed instructions exactly, not adding any more ingredients or changing proportions at all), you would pressure can it using the instructions for hot peppers. For tomato products with nothing else in them, add two teaspoons of lemon juice per pint, or four per quart, or the same amount of vinegar, to ensure their acidity stays below minimum levels. This might also be wise if you are canning very overripe fruit.

Equipment

You need a few things for canning. You need a large pot with a lid — canning kettles with racks are great, but you can use any big pot with a lid, and something to keep the jars off the bottom of the pot so they won't break — a steamer, a baker's rack, anything that will lift the jars off the bottom and allow water to circulate. Ideally, you will also have a canning kit. This comes with a jar lifter (big tongs designed to lift full canning jars), a magnet (for pulling the lids out of boiling water) and a funnel the right size for pouring hot things into canning jars. You don't actually need these things — they are merely convenient — but they are *really* convenient, and nice and cheap, so I recommend them. You can take the jars out with regular tongs — I have done this. I've also had one splash back and send boiling water at me. Your choice. You can fill the jars without the funnel, but why struggle? The stuff is also available used at your friendly neighborhood yard sale.

I have never bought a new canning jar. I get them constantly for a buck a box or sometimes three dollars for five boxes. They usually come in boxes of a dozen pint jars or a half dozen quarts and new they can cost up to one or two dollars per jar. They are one of those things most people seem to have in their garage. Put out requests on freecycle or Craigslist, and see what you can find before you buy them. If you live in a city or if canning suddenly becomes the new black, you may have to buy them, and they aren't cheap new. If I had to buy canning jars, I'd probably can less. The jars and the metal rings that hold down the lids can be reused almost indefinitely, as long as they are not damaged (check carefully for little nicks or cracks that might cause a broken jar or a lid not to seal), but you need new lids every time.

The only canning jars that are really considered safe to use are the newer kind, that have two-piece, screw-on lids. The old ones with the jar rubbers can technically be used for high-acid foods, but they aren't recommended, and can only be used with new rubbers. I'm not going to explain how to can with these, because there's a lot of controversy about whether it is safe. If you have the old zinc lid or wire and rubber canning jars, use them to display stored food, or store dehydrated stuff. Don't can with them.

You also don't need to buy new rings. As long as the rings aren't rusted through, and as long as they fit on the jar (used canning jars often come with the rings), you can reuse them. I occasionally do buy new rings, as not all jars come with them. You also don't need as many as you do jars. Once the jars are sealed, the rings can and should be gently removed and the lids themselves are sufficient. If you don't, the rings can rust on. So you shouldn't need tons of them.

You do need a new lid every time. Because jars come in two sizes, regular and wide-mouthed, you not only need a new lid, but an appropriately sized one. I buy my canning lids by the case, because I do a lot of canning. They store for quite some years as long as they are kept cool and dry, and are much cheaper if you can afford to buy them in bulk. Those who don't do enough canning to justify this themselves might split a case with several friends.

Now in a real crisis, where you could not get any more lids, it is technically possible, *although not recommended* to reuse lids that have been carefully pried up and checked to ensure there are no dents or damage to the rubber inside — *but only on very high acid foods.* I am telling you this because in a real crisis, it might be useful knowledge. I do not advise it — you do it at your own risk. At a minimum I would use it on pickles and acid fruit jams only — never, ever, ever on any low-acid or even borderline food — and add some extra lemon juice or vinegar to be sure. The best use for used canning lids is for jars of food that you are dehydrating and storing, or for mason jars you fill with beans and grains that aren't canned.

Instructions

So what do you do? Let's say you want to make raspberry jam. You would take fresh raspberries (you really don't want to leave your stuff sitting around too long before you can it — off flavors can permeate your whole batch), add sugar to taste or to meet the requirements of the brand of pectin if you are using any (we use low-sugar pectins only because we find regular ones make a jam that is simply too sweet for us), and follow the instructions for the pectin (there are several kinds, and each one has slightly different requirements, so follow the manufacturer's instructions).

In the meantime, wash your canning jars and lids carefully and check the jars for tiny nicks on the top that can ruin your seal. Then submerge the jars in a pot of boiling water that comes up at least two inches above the top of the jars. Bring the water to a boil and boil the jars. Meanwhile, boil the lids and rings as well, in a separate pot. When your jam is hot and ready to be ladled in, use the jar lifter to take out the jars, and put them upside down on a clean dishtowel to drain. Then flip them, and use a ladle or spoon and the funnel to fill the jars to the recommended level of headspace.

Headspace is the amount of space between the food and the lid that you need to create a good seal. Often it is one inch, but check the recipe every time, because it may be more. When the jar is filled to the appropriate level, wipe the rim of the jar with a clean dishcloth to remove any food that might prevent a good seal, put the lid on, put the ring on (not super tightly — just enough to hold the lid firmly in place), and use the jar lifter to put the jar in the canning kettle. Process for the amount of time listed for the ingredient — jams are usually 15 minutes. Processing time begins when the water returns to a rolling boil — start timing then.

When you are done, use the lifter to take the jars out of the boiling water bath, and put them carefully (don't bang them around) on a clean, dry dishtowel. You will hear a seal being formed within a few minutes — a "thwuck" sound. Some will seal right out of the kettle, others a few minutes later; this is normal. Allow the food to cool without being disturbed. When the jars are cool enough to touch, press down on the lid. If it is suctioned down and has no give, it is sealed. If you can push down on it and it pops up again, it isn't. If it isn't sealed, you can either reprocess with a new lid for the same amount of time, or you can stick it in the fridge and use that one first.

You may have been taught to can by someone who did oven canning (jars are baked), inverted the jars to create a seal, or did open kettle canning (poured hot food into jars and put on lids and let them seal themselves). These are not safe. *Don't do them!* Or do weird things like putting an aspirin (ugh!) in the jar. Yes, people did this and most of them didn't die. But a few did, and why on earth would anyone risk their lives for something so silly? None of this means that you can't use Mom's wonderful pickled beet recipe that she used to oven can. You just have to use current techniques to can that old recipe.

That's really all there is to water bath canning. It is very easy, and very convenient, as long as you do it wisely.

Pressure Canning

Some of you may read what I just wrote about water bath canning and think, "I've been doing it forever, but just slightly differently, and no one died. She's being so anal about this!" Well guess what — you ain't seen anal yet. With water bath canning, there are a few things that can be dangerous — you might make yourself sick by eating spoiled food but mostly the acidity will protect you from botulism and death. With pressure canning, by definition, most of the foods you will be canning can support botulism toxin. If you do it wrong, you and anyone who eats your food could die horribly. There are only a few cases of botulism each year, but you definitely don't want to be one of them — or worse, have someone you love be one.

Now I can imagine that some of you are just plain terrified by the heavy repetition of the word "death" here, and don't ever want to pressure can. But if you eat any food from cans, you are eating food preserved with the very same processes. The canned green beans or soup you are eating has precisely the same risks and benefits that home pressure-canned food has (and, in fact, there was a botulism outbreak involving commercial foods in the year I wrote this). So the issue here is not, "I should be afraid of pressure canning?" but, "I should be very wary and respectful of pressure canning, and make sure I do it *exactly* correctly." Because the truth is that properly canned food is safe. What I want to make clear is that cutting corners, or using older techniques your Grandma taught you, or just estimating is not sufficient in this case. I'm one of those estimating type of people who tends to be casual about things — but *not* when I pressure can.

Six Rules and Six Warnings for Pressure Canning

1. No one pressure cans until they have water bath canned. Until you learn the basics of handling jars, filling them, creating a seal, etc. don't start pressure canning.
2. Make sure you are up to date on your canning information. Use only *current* canning instructions. You can use older recipes — or any recipe — but make sure that when you can the food, you can it using currently appropriate techniques for the ingredient that has the *longest* canning time. If you have a family recipe for meat sauce, can the recipe based on the meat, which is probably the thing that requires the longest canning time.
3. You should have a current copy of the Ball Blue Book guide to canning, usually available any place canning supplies are sold or online. Canning books written before 1994 are not safe! I also suggest you take a look at the University of Georgia website (see Bibliography) for up-to-date canning information, but I really want you to get an

actual paper book because I think that when you are in the middle of a big project, with your hands covered with squash and water steaming out of a pressure canner, you might not stop to go online and confirm that it was, indeed, 12 pounds pressure, not 10. This is not acceptable — have the book so you can just look it up. This is not a place to rely on imperfect memories.

4. Please make sure you read through the instructions for pressure canning and genuinely understand them before you do it. Take no shortcuts. Don't just wait until the steam is kind of puffing out, wait until it is steady. Don't estimate times. Don't decide that a lid that doesn't quite fit is good enough. Do what they tell you.

5. Make sure your pressure canner (*not* a pressure cooker — you cannot safely can in a pressure cooker) has an accurate gauge. This is not a big deal if your pressure canner has a weighted gauge (the kind that jiggle and make tons of noise), but it is absolutely essential if you have a dial gauge. Take it to your county extension office and have them check it once a year, and make sure you know your elevation and use appropriate pressure for that elevation. And if you have a dial gauge pressure canner, a study found that the standard should be not 10 pounds pressure, but 11 pounds. If you see a recipe, even a recent one, that says "10 pounds pressure" — put it at 11 pounds.

6. If you buy a used pressure canner (and there are a lot of used ones out there), make sure you get a manual. While old pressure canners are much safer than old pressure cookers, there is still a lot of pressure built up, and if you don't use them as instructed, not only could your food not be safe, but you could get a face full of hot steam or even be injured by flying parts. The companies that make pressure canners will have old manuals available, so if you buy a yard sale canner, the first thing you need to do is call the company and order the manual. The second thing is to have the gauge checked (worth doing once even if you have a weighted gauge) and to make sure that the gasket still fits tightly. If you see or feel steam persistently coming out along the gasket, you need a new one. You can order a kit from the company to fix it, or find a different pressure canner.

Here six things you absolutely must not do when pressure canning:

1. Use no jars larger than one quart. The food can't get hot enough to be safe.

2. Never reuse jar lids when pressure canning — ever. Make sure the bands aren't too rusty and aren't bent, because the jar won't seal. Check the rims of the canning jars very carefully. Nicks or bumps will ruin your seal.

3. Don't use rubber jars or anything other than the two-piece canning lids. *Test your dial gauge canning kettle annually. Don't can until you have tested.* Test a new kettle *before* you use it. Read the manual — details vary a lot by brand.

4. Don't raw pack unless you are sure it is safe. "Raw pack" means putting food in the jars that has not been cooked. There's a general move in canning towards hot-pack only. That means that the food should go into the jars hot. You'll see mixed recommendations about this, but it is *always* unsafe to raw pack beets, greens of any kind, potatoes, sweet potatoes, squash, pumpkin, okra, tomato/okra mixes and stewed tomatoes, and honestly, it is safer not to raw pack at all. Research has found that hot packed foods are often better textured and flavored as well.

5. Make sure that your heat remains even (especially if using a wood stove), that your stove is safe to can on (if using glass-topped stoves), that you don't begin counting time until the steam has been exhausting for ten full minutes and that you are present to ensure that there are no sudden drops in temperature or other mishaps.

6. Remove jars carefully. Don't bang them or tip them. Wait until they are fully cool to test seals.

Honestly, if you find all this too overwhelming, no worries — human beings didn't have pressure canning until fairly recently. You can preserve a lot of food by root cellaring, season extension, water bath canning of high acid foods, dehydrating, lactofermenting, preserving in salt, alcohol and sugar and freezing. I encourage people to pressure can, but if you don't think you can do it correctly, you will be fine without it.

Instructions

Here's how you pressure can.

Most of it is the same as water bath canning—you check the rims, you make sure the jars have been cleaned in scalding water (boiling the jars is necessary if you are pressure canning for less than 15 minutes, and recommended anyway) and that lids have been simmered.

Make sure the food you are canning is really clean and dirt free. This reduces the chance that you are putting a big helping of botulism, which lives in the soil, in your food. Use the recipe you have chosen carefully. You *can* safely reduce salt quantities when pressure canning, but not when water bath canning.

Pack hot food into clean, hot jars—if you put it in cold jars you could have one explode on you. Run a clean spatula (plastic or wood, not metal) along the edge of the jar to reduce air bubbles, and add more liquid if need be to compensate after the air comes out. Wipe the rim with a clean cloth to make sure that no food gets under it. Leave the recommended amount of headspace (i.e., room for the seal to be made)—always a minimum of one inch when pressure canning, unless a current recipe says otherwise.

Put on the hot lid, put the clean, hot metal band on, and screw down firmly, but not so tightly that no air can escape.

Put in the rack and add the relevant amount of water (this varies by the brand of pressure canner, so read the manual) in the canner. Put the filled jars into the canning rack (never put any jars, using any technique, directly on the bottom of the canner). Screw the lid on the canner tightly.

Make sure the petcock valves are open. Turn up the heat—and *pay attention*. This is not something you can do while you do other things. Watch for the steam, and then start timing when the flow is steady. After ten full minutes of steam steadily and rapidly coming out, the air trapped in the jars and canner should be exhausted. If the air isn't properly exhausted, the pressure may be inaccurate and the food may not be safe.

After ten minutes of steady exhausting, close the vent. Watch the pressure gauge until it reaches the correct pressure *for your altitude*. If you live more than 1,000 feet above sea level *you must adjust the canning pressure* to compensate. Confirm your elevation before you begin canning and refer to the USDA chart for what is appropriate for your canner. If you have a weighted gauge, you can't adjust it finely; this is completely normal. If you have dial gauge, you can, so it matters both where you live and what kind of canner you have.

When you reach the desired pressure, adjust the heat on your stove to keep it at the same level. If it goes over, turn the heat down (or bank the fire) a bit, if it is under, turn up the heat. Keep an eye on the gauge. I do dishes or other light work, but nothing very distracting.

Do not begin timing until your canner is at the recommended pressure, and stay close to make sure that it remains at the same pressure level during the entire processing time. When you have processed for as long as required, take the canner off the heat, and let it cool. Leave the canner alone otherwise — don't vent pressure or do anything else. It will take an hour or so to get down to normal pressure.

Do not open the canner until there is no steam coming out, even when you poke the regulator with a stick (not your hand). A face full of hot steam can seriously burn you. Don't mess with it — make sure there is no more left.

Open the petcock valve *slowly and carefully*. Wait a bit, until the canner is even cooler, then unlock the canner lid and remove it carefully. Leave the jars alone for ten minutes with the canner open, and use the jar lifter to carefully transfer the jars to a clean dishtowel, without tipping them. Allow them to cool undisturbed. You should hear the "ping" as the jars seal.

When the jars are entirely cool, check them for the seal. If you press down on the center of the lid and feel any give or movement your jar is not sealed. You can either reprocess the food (go through precisely the same procedure again *with a new lid*) or you can put it in the fridge and eat it soon. You will lose a lot of nutritional value reprocessing, so I wouldn't do this with anything like greens.

After 18 to 24 hours, wipe off the jars, remove the rings, label them and put them in a cool, dry place.

Check pressure canned food when you open the jar before you eat any. If there is any reason for you to seriously doubt the safety of the food — if you don't hear the popping sound that goes with a breaking vacuum when you open it, if there is an off smell, bulging around the lid, a vent of gas — throw it out, and not on the compost pile, but in the garbage. *Don't taste it!* Botulism has no taste or smell; it sometimes causes bulging, but can exist simultaneously with other kinds of spoilage. *Throw it out if there is any doubt.* Throw the whole jar out — don't try to reclaim it and don't give the food to animals.

Some things — darkened bottom lids, discolored peaches, a pinkish color on some fruits — are normal. They are chemical reactions to canning and are not signs of trouble. I won't list them all. I reiterate, this is why you should read the Ball Blue Book or recommended websites carefully and several times until you are familiar with the information.

The USDA recommends that you boil any food that has been pressure canned, or anything that might conceivably support botulism (including tomato products without added acid) at a rolling boil in a covered pan for ten full minutes and one additional minute if you are more than 1,000 feet above sea level for each 1,000 feet or fraction thereof (i.e., if you live at 2,200 feet you would boil your for 12 minutes). They recommend that you do this every time, and definitely if there is any doubt about your having used a safe canning technique. It should not be necessary if you have done everything carefully and precisely, but it provides a measure of security. I personally don't always do this, but if I were in the slightest doubt, I would.

Canned food will keep for many years, as long as the seal is intact, although there is a gradual loss of nutrients. Jackie Clay at Backwoods Home regularly tests and uses canned food that is more than a decade old, but the general recommendation is no more than three years. I wouldn't hesitate to eat anything older, as long as the seal seems intact, and there are no problems, but more than five years out, I would boil it for the recommended time, just in case.

OK, I know that was a little scary and overwhelming, but think about it this way — you learned far more rules and regulations when you learned to drive, but you probably do that all the time. So just be careful and wise.

Making Good Use of Canning

Canning is a great technique for some foods, and really rotten for others. Personally, I don't much like canned green vegetables of any kind. I know Americans are crazy about their canned green beans, but they don't do much for me. You can can just about anything, but if you try to can everything, you might make yourself a little nuts. You'd need thousands of jars, which would represent hundreds or thousands of hours of labor to feed a family entirely with canned food. So it makes sense to be judicious about how you use canning, just as it does with any techniques.

The Best Canned Foods

To my mind, the best water bath canned foods are:
- pickles of all sorts
- jams, jellies, marmalades and fruit butters
- some juices (not all juices taste good canned — most berries, rhubarb, peaches and apricots make excellent canned juice; others, like apple cider or orange juice just taste awful)
- fruit sauces (apple, rhubarb, strawberry, cranberry)
- some pie fillings (pie cherries are the best, but blueberries and elderberries can surprisingly well and make a great summer pie in winter)
- tomatoes
- tomato juice

The best pressure canned foods are:
- tomato sauce
- salsa
- meat stocks
- canned soups and stews
- meats if you don't have a freezer

If you don't have a freezer or electricity, canning may be a better option for more things, but generally speaking, most vegetables, taste much better root cellared, dehydrated, fermented or season extended.

Recipes

Crunchy Chicken's Raspberry-White Chocolate Jam with Coffee Liqueur

Deanna Duke who blogs as Crunchy Chicken (thecrunchychicken.com) is a friend and one of the smartest and funniest women I've ever met. She also is one heck of a jam maker. This recipe was originally published at *The Mother Earth News* website. Not being a coffee person, I've experimented with making this jam with amaretto, instead of coffee liqueur, and it is awfully fine that way too. Makes 10 pints.

- 5 cups raspberries, crushed (use a potato masher or other implement to crush the berries)

- 6 cups sugar

- ¼ cup coffee liqueur (Starbucks or Kahlua)

- 1 cup white chocolate chips (spring for the Guittard or other gourmet chocolate if it's available in your area)

- 1 pack pectin

Heat raspberries while slowly adding in the pectin. Once the raspberries are at a full boil that you cannot stir down, add in the sugar. Return to a full rolling boil, stirring for one minute. Take the raspberry mixture off the heat and add in the white chocolate. It will take a while to melt, so be patient (unless you want chunks of white chocolate in your jam). After the white chocolate has melted, add the coffee liqueur and stir until well blended. Because the raspberry jam is quite hot, the alcohol will burn off, so if you want to have more of the alcohol flavor, add it in at the very end. Pour jam into sterilized canning jars and process in a hot water bath for 10 minutes. That is, assuming you haven't eaten half of it already. Yields 10 pints.

Vanilla-Amaretto Strawberry Jam

OK, I realize I'm going to have to send La Crunch a check or something out of the royalties from this book, but this is so good I can't resist including it. Deanna is the goddess of great jam making, and you deserve to have these recipes (there are more at her blog, so go worship at her feet). Makes 4 pints.

- 5 cups crushed organic strawberries, washed and hulled
- ¼ cup lemon juice
- 7 cups sugar
- 1 tbsp quality balsamic vinegar
- 1 vanilla bean, cut in half and split down the middle
- 1 package pectin
- 2 tsp lemon zest
- ¼ cup Amaretto (or Disaronno)

Add the lemon and lemon zest, Amaretto, vanilla bean and balsamic vinegar to strawberries in a non-corrosive pot and slowly add the package of pectin. I use a wooden spoon, but you can use any non-reactive implement you like. Bring the mixture to a boil on high heat and then add the sugar. Bring this mess up to a rolling boil, wherein you can't stir down the boiling action and, most likely, are getting bombarded by spattering molten lava strawberry bits. Boil for one full minute.

This concoction smells absolutely heavenly while on the stove but avoid the temptation to throw yourself into the pot headfirst lest you suffer third degree burns on your face and mouth.

When the jam is finished cooking, take it off the heat and let it rest for about 3 minutes. Stir the Amaretto into the prepared strawberry jam and ladle into hot jars. Seal and hot process jars in a boiling water bath for 10 minutes.

Don't get greedy and eat these right away. The flavors in the jams will mellow out and become quite subtle. Even a few days maturity will improve the flavor of these jams immensely.

Salsa Verde

Tomatillos go crazy in my garden every year. Fortunately, I love salsa verde, the perfect use for the tomatillo. Most recipes call for cooking the tomatillos down on the stove, but I find that roasting them actually gives a wonderful flavor. Makes 6 pints.

- 20 tomatillos, husked
- 3 hot Serrano peppers (only if you like things hot)
- 12 cloves garlic

Throw all the ingredients in a pan together and roast at 400° for 1½ hours. Puree with a blender or run through a food mill. Add ¼ cup lemon juice and 2 tbsp brown sugar, and stir over low heat to dissolve sugar. Pour hot sauce into hot pint jars, with 1-inch headspace and process for 20 minutes in a boiling water bath.

Bestest Everything Pickles

My son Simon gave these their name a few years ago, and they are pretty terrific. Why limit yourself to cucumbers when you can throw everything in the garden into your pickles? Makes 5 pints.

- 2 cups carrots, finely chopped (about 4 large)
- 4 cloves of garlic, finely chopped
- 1½ cups cauliflower, finely chopped (about ½ medium head)
- 2 medium apples, finely chopped (about 1⅓ cups)
- ½ lb dark brown sugar
- 4 tbsp lemon juice
- 1 tbsp mustard seed
- 2¼ cups rutabaga (1 small)
- 8 pickling cukes cut into slices
- 2 onions, finely chopped (about 1⅓ cups)
- 2 medium zucchini (unpeeled), finely chopped (about 1½ cups)
- 1 tsp salt
- 1½ cups apple cider vinegar
- 5 dried chile peppers

Combine all ingredients in a saucepan. Heat to boiling, then reduce heat to a simmer and cook until rutabaga is cooked but still firm, about 1½ to 2 hours. Can in a boiling water bath for 25 minutes. Yields 5 pint jars.

Apple Cider Syrup

We love this on pancakes instead of maple syrup, particularly with a few sautéed caramelized apples on top of them.

- 1 gallon apple cider

Put apple cider in a heavy pot over low to medium heat, and reduce until it is about ⅓ of its original volume. Ladle into hot clean quart jars with 1-inch headspace and water bath can for 20 minutes. It will thicken at room temperature and make a wonderful apple-y pancake syrup.

Canned Meat Broth

Most commercial canned meat broths are disgusting watery things that taste mostly of salt and are made from industrially produced meats. But they are awfully convenient too. My absolute favorite use for a pressure canner is canning stock made from bones. It is just so lovely to have on hand, and so much richer and tastier than the commercial versions. Makes 4 quarts of stock.

- 3 lbs of chicken, turkey or beef bones, ideally with a bit of meat on them
- 4 quarts of water
- 1 tbsp white peppercorns
- 2 stalks celery
- 2 onions
- 3 bay leaves
- 3 big sprigs of thyme
- 1 tablespoon of salt

Combine all ingredients, bring to a boil. Reduce heat and simmer 2–3 hours, skimming foam occasionally. Remove from heat, reserving any meat for other uses, and strain through a fine sieve. Chill, and remove fat from stock. Bring stock back to a boil and ladle hot stock into hot jars, leaving 1 inch of headspace. Put on lid and tighten ring carefully. Process in a *pressure canner* for 20 minutes for pints, 25 minutes for quarts at 11 lbs pressure. Yields 8 pints or 4 quarts of stock.

The Best Beef Stew

This is an adaptation of a recipe for "Slow Cooked Beef Stew" from Sarah Leah Chase's *The Cold-Weather Cookbook.* It is one of the coziest recipes I know of, and after years of making it, it suddenly occurred to me that it could be canned and be around for those days when you need comfort food but don't have time to cook. Makes 7 quarts.

- 4 lbs beef stew meat
- 10 medium potatoes, peeled and cubed
- 5 large cloves of garlic, minced
- 2 tbsp red wine vinegar
- 1 tbsp salt
- 1 tbsp dried thyme
- 1 tbsp brown sugar

- 6 medium onions, chopped
- 12 medium carrots, sliced and cut into chunks
- ½ cup red wine
- 2 tbsp mustard
- 2 tbsp Worcestershire sauce
- ½ tbsp black pepper
- 5 cups V8 juice, or homemade tomato or vegetable juice

Prepare meat and vegetables, removing excess fat from meat. Mix vegetable juice, wine, vinegar, mustard, salt, Worcestershire, sugar and spices together and pour over meat and vegetables in a large, oven-proof pot. Stir to cover and add water if needed. Cook in a 350° oven for 2 hours, until liquid is bubbling hot and meat and vegetables are cooked through. Ladle hot liquid (turn a burner on under it if necessary to keep it sufficiently hot) into hot, clean jars, leaving 1 inch of headspace. Remove air bubbles, adjust lids. Process pints for 75 minutes, quarts for 90 minutes at 11 lbs pressure. Yields 14 pints or 7 quarts.

old ways
and New

I think there are a lot of us who have become disconnected from our past. We've been so busy living in the modern world that a lot of the time we've barely noticed the passing of old ways. Or perhaps we were glad to see them go — glad to lose the things that marked us as from the old country or as a hick or a country person. Those things, we were told, were of no value to the new people we were. And so what our grandmothers and grandfathers knew was lost. How frustrated they must have been to see generations arise who didn't value their thrift and work, and then, how frustrated we all were when we realized we did need to know these things, and the grandparents who could teach us were gone.

I'm one of those people who waited too long. My grandmother Barbara and her sister Helen lived together for more than 40 years. The two women gardened, cooked, knitted, sewed and tended to their community. They brought over food when a baby was born, or flowers when someone died. They were raised when women learned certain skills. My grandmother had had only sons, and my aunt no children at all, and they pounced on my sisters and I as the recipients, at last, of all this collective womanly knowledge.

When we were small, we soaked it up, the names of the garden plants and the loops of the crochet hook. They spent themselves freely on us, and we wanted to be like them. But when we grew older, nearly ready to begin to really learn from them, other things got in the way. Their notion of what a woman's life should be was caught up with their desire to pass knowledge along. My sisters and I were determined not to be caught in what we saw as the trap of a too-close attention to femininity.

I was perhaps 12 when I told my grandmother I wasn't going to be a sewing sort of a person and she told me what mattered about this work and why she did it all. She said, "You have to have something that lasts. You cook food and it gets eaten. You wash the dishes and they get dirty again. You tend the babies and then they need the same again. You need something that lasts past the end of the day."

I thought she was crazy. Of course, my life was going to be filled with things that lasted, filled with art and beauty. I was never going to be a woman tied to my home, cooking and cleaning only to do it again. I rejected all the gifts they tried to give me, all the lessons they could have taught. It is too late now to have those lessons back.

Fast forward 22 years or so, and I do make things — words, mostly — that go on past the end of the day. But I also live in a world where the dishes get finished, only to be started again, where laundry piles up, is washed, put away, and the next day the pile is the same. I live, not because I am a woman, but because I have children, in a world of endless repetition. (Unlike them, though, I share the workload with my husband.)

And now, I take great pleasure in the things that last longer than a day. I put away my jars of food on the shelf, and each one takes on a new role when I can say, "And this is what I did today that will outlast the moment." Painfully, and with many errors, I have learned to garden, knit, sew, cook, can as they did. Painfully, and with every error, I have discovered my own failure to understand what they meant and what they were offering me.

I wish more than anything that my grandmother and aunt could have taught me. I wish I had understood that the old ways were not of a piece — that one false piece (the idea that this is only women's work) need not contaminate the gift of skills, and love, and old hands that try and give when they can to young ones.

11

Fermentation

Fermentation in General

I SUSPECT A LOT of my readers think that fermentation sounds weird and that they don't like or might not like fermented foods. So let me reassure you — I suspect you do like fermented foods and you probably eat them quite a lot. What are some familiar fermented foods? Well, beer, wine, hard cider and vinegar to begin with. Have you eaten yogurt, sour cream or crème fraiche? Cheeses are fermented, as is sourdough bread. Tempeh and soy sauce are both fermented soybean products. Black tea leaves are fermented before you drink them. If you've ever eaten a kosher dill pickle, sauerkraut with your hotdog or kimchi at a Korean restaurant, you've enjoyed fermented foods.

Fermentation involves taking natural wild microscopic creatures, found all around us in the air, in the water and on our bodies, and putting them to work to create delicious food. Most commercial versions of the foods I listed involve reproducing the same microbial culture over and over again in a lab and injecting it into our food to produce one particular taste in, say, your yogurt. This is pretty much the equivalent of monocropping, growing, say, the same corn variety over and over again for thousands and thousands of acres. Not only does it look boring, it has ecological costs and it tastes boring.

Home-scale fermentation, however, creates tastes that are truly local, since no one else has precisely the same microbial cultures around. Just as with other kinds of preservation, this is food that money pretty much can't buy. You can make things that taste wildly, wonderfully different using very simple, very safe processes. Sandor Katz, the fermentation guru of our times, writes on his website:

> By eating a variety of live fermented foods, you promote diversity among microbial cultures in your body. Biodiversity, increasingly recognized as critical to the survival of larger-scale ecosystems, is just as important at the micro level. Call it microbiodiversity. Your body is an ecosystem that can function most effectively when populated by diverse species of microorganisms. By fermenting foods and drinks with wild microorganisms present in your home environment, you become more interconnected with the life forces of the world around you. Your environment becomes you, as you invite the microbial populations you share the earth with to enter your diet and your intestinal ecology.
>
> Wild fermentation is the opposite of homogenization and uniformity, a small antidote you can undertake in your home, using the extremely localized populations of microbial cultures present there, to produce your own unique fermented foods. What you ferment with the organisms around you is a manifestation of your specific environment, and it will always be a little different. Do-it-yourself fermentation departs from the realm of the uniform commodity. Rediscover and reinterpret the vast array of fermentation techniques used by our ancestors. Build your body's cultural ecology as you engage and honor the life forces all around you.
>
> The prized cultures of a San Francisco sourdough, or the finest Bleu cheese, have their roots in wild fermentations that took place in someone's kitchen or farmhouse long ago. Who knows what compelling healing flavors could be floating around in your kitchen?

Many fermented foods are extremely expensive when purchased. A good blue cheese or a nice bottle of wine can set you back quite a bit. But these are cheap foods, in many cases, when you make them yourself and the quality is so much higher. For example, my family doesn't drink much in the way of soda, but it is a nice treat for birthday parties. We make homemade ginger ale and fruit sodas, using our homegrown fruits. They are less sweet and far tastier — the ginger ale tastes like ginger, instead of sugar water, the strawberry soda recipe, taught to us by a friend, is the nectar of the gods.

The flavors are unique, complex and remarkable — exactly the opposite of industrial food flavors. Generally speaking, making fermented foods is simple. They take some time, but not the sort of time where you have to sit over them and pay attention. You might spend ten minutes putting together brine and chopping vegetables or warming the milk and adding the sour cream culture, and then you can ignore the food for several days until it comes time to simply bottle it and put it in a cool place until you want it. While some fermentation projects require a bit of investment in time and equipment, most are quite simple and don't require very much of either. If you are just getting started in home preservation, many fermentation projects allow you to dip your feet into the water easily.

Lactofermentation in Particular

Lactofermentation is pretty simple — a salt brine is created, strong enough to kill off unwanted bacteria, mild enough to encourage lactic fermentation, which makes things sour and yummy. Fermentation is faster in warm weather, slower in cool, so you want to watch it closely if you do it in the summer time — otherwise, easy peasy. And the food is delicious, nutritious and amazing — I can't say enough good things about most lactofermented foods. Best of all, they are alive and contain enzymes that are good for you. For example, kimchi contains a natural antibiotic specific to *E. coli*, as may other lactofermented foods, making them good to eat with meats.

My own passion for this stuff comes in part from a real liking for the taste and in part because during each of my four pregnancies, I threw up constantly for four straight months. The category of things I could eat without throwing up was very, very small and kimchi, sauerkraut and brined pickles were among them each time. They were one of the few things that made me happy during those 16 months of hell. I am not the only pregnant woman who could eat these things — they are a classic remedy for morning sickness in many countries. Thus, for me they can do no wrong. I have only happy memories associated with them.

Add to this that lactofermentation is the only form of food preservation that actually makes the food more nutritious than if it wasn't preserved. Fermentation makes nutrients available and foods more digestible, so we get more benefits. Napa cabbage, made into kimchi, is more nutritious than fresh napa. Regular cabbage transformed into sauerkraut has more accessible vitamin C, is more digestible and doesn't cause gas in most people the way regular cabbage does. There's really not a downside.

Now you may think you hate all these foods, but if you've only ever eaten canned sauerkraut, you have no idea how delicious the real thing is. Fermented foods don't even have to be that sour. Because these are living foods, you can adjust their sourness to taste. A lot of my favorite kimchi panchan (small dishes) are very mild, even sweet and tangy. Others are flaming hot (which I love). So they are worth experimenting with.

The best books on this subject are Sander Katz's great *Wild Fermentation* (he has a website with a bunch of recipes and a lot of information on it at wildfermentation.com), Sally Fallon's book *Nourishing Traditions* and Linda Zeidrich's *The Joy of Pickling*. The Katz book is so superb I'd recommend it for everyone's library — he's a wonderful and engaging writer.

Lactofermentation Basics

OK, here's the basic project. It works for making fermented (often called kosher-style) pickles, for pickled grape leaves, sauerkraut, kimchi and a host of other good things. You make a brine with some salt and water — for kimchi a bit more, for pickles a bit less. For kimchi, I use three tablespoons of salt to a quart of water, for pickles two table-spoons. If you are fermenting in warmer weather, a stronger, saltier brine will be useful to retard growth and bacteria, while if you are fer-menting in cool weather, you can use less. It isn't a very picky process — I've used quite little salt too. But two or three tablespoons are about standard.

Chop up your vegetables (if chopping is called for) and dump them into some kind of non-reactive pot, crock or container. Make a brine by mixing the salt in the water until it is dissolved. Let the veg-gies soak overnight if fairly finely chopped, or 48 hours if you're using whole cukes. Weigh it down with a plastic baggie full of water or a plate covered with a weight — you want minimal to no exposure to air, but enough leakage to let gasses out. This is super-important with dai-kon radishes, because they make explosive gasses — ask me how I know. Take the vegetables out, reserving the brine, and then pack them into the container that you plan to store them in, but now add spices and flavorings. Pour enough brine to cover, and leave it in a reasonably cool spot, no higher than 68 degrees, until it tastes like what you want taste.

The easiest way to ferment kimchi is to pack the cabbage into mason jars after the initial brining, leaving a little headspace. Add hot peppers, spices, ginger and garlic, and put two-piece mason jar lids on very lightly, so that the gasses can vent. You can also make these in a barrel or crock with a lid that's fairly tight fitting but with enough air transfer to let the fermenting gasses out.

How long to ferment? Kimchi usually takes about a week, depend-ing on how strong you like it. Pickles can take several weeks, so can sauerkraut. The key is to keep tasting it. The warmer the weather is, the faster the fermentation, so keep an eye on your pickles if you are mak-ing them in hot weather. We generally only do large-scale lactofermen-tation (more than a few jars we are going to eat immediately) in cool weather.

What's the downside of fermentation? Well, these are living foods. They don't keep forever, unless you can keep them very cool (fridge temperatures) or unless you can them. And the bad part of canning fer-mented foods is that you kill many of the living organisms that make them so wonderful—and some of the taste. At really warm temperatures, they can develop mold quite quickly, while in a fridge or cold spot they will last several months, although they will get sourer, so keep tasting them to make sure you like them. Do not freeze them, as they turn to mush. My kimchi and sauerkraut keep for about four months in my root cellaring space, which averages about 35–45 degrees.

On the other hand, they are unbelievably delicious—stuffed pickled grape leaves, dill pickles, mustard pickles, kimchi of all sorts, sauerkraut with dried cherries, juniper sauerkraut...the tastes are infinitely varied, and absolutely lovely.

What do you do with them once you have them? Well, we like sauerkraut in lots of things—with meats, in eastern-European style pies, etc. Kimchi we eat in soup, and also stir-fry with garlic and tofu or meat. Pickles we just plain eat—and all four of my kids can keep up even with me. Grape leaves we stuff.

Salting

Another "oldest method" of preserving food is salting. It is comparatively rarely used now, and for fairly good reasons—some people are salt sensitive, and experience blood pressure rises if they consume too much. Eating lots of heavily salted foods has been linked to stomach cancer. And salted foods are *salty*. They have to be soaked to remove the salt and be palatable. But that said, salt brines were the standard method of preservation for many meats and fishes for centuries, and this technique is potentially useful for many of us. Salt is inexpensive, and its replacement came with the era of refrigerated shipping, which is probably getting close to over. And salt foods have their place in various cuisines and cultures. Baccalao, or salt cod, is a traditional food for the large Portuguese populations of coastal Massachusetts where I grew up—and it is delicious. Salt pork was the staple meat of most pioneers, simply because it could be transported, and is still commonly used in baked beans.

The theory is very simple—enough salt and microorganisms can't live. They can't tolerate an extremely salty environment. The recipes I'm using have not been USDA approved—I can't find any useful

USDA information about salting at all, except in collaboration with smoking. I don't think anyone recommends it. But in *Keeping Food Fresh: Old World Techniques and Recipes* there are recipes from French gardeners and farmers that have been used for centuries. They suggest that fish should be essentially buried in salt. That's what is done with salt cod. The fish are cleaned and layered with a thick layer of sea salt (sea salt has a better flavor than most kitchen salts). At room temperature, salted fish will keep a full year, although use your nose and eyes for signs of spoilage.

More to my family's taste is a salt-herb stock base we make, which can be added (in small quantities, it is very salty) to broths or used as the base of a quick soup. Half a pound of sea salt is layered with two pounds of mixed green vegetables and herbs. We like basil, tarragon, parsley, scallions, chives, rosemary and cilantro in this, but any herbs will do. Just chop up the herbs and toss them with the salt, put it in a jar and ignore. It lasts forever and tastes fabulous.

Preservation in Oil and Alcohol

Preservation in oil and alcohol are old traditions for preserving food. They have the downside of being expensive for most of us who don't own a vineyard or an olive orchard. Moreover, these aren't the best techniques for staple foods. But they do make some wonderful foods for special occasions or gifts.

Preservation in oil is very simple. You put the food that you want to preserve in a container and cover it with enough oil that air can't get at it to spoil it. The added plus is that the oil is flavored with the contents — but botulism has been found in some oil items, including homemade garlic oil, so this is something to be quite careful with. If you are going to use this technique, make sure you have a mechanism of keeping food cold lest botulism spores develop. Either refrigerate it, keep it in a cold cellar or do your oil preserving only when the weather is chilly.

One of my favorite foods preserved in oil is homemade yogurt cheese or labneh. This is the simplest form of cheese making and produces something that is like a much tastier version of cream cheese.

You take yogurt — this is a great use for your homemade yogurt — and put it in a fine mesh colander or bag of cheesecloth, and suspend it over a bowl. The liquid will gradually drip out, leaving you with the milky solids. After 24 hours or so, you'll have something that looks rather like cream cheese, but is tarter and tastier. You can just eat it straight, but if you'd like to preserve it, one good way is in olive oil.

Take the cheese and mix in some fresh herbs. We like thyme, oregano, zaatar, sage and garlic chives, but you can use anything that you've got. If you don't have fresh herbs, you can use dried. This is a forgiving substance, this cheese. You could add a little lemon zest, or some chile peppers as well. Roll the herbed cheese into balls and pack lightly in a clean mason jar. Add a couple of sprigs more of fresh herbs, chile peppers or a cinnamon stick if you like. Then pour oil over the cheese balls. Leave for a few days for the flavors to develop, and then eat on crackers, fresh biscuits or pita bread. Yum!

Alcohol is a great way of making things last, and kills most of the microbial bad guys that spoil food. The downside (or upside depending on your tastes and whether you are over the age of consent) is that whatever you preserve is imbued with alcohol (and the alcohol flavored with the food preserved). Now this means that while it was once considered reasonable to preserve meat in wine, this is no longer in fashion, because neither winey chicken (not coq au vin, but really, really winey chicken) or chicken-flavored wine is in favor. But there are many, many good ways to make this work for you.

The simplest way to do this is to buy inexpensive vodka and imbue it with the flavor of something you like. You want something palatable, but it doesn't have to be fancy. I'm told, but have not tried it, that running very cheap vodka through a Brita filter improves its taste considerably, so you might experiment. Thus, cheap vodka is transformed into something kind of fancy, you get a flavoring or a beverage, and people get gifts. For example, every year I make about a gallon of raspberry-cinnamon vodka. I take a half-pint of raspberries and two cinnamon sticks, and a cup to a cup and a half of sugar, and put them in a clean half-gallon glass jar. I pour vodka over it, cap it and occasionally shake the jar a bit to dissolve the sugar. Three months later I have something that friends of mine have actually tried to steal from me. You can do this with just about any fruit, and while the results vary a bit (raspberry-cinnamon is my favorite, but black currant-vanilla is awfully good too), they are never that bad.

If you leave out the sugar, you will get more of a fruit brandy taste, but this takes a bit longer to infuse. You really can use any high-proof liquor, but it will taste more of the liquor and less of the stuff you add if you use, say, rum. Gin is already flavored, so you might not want that — or maybe you do. The better the quality of the liquor you use, obviously, the better things will be. That said, however, the beauty of this method is its power to transform cheap liquor into something better than you paid for.

You can do much the same thing with brandy, either pure brandy or a pint of good brandy to a pint of cheap vodka. Any fruit will do. One of my goals is to remember to take some glass bottles and put them carefully over growing peaches, apples and quinces while they are forming on the tree. You slide the jar down so it covers the tiny fruit, and then the fruit grows inside the jar, and you have this cool, fruit in a bottle effect and everyone wonders how it got there. Then you can soak it in homemade pear or apple or quince liqueur and make something truly fancy.

One of the best forms of alcohol preservation is making home-made vanilla. We use vodka, but brandy is good too. Macerate one or two sliced vanilla beans in the brandy for some months. You can make almost any flavor extract this way — mint, nut flavors and maple are just a few examples.

Herb liqueurs are good too. I like mixed fruit and herbs — apple-thyme, citrus-lemon verbena, peach-mint. But plain herbs are good, both as flavorings for baked goods and also as dessert drinks. A glass of rosemary-thyme liqueur is very palate cleansing. There is something of a fine line between this and herbal tinctures — but what a pleasant way to take your medicine!

In his wonderful, wonderful book *Good Spirits* Gene Logsdon suggests making lemon liqueur, getting it really cold, making lemonade and mixing the lemon liqueur half and half with the lemonade. I've tried this, and it is very, very good.

Other than finding new and improved ways to get drunk (and this is no bad thing), what else can you do with alcohol? Well, you can make rumpot.

A rumpot (or Bachelor's jam) is a bunch of fruit put together with alcohol to meld and make something that is syrupy, good and alcoholic. You want a large stoneware crock or something similar that is reasonably airtight but allows the venting of fermenting gasses. Quart mason jars will do, if the lids aren't put on very tightly. Use whatever fruit you have — peaches, plums, berries, currants, apricots, pears… Chop the fruit, layer it in, add a layer of sugar (enough to cover) and pour cognac or brandy over it to cover. Keep adding fruit as the season progresses, and then leave for three to six months minimum. It is great on toast for breakfast, if you are the sort of person to eat this for breakfast, or it is wonderful over ice cream.

Any kind of dried fruit can be packed into brandy diluted with one quarter water and will keep indefinitely that way. The fruit is good to eat, and the now flavored brandy will be good too. Nuts can be put away this way as well.

Cheeses can be preserved in good quality wine — put the cheese in a jar, pour the wine over it, cover and store at room temperature. The only problem with this method is that you might not want to drink the cheese-flavored wine, and the cheese does get a strong wine taste. But you might like the taste involved.

Finally, there's the making of alcohol itself, for food, medicine, fun and fuel. This is a bigger subject than I have any intention of dealing with — I'm still new to home brewing and winemaking, and wouldn't presume to teach others. Still, I'll end this section with a neat trick my father claims works well — making Applejack. I have not tried this, but I plan to. You need unpasteurized apple cider. New York state recently went to all-pasteurization, but you can still make your own or buy it occasionally if you plan to use it for "cooking." I get mine from a neighbor.

Let the cider sit in a place warmer than a fridge but cooler than a sauna. Keep a close eye on it — when it starts to go fizzy, check it more often or put it in the fridge, and keep testing it until there is a faint, sour taste that suggests it is about to go to vinegar. Then freeze it. Because the alcohol freezes at a much lower temperature than the water, this operates as an entirely safe method of distillation. Check it regularly and skim off the ice. You can put it in a freezer or leave it outside in cold weather. The latter is traditional. Skim off the ice two or three more times, until it is hard to get any water at all. You now have an apple brandy that's probably around 80 proof and you may do with it as you will. You'll probably want to age it a little, and I've been told it can leave you with something of a hangover, so be careful.

Recipes: Fermentation

Homemade Kimchi

I love kimchi, and we eat a lot of it. Not as much as most Koreans, who eat several hundred pounds a year on average, but quite a bit. We make it out of a host of greens and roots, but this is a recipe for classic style kimchi, made with napa cabbage, daikon and carrots. If you don't have these ingredients, consider experimenting — grated turnip is good instead of carrot, and almost any green can be fermented well. Here's a typical version for my house. Makes 1 quart.

- 2 tbsp pickling salt
- 1 lb napa cabbage or other greens
- 2 carrots, grated or sliced thinly
- 3 tbsp minced fresh ginger
- 3 tbsp Korean hot pepper or cayenne (or less, if you like it milder)
- 6 cups water
- 1 lb thinly sliced daikon
- 10 cloves garlic, sliced finely
- 3 tsp sugar

Dissolve salt and water together, combine cabbage, daikon, carrots, ginger and garlic together, and pour brine over them. Weigh the kimchi down with a plate until completely covered and wait 24 hours. Then drain vegetables, reserving brine. Put 1 tsp sugar and 1 tsp hot pepper paste into a clean mason jar. Fill with vegetables, and cover with reserved brine. Screw the lids on tightly enough to not allow much in, but loosely enough that gasses can escape. Ferment for a week, tasting every couple of days, until it tastes good to you. Then put somewhere cold until you eat it.

How to use it? One of my favorites is as kimchi tofu soup, which is wonderfully warming on a cold winter's day. You can use any kind of kimchi here, but the traditional one will certainly clear your sinuses if you are sick.

Kimchi Tofu Soup

- 5–6 cups chicken, beef or vegetable stock
- 1 tsp ginger root, finely grated
- 1 cup mushrooms (fresh, canned or dried and reconstituted—we like Chinese black mushrooms, which are stored dry), thinly sliced. (This is traditional, but any veggie will do.)
- ½ cup scallions (or onions, or chives or leeks), thinly sliced
- 8 oz firm tofu, cut into cubes (you can use meat or stir a beaten egg in if you don't have tofu)
- 1½ cups kimchi, chopped into bite-sized pieces
- ¼ cup soy sauce

Put stock and soy sauce in a soup pot and bring to an low boil. Add kimchi, tofu, mushrooms, scallions, and ginger. Simmer for about 15 minutes and serve. Serves 4.

Wine Sauerkraut

Linda Ziedrich's excellent *The Joy of Pickling* gave me the idea for this sauerkraut. She points out that wine was a common flavoring for kraut, and suggests using a dry white. But it occurred to me that a sweet German wine might be even more appropriate, and that some fruit might go nicely. Boy, was this good.

- 2 cups sweet white wine—ideally a Gwertztraminer or sweet Riesling.
- 6 tbsp pickling salt
- 2 tbsp juniper berries
- 5 large apples, chopped finely (you can peel them or not, the skins add a nice color)
- 6 tbsp caraway seeds
- 10 lbs chopped, washed green cabbage, sliced thin

In a huge bowl, mix all ingredients but the wine together, and then pack in jars or a crock and weigh down with a heavy weight, and place somewhere that stays under 70 degrees. Wait 24 hours and then add wine and mix thoroughly.

Check kraut every few days, and taste to see how you like it. If any white scum develops, skim it off and rinse the weight before replacing. Depending on how warm it is (it ferments faster in warmer temperatures), it should be done in 2–6 weeks. Then pack in jars and put in a cold place.

Japanese-Style Rice-Fermented Greens

One of my first food preservation class members was a woman named Susan who was partnered with a Japanese man. She mentioned that they ferment greens using rice, and I couldn't wait to get a recipe. I've tried it several times, and these are absolutely delicious. The ginger is my own addition because I like it, but you could leave out.

- 1 lb of strongly flavored, sturdy greens—kale, mustard greens, radish leaves, turnip greens, etc.
- 2 cups rice, left out for a couple of days (should have a slight fermented smell, but not smell at all yucky or off-putting)—you can add a little water if it has dried up at all
- 1 tsp minced ginger
- 1 tsp salt
- a handful of raisins

Wash and chop the greens into manageable pieces. Add a little warm water, the raisins, salt and ginger to the rice, and cover the greens with it, spreading it around to cover. Put something heavy on top to weigh it down—another bowl filled with something is a good choice. Leave for 2–4 days, tasting the greens periodically (just wipe the rice off) until they are lightly soured. Use in sandwiches, over rice or add to soup.

Salting

Preserved Lemons

These are wonderfully delicious, rich, salty, sour and perfect. My favorite way to use them is in salad dressings—a tablespoon of chopped preserved lemons in vinaigrette. I also like them with chicken, in carrot salad and mixed with dried fruit in fillings for stuffed cabbage. Make sure you use organic lemons here since the peel is what you eat.

• 6 large lemons	• 1 cup sea salt
• 2 tbsp mixed colored peppercorns	• 2 cinnamon sticks
• 3 bay leaves	• 2 cups additional lemon juice

Wash lemons and cut them into eighths. Toss the lemons with half the salt in a bowl and weigh the lemons down with a plate or something similar to extract the juice from the lemons. After 4 hours or so, put a thin layer of salt in a large jar, add some lemon quarters, then a bay leaf and a few peppercorns, another layer of salt, some lemons and a cinnamon stick until everything is used up. Add the additional lemon juice until completely covered. Shake jar to dissolve salt.

Put in a cool, dark place for several weeks, shaking and turning the jar over every few days (make sure the lid is tight). Then eat. You can eat the lemons straight (they are very salty and very sour) or soak them in a couple of changes of cold water to make them a little milder.

Salt Pork

My family doesn't eat pork because we keep kosher and yet wanted to include this recipe. I grew up on classic New England cooking, much of which involved salt pork for flavor in things like baked beans and clam chowder. It was an intensely flavorful meat, that could be kept and added in small quantities to transform foods. Salt pork isn't used much these days, but since small-scale pig raising can produce so much food mostly on our scraps, perhaps it should be.

- 10 lbs pickling salt
- 5 gallons of water

- 5 lbs pork backfat
- Non-reactive crock with lid or plate to press down

Cut backfat strips into 1-inch chunks. Pour one pound of the salt into the bottom of the crock and smooth to cover. Lay the backfat chunks on the salt. Lay the platter or other flat object over the meat. Add a heavy weight (big cans or something) on top to hold the platter in place. Dissolve the remaining salt in 5 gallons of water. Pour over the contents of the crock. Make sure you have enough water to completely cover the backfat and platter. If more is needed, add up to 2 more gallons of water.

Cover and place in a cool place (under 45 degrees), or the bottom of the refrigerator, for up to 2 months. Freeze if longer storage is wanted.

Preservation in oil

Grilled Vegetables in Oil

This recipe is potentially risky, since botulism can grow in an anaerobic environment like oil with non-acidic things like veggies in them. If you do make these, eat them fairly quickly and keep them quite cool. The lemon and salt here do provide some help retarding the growth of things you don't want. Store in the refrigerator.

- 2 lbs mixed vegetables — eggplants, zucchini, onions, sweet or hot peppers, anything that grills well

- ¼ cup soy sauce
- olive or other tasty oil to cover
- 4 tbsp lemon juice or vinegar

Marinate the vegetables for 2–8 hours, and grill vegetables until they reach the desired level of carbonization. Remove, cool and put in a jar. Cover with good oil. Keeps several days in a cool place, and the oil can be used for salads — both vegetables and oil are absolutely delicious.

Alcohol

Grandpa Orlov's Vodka

This is a recipe by the great Dmitry Orlov, whose wonderful book *Reinventing Collapse* describes the history of the Soviet Union's fall and its relevance to the crisis of empire the US is having now. It is a brilliant, readable and enormously funny book, and I recommend it to everyone. Dmitry is a great writer and a wonderful person, and when he wrote down his Grandfather's Vodka recipe on his blog, I knew I had to have it for this book. This is just a small sample of his writing — do read more of it!

Just as a point of reference, there are some legal issues with making your own liquors in the US, so be careful about what you are doing and who you tell!

Now, "Man doth not live by bread alone…" [Deut. viii. 3] This becomes especially apparent at the onset of cocktail hour, and, in circumstances both dire and not-so-dire, having a source of homemade "spiritual sustenance" can often spell the difference between miserable company and amiable companionship.

When it comes to food, waste is a fact of life. Almost always, there is fruit left rotting on the vine or on the ground, and it usually goes straight into the compost. But there is something more useful that can be done with it: it can be made into alcohol. Anything that has sugar in it can be fermented and distilled.

For years, my father made vodka in our kitchen in an apartment in Leningrad, using the technique I am about to describe.

This made him a popular man: he would pour it into brand-name bottles and bring them to parties. Most people probably just wondered how he managed to get his hands on such fancy imported booze. Due to certain official restrictions, the fact that it was moonshine was communicated on a need-to-know basis. And since the substance in question was effectively identical to the brand-name substance (alcohol is alcohol) plausible deniability was maintained.

Store-bought alcohol, with the possible exception of certain low-grade products, is made from high-quality inputs: grains, grapes, and so forth. But here is the shocking good news: you can make excellent quality vodka, something you can proudly serve in a martini glass, out of stuff that would otherwise go into compost. The key fact is that vodka is just alcohol diluted with water; the better the vodka, the more pure the alcohol. Its good taste does not come from the ingredients that were used to make it but from the complete lack thereof in the final product.

To make it, whatever it is you can get your hands on (rotting apples, pears, grapes, berries, and so forth) is mashed and soaked in hot (but not boiling) water to dissolve out the sugars. The result is strained, to get rid of the solids, then boiled to kill everything in it and poured into a large bucket with a tight-fitting lid. After it cools to lukewarm, yeast is "pitched" into it and an airlock (bubbler) is placed on top. Any book on making wine or beer will tell you how to measure and adjust specific gravity, to make sure that wild yeast (which can cause runaway frothing) is kept out, and that fermentation has a chance to run to completion before the yeast gets too drunk to do its work.

After the bucket is allowed to sit for some weeks in a warm place, the result can be distilled. Distillation requires some equipment, such as a pressure cooker fitted with some sort of cooling apparatus (glass or metal tubing submerged in cold water) to turn alcohol vapor into condensate before it escapes. Again, there are plenty of resources, on the web and in the library, on how to do this.

Now, here is the magic step that turns cloudy, stinky, low-grade moonshine into something that is indistinguishable from Stolichnaya, Finlandia, Absolut, or any other high-quality commercial vodka. Sprinkle in potassium permanganate crystals (available in bulk from pool supply stores) and agitate until the liquid turns slightly pink. Label it "Poison!" to make sure nobody drinks it, and let it stand overnight. (It won't kill you if you drink it, but it will wipe out your intestinal fauna and give you really bad diarrhea, so it's important to make sure that nobody drinks it at this stage. If some fool does drink it, just feed him some yogurt or acidophilus tablets, plus something for the fierce hangover.)

A day or so later, the solution will no longer be pink (or toxic), but it will be cloudy, and there will be some dark precipitate at the bottom. Take a funnel, pack it with cotton, lay down a layer of charcoal (either commercially available activated charcoal or wood charcoal knocked off a partially burned log), and pack it down tight. Drip the distillate through the filter, changing the stuffing every gallon or so. The result will be clear and have no taste or smell other than the taste and smell of alcohol. Add water to bring it to 80 or 100 proof, and consume responsibly.

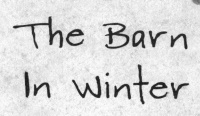

The Barn
In Winter

We're having our first serious blast of winter here — bitter cold, snow, winds. It is the kind of weather that makes you want to be indoors drinking cocoa in front of the fire. So why am I so drawn to the barn, when I could be inside?

I think it is because the barn in winter is one of the loveliest places imaginable. The animals huddle together on the coldest days and they are delighted to see us as we come and bring treats, replace frozen water with fresh and make sure all is well. During the warm months, the animals are often busy doing their things. They are hunting bugs and grazing, and while they do stop a moment and interact with us, they, like us, are attempting to get the most out of the time they have on those lush, sunny days. And then suddenly winter comes, and the animals have time and so do we. Shut up inside (not always, but on the coldest and stormiest days), we have a shared sense of endurance and the knowledge that friendliness passes the time and warms us up.

Thus, the angora bunnies come hopping up to be held. They are as soft as anything you can imagine, and surprisingly small — their halos of fluff make them look far bigger than they are. In summer, I pick them up, and they tolerate my strokings, but are clearly thinking of the green grass underneath their bunny tractor. Today, they nuzzle against my jacket and nibble slices of pear from my fingers.

The chickens make soft winter noises as they roost around the barn. They call softly to one another, and allow me to stroke their feathery heads. There are only a few eggs since it is the darkest season and hens lay by light, but what there are must be collected regularly, lest they freeze, and the cochin must have her eggs taken away, for we want no hatches in this bitter season. She pecks at me, but gently, displeased but nowhere near as protective as she will be in the springtime, the right season for raising babies. I bring the scraps from the house early, since it is too cold for them to be out hunting for bugs. Even the duck who thinks he is a chicken, and the two hens who reside with the goats, will come out for cabbage leaves and plate scrapings.

The goats, of course, think they are people. Their preference would be to spend these days in the house with us, alternating between sitting on our laps and climbing on the furniture. Since we are so cruel as to deny them our company there, they are thrilled by it when we come out to milk or bring them a handful of sunflower seeds or a slice of apple. They eat hay from my hands, and rest their bodies against mine, warming me and themselves. At milking time they bounce and leap, shaking out the energy that they can't burn in the pasture on this icy, snowy, frigid day.

Zucchini, our barn/house cat has taken a break from the space behind the cookstove, where he absorbs heat, to come radiate it in the barn and keep an eye out for mice. He hangs out on a bale of hay, leaping off occasionally to chase a hen, pouncing at her and enjoying the sudden outraged clucks of a chicken confronting a half-hearted predator no larger than herself. He does them no harm, and the chickens probably know this deep in some small segment of their none-too-large brains, but just as my five-year-old can't resist rising to the bait when his toddler brother teases him, the chickens never fail to give a satisfying bit of panic to a bored cat. Angus, who is mostly a house cat but occasionally joins Zucchini in the barn, no longer plays this game, since a particularly assertive hen he annoyed suddenly noticed that she was as large as he was, turned around, and began chasing him around the yard this fall. It took weeks before poor Angus, who is about as fierce as your average marshmallow, could get near a chicken.

All this life together is surprisingly warm. The barn isn't very airtight since it is better for their health to have more air circulation and less warmth. But the combination of creatures all lending their body heat — and I mine — means that the barn is surprisingly pleasant. Nor does it smell bad, if your nose is accustomed to animal smells. The shavings and bedding absorb much of the manure smell, and it is earthy rather than unpleasant, at least to me.

Sometimes the children come out and nestle down in the new bedding with the goats, or settle on a bale of hay, and wait for a hen to come and sit next to them, so they can feel the feathers under their hands. Somehow, we fellow creatures, we animals all, human, hen, cat, goat, duck, rabbit — we are all quietly settled, waiting for spring, and in the meantime, taking comfort in fellowship. And so I find myself strangely drawn to the quiet — and the noise, the cold and the warmth, all the pleasures and contradictions of the barn in winter.

Replenishing Stores: Gardening, Seed Saving, Raising Animals

*Cause and effect, means and ends, seed and fruit cannot
be severed, for the effect already blooms in the cause,
the end preexists in the means, the fruit in the seed.*

— Ralph Waldo Emerson —

SOMETIMES WHEN discussions of stored food and gardening come up, the two are treated as opposed to one another in some way. One person will observe that sooner or later stores will run out, and claim this means there is no point in storing food, since it will not last forever. Others note that there are times of the year when the garden is not producing, and that bad harvests happen, so gardening is not a priority. In fact, there is no real opposition—both perspectives are true. Any food security we have is based on putting aside during times of bounty and also replenishing stores consistently. Most of us can do a surprising amount of replenishment simply by making good use of the space around us.

Now not everyone can garden, raise livestock or save seeds. But most of us can do a little, whether it's some herbs in a pot on a windowsill, or some mushrooms (really!) under the bathroom sink or an acre or more of garden and pasture. I know people who grow huge amounts of food in containers, on rooftops, in community gardens, in their neighbor's yard, on church, synagogue and mosque lawns, or at their office. City folks may feel they can't grow food, but many of the most densely populated cities in the world produce 20 percent or more of their produce and meat within city limits. There are ways for the busy, disabled, elderly and children to grow and be involved with replenishing stores. We must all take some real responsibility for our own food security.

I don't have the space here to offer a full primer on gardening, raising livestock and seed saving. Instead, I want to talk about how to get started and about some common mistakes and assumptions about food production. And I want to talk about seeds as objects to be used, stored and saved because the tiny seed is, in fact, the repository of a great deal of our hope, and there are reasons to be concerned about supplies of seeds for a nation that really needs to feed itself.

Ten Mistaken Assumptions About Growing Food and Keeping Livestock

1. **I need a big sunny yard to grow enough food to matter.** It is true that plants take up space, and most food plants need at least four to six hours of sun a day — some need more. But even without a yard, many people produce a lot of food in small spaces. If you have four hours of sun a day, you can grow lettuces, spinach and other greens, rhubarb, currants, gooseberries, raspberries, and many herbs. If you have a sunny spot, but no ground, consider growing in containers. One possibility is conventional pots, but you can build containers including self-watering containers (also known as "earthboxes"), that will produce a lot of food. Edible container gardening can be remarkably productive, and make excellent use of small spaces. In shady spots you can produce medicinal herbs of high value, and mushrooms with nutritional and healing powers.

   You don't have to have land at all — could you talk to a neighbor about growing in their yard and splitting the produce, to your church/synagogue/mosque or your business about using some of their open space? Lease a vacant lot or a bit of unused land for a garden? Join an existing community garden or start one? Ownership is not the only way to find land.

2. **Growing food is only for young, healthy people — it's a lot of work!** Remember my friend, Pat Meadows? Pat is over sixty and disabled by lupus and arthritis, and her husband is also disabled. If anyone has a reason to take it easy, it is Pat. And yet, Pat produces hundreds of pounds of fresh produce every year in containers on her deck. She takes her time, plans ahead to minimize heavy work, barters or hires out the few jobs that really do require heavy lifting, and stops when she is in pain or feels tired. There are gardeners who garden in wheelchairs from specially designed homemade raised beds. Gardening is for everyone. The reality is that many more of us can grow food than do. Techniques like container gardening and mulch gardening (which garden writer Ruth Stout did into her 90s) and lots of tricks for working "smarter not harder" are useful not just for those who are elderly or disabled, but for all of us.

2. **A garden is rows of tomatoes, peppers and eggplants laid out neatly, and I just don't want that.** The typical North American garden is made up of annual plants, often in straight rows. There's nothing wrong with this kind of garden, but it isn't the only option. For those who want to have a different kind of garden, think about perennial plantings, fruit trees, food gardens modeled on English cottage gardens or even about partly cultivating wild spaces. The first human gardening was probably mostly creating the conditions for desirable wild foods to grow.

My front yard has three very tall spruce trees in it. When I moved here, I planted cultivated raspberries in the backyard, which did OK. But I noticed that under the spruce trees, wild raspberries proliferated. Gradually they came to fill the whole understorey of my beautiful spruces. We pulled out weeds and made space for them, but did little else and now my children graze on raspberries under the trees, which require no effort at all from us, unlike my laboriously nurtured raspberries in back.

If you have shade, try herbs. You may even be able to grow some woodland medicinal that you can sell or barter for food. If you have wet ground, plant things like blueberries and highbush cranberries that like wet ground. If you want beautiful, well, there are few flowering plants more lovely than a blueberry flaming red in autumn, a pomegranate in bloom or the hibiscus flower of an okra plant. Gardens are various and wondrous.

4. **You can't really grow enough food to make a difference in your budget.** A lot of the reasons people think this is because most American gardens are salad gardens. That is, they grow a few typical crops — lettuce, green beans, tomatoes, peppers — that mostly feed us what we think of as "side dishes." But while these are tasty, they aren't a major contributor to our caloric needs. So in a sense, it seems like vegetable gardening might not matter much.

But consider how that changes if you start raising small livestock for some of your meat, maybe using your garden scraps and weeds to feed them, or if you start growing potatoes and sweet potatoes along with your lettuce and peppers. These are dense, calorie-intensive crops that can really make a difference in your diet, reducing your dependency on the grocery store. And if enough people do this, well, the three hens and the 100 x 20-foot bed of potatoes can make a real net contribution to the food security of a city or region.

5. **Nobody here has chickens (or rabbits, or bees).** That might not be true. Until you start looking for them, you may not see them, but livestock shows up in remarkable places — there are beehives in London, meat rabbits on balconies in New York City, and chickens in Seattle backyards. I've heard stories of goats in Oakland, Portland, Oklahoma City and Los Angeles, pigs in Cambridge, Massachusetts and Miami, and someone whose cow wandered down the street in a suburb of Philadelphia.

Backyard livestock keeping is more common than you'd think. It's been brought by country folks and immigrants who always kept livestock, by people who have come to understand the relationship between small-scale husbandry and local food security and by those who simply want some contact with animals. Really, three chickens are a heck of a lot easier than a dog, and I'm going to bet some of your neighbors have them.

6. It isn't allowed. This is sometimes true, and sometimes not. Sometimes we just assume that because no one has a front yard garden or because we don't see chickens in the front yard, that no one has them in the back. Often the local zoning laws are friendlier than most of us would guess. But what if you live in a subdivision or a city with really draconian laws?

Well, those laws are going to have to change. They come from our assumptions about class and culture, and they are being challenged all over the US — people are playing civil disobedience and planting front yard gardens, hanging laundry where it has been forbidden and fighting to bring chickens into their community. And if you care about this stuff, there's a decent chance that someone else does. So now is the time to talk to your neighbors, your zoning board, and sweep away those old false assumptions.

7. I need a lot of expensive equipment like a rototiller or a tractor. If you are going to start farming 20 acres, yes, you'll need some tools. But if you just want to start gardening, well, that couldn't be easier. The simplest way is to collect cardboard or newspaper and do something called sheet mulching. This means laying a layer of cardboard or about 10 layers of newsprint down where you want a garden. Wet it down well until soaked On top of that, put some manure, some grass clippings or old leaves (shred them first), some compost, a little bone meal and a handful of greensand, topped with a couple of inches of some kind of mulch — straw, leaves, bark, etc. and a sprinkle of blood meal to get it moving. Build it up a couple of inches, and then plant anything but root crops into the stuff. Over the course of the season the mulch will begin to break down, but the weeds will be smothered, and you will have a beautiful bed, all ready to use. You can even do root crops if you start the fall before.

8. No one in my family will eat fresh vegetables. Well, that's a problem, isn't it? I mean fresh vegetables are pretty much the best thing in the world for us, and we need to eat them. So the question is how to enlist people you love in eating those scary green things. And the two best strategies I can think of involve those people in growing and cooking them. Kids, particularly, love to eat what they grow, and love to pick food directly from the garden. I will never forget the day I told my then four-year-old, Isaiah, that he and his brothers could each pick something to bring to visit Grandma. My son took a bowl and went out into the garden, and brought back a salad of mixed greens, cherry tomatoes, herbs and edible flowers, which he proceeded to transport with him to Grandma's in New York City.

Now I have normal children, who don't ordinarily consider salad the dream food. But salad you've picked yourself, salad you proudly showed to Grandma as your own, well, that's a very different thing. The same is true for both children and adults with food that you have a personal investment in, that you helped grow, helped cook, helped come up with recipes to use. The first key to eating it is getting to know it. For more help with this one, have another look at my advice in Chapter 5.

9. **I don't have a green thumb.** Neither do I — and I run a farm. Seriously, I've killed plenty of plants over the years, particularly houseplants, which I tend to forget about. Really, gardening is much less about a green thumb than about the willingness to experiment, and a passion for food. If you like to eat, you can learn the basics of soil and roots and harvesting.

"Green thumb" is usually just a code word for "pays attention." And that mindfulness is, I think, the whole key to the garden. Pay attention to the instructions in your garden books. Pay attention to the soil and water. Visit your plants and look at them. Pay attention to how they grow and what they like. All that attention will pay off.

10. **I don't have time to garden.** This may well be true. But there are a lot of balancing issues here. If you care enough, maybe you'd have time if you let something less urgent go. Maybe if you could get a loved one involved, you'd have time because you wouldn't have to do everything yourself. Maybe you have time for one fruit tree and a potted tomato, but not a 30 × 50-foot garden. Or maybe you could start small, with one bed, and build up from there. Maybe shifting your thinking would help. If you could do it with your kids,

maybe it wouldn't be "time away from the kids or work" but "an enjoyable family activity" or maybe you could give up your gym time and spend the time working out in the garden, getting exercise that way.

We're back to Carla Emery — life is a struggle, and you have to choose what you'll struggle for. For people who are working every minute until they fall into bed, there probably is no time to garden, no time for animals. I understand. That's a hard reality for many of us, and you know what you can do better than I do. But if you do have a little time to devote to replenishing your stores, well, that's good too.

Seeds

I think a lot of us imagine that if times get tough, we'll grow food. And there are good reasons to do this — in fact, it will go a lot more swimmingly if we start practicing soon. But implied in "I'll plant a garden" is the assumption that we will have plenty of access to good, viable seeds that will help us grow the food we want. And for the moment, that's true. But if gardening becomes necessary for you, it may also be necessary for your neighbors, and the current mail order seed industry would have a tough time handling a massive influx of new gardeners.

Thus, they will need open pollinated seeds, that is, seeds that come true to type, rather than more expensive hybrids that have to be bought year after year. They will need to learn how to produce enough seed for next year's crop, store it and keep it viable, as well as growing enough to feed themselves. If they do rely on hybrids they will need to find the money for more seeds, but with millions or tens of millions of people competing for available seed sources, we can expect predictable rises in seed prices.

It may well be easier to teach a hundred million Americans (and a similar proportion of folks in other nations in the Global North) how to grow food than it will be to find enough seeds for them to plant if a large percentage of the US is forced to grow food to feed itself quickly.

There are a number of issues here. The first is the total supply of seed, the second the vastly smaller supply of open pollinated, non-genetically modified seeds. There are concerns about the time needed to ramp up commercial seed production, and the time needed for home gardeners to become a successful seed savers. There are issues of seed quality that are likely to become more critical when we depend on our garden seed to eat — that is, when a seed failure means that we do not have any peas this year. There are critical issues of genetic diversity and disease vulnerability, and particularly the vulnerability of staple food crops like corn and potatoes.

I think most of us have underestimated the potential limits created by our current seed production model when faced with a crisis. There are also solutions to these limits, and the most important one is a radical expansion of home seed saving. The more people who produce seed, and the more diversity we protect, the more secure we will be in the long term.

It is helpful to begin by describing the seed trade as a whole. The vast majority of seed production in the US is focused on a fairly narrow range of crops for professional, industrial-scale farmers. A majority of these seeds are either hybrids, that is they generally do not "come true" if you save seeds from them and replant. (Some plants labeled hybrids have actually stabilized genetically and do come true, but this is comparatively uncommon — more on this later.)

If you take an open-pollinated seed, plant it, grow the plant out and save its seed, you'll get something pretty much like what you planted, as long as you take reasonable care to prevent cross-pollination. If you plant a hybrid, you'll get a mix of "off-types" that resemble the plant's parents, not the actual plant you want. Some of these may be fine, some may be nigh-on inedible — you simply don't know. You can replant seed from hybrids, but the plants will be less vigorous, lower yielding, less tasty or inferior in other ways. If you have time and patience, you can grow these hybrids out, get rid of any ones you don't want, and select until you get something you do want, but that takes some years, and does not offer short-term solutions.

The home garden trade is a small subset of the seed trade, and the serious home gardening/small farming trade is a vastly smaller subset even of that. The majority of home gardeners start comparatively few seeds. They purchase pre-started flats of vegetables instead of seeds. I'm consistently amazed to see plants that are grown from seed incredibly easily—lettuce, for example—in flats, and being bought like wildfire. So the majority of home gardeners have little experience planting seeds at all—carrots, perhaps, and peas, and that's probably about it. Although slightly off my main topic, this is something worth noting—even most experienced gardeners may have almost no experience growing food from seeds.

Of gardeners who do start seeds, the vast majority—more than 90 percent of them—do not order from seed catalogs and companies that specialize in home garden seeds. They get their seeds from seed racks in garden centers, supermarkets, Wal-Mart's and other places. And the majority of seed companies that sell through these seed racks are not deeply invested in producing high quality seed. According to Steve Solomon, founder of Territorial Seeds and author of *Gardening When It Counts,* the vast majority of seed sales involve simply the purchase of bulk seed, often from foreign distributors, and repackaging of that seed without variety trials, often without germination tests, and with little consideration of what is adapted to particular regions.

In many cases, the cheapest varieties of bulk seeds will have off-types, because hybridization often requires labor-intensive hand pollinating in the field, and high cost isn't what such companies are after. Solomon also notes that many companies use extremely poor quality seed, even sweepings from the seed floor for those cheap packets that are sold in commercial garden centers. Those ten-cent packages of seed you see in various places may not even have ten cents worth of seed in them.

Only about ten percent of the home garden seed trade is focused on high quality vegetable seed production, mostly by mail order. These are the seed catalogs whose seed will have the germination percentages they claim. These are the people who will replace your packet that does have poor germination, and who will ensure vigorous seed with varieties tested for your region—but it is important to remember that they are not necessarily prepared to serve a vast increase in need.

That is not to say that high quality mail order catalogs are the only place you can get decent or viable seed—but they probably are the best source for home gardeners. Seed saver organizations are also a good, reliable source. In an agricultural transition period, with millions more people gardening, new gardeners will want seeds that are viable (that is, they are not too old and have been stored well, and thus, will grow), vigorous (that is, they grow well and don't produce weak plants vulnerable to disease and pests), high yielding (that is, they produce a lot of whatever crop we are seeking), adapted to their climate and to small-scale food production (that is, they weren't selected for commercial production or shipping ability and will grow well in our climate), available in fairly large quantities (most home gardeners buy a packet or two of each thing, but if you are feeding yourself from your garden, or making succession crops, or selling at market, you'll find you need much more seed), and reasonably priced.

With increased demand, seed suppliers initially would be unable to meet demand. They have been expecting less than five percent of the American population to plant any kind of garden, and most of those are flower gardens, and they simply don't have enough spare production capacity to meet present needs. This is particularly likely if the biofuels boom continues and there is no leeway in the demand for seed among commercial farmers that might be sold to home gardeners.

Indeed, early signs of failure to meet growing demand are already showing. The annual Fedco seed catalog for 2009 included this message from founder C. R. Lawn, explaining rising prices and the absence of some varieties from their catalog.

> And now seed prices. I've been 30 years in this business and these are the highest increases to us I've ever seen. The ethanol boom diverting land to corn production has had a tremendous impact on farm commodity prices, including vegetable seeds. Wholesale prices for pea and bean seed are up 30–50%, for corn and squash 20% or more. Even so, wholesalers could not find growers for all crops so several varieties are missing from our catalog. Horrible growing weather this summer has exacerbated the shortage.

If many more people began gardening for food, we would see seed prices skyrocket, availability fall, and many people would have to rely on seed packets that don't meet the above requirements — that is, seed packets that have been kept in heated supermarkets and thus have reduced viability, or those routinely placed outside where they get wet and are exposed to repeated freezing and thawing, or were of low quality to begin with. So not only will the seed trade come up short, but much of what will be sold will be seed that was never of a quality likely to feed those who depend on them.

Seed production obviously requires at least one year to ramp up, and two years for the large number of primary vegetable crops that are biennials. Many of these are staple foods in difficult times (carrots, cabbage, etc.). In some cases, this will be perfectly possible. Existing seed farms may be able to ramp up their production. Large companies may be able to outsource seed production to poorer countries, where the labor-intensive process of hybridization can be done cheaply. But assuming that the biofuels boom is still in progress, we may see difficulty finding land to triple or quadruple seed production.

Seed companies will probably look to farmers who have not grown seed before — and this is potentially a good business for them. But the need for expanded seed production will become obvious in the late winter and early spring of a year in which many farmers will have already planned for their crops. It may not be easy to convince a farmer to begin growing a field of carrots for seed production when he may have planned to grow watermelons for market instead. A high price may have to be paid for the seed — more than the watermelons would have generated — which is likely to raise the price of seed further.

Seed saving on a large scale is quite difficult for some crops. With inexperienced farmers it is not unlikely that off-types and some cross-pollination will occur, particularly for wind pollinated crops that are difficult to isolate, such as corn. Since seed production also requires adequate equipment (for winnowing, drying etc.) and storage facilities, it is likely that there will be some more losses in production, even if seed sellers can find enough farmers to produce the seed so quickly.

Most biennial production in the US takes place in fairly warm areas where it is not too difficult to overwinter chard or carrots in the field. If it is necessary to localize seed production, this may require more capital investment in greenhouses and other heat retention aids. Some crops may not be able to be produced on a large scale in some regions. For example, production of cabbage seed in the cold Northeast generally involves digging up the cabbages, planting them in buckets of sand and replanting them. This is enormously labor intensive and large-scale cabbage seed production may be impossible, or prohibitively expensive in many climates. Also, a biennial crop that stays in the ground must compensate the farmer for extended periods in which she can't plant anything else. Again, prices can be expected to rise.

Meanwhile, new seed savers are likely to have similar difficulties with keeping seed pure and overwintering some crops. Learning to save a new variety of seed often takes a year or two of practice. It is extremely easy to save lettuce, bean and pea seeds, but a bit more challenging to master squash, corn and beets, especially in a neighborhood where lots of other gardeners are creating opportunities for cross-pollination. Again, this is not necessarily a disaster. The results of cross-pollination are often edible. But sometimes they aren't — or just barely — as you'll know if you have ever eaten the results of a badly isolated squash cross.

If we ever see a major shift towards mass gardening, we can expect that increasing seed production for home gardens will involve quite a lot of low quality seed in the first year or two, either from grower error, or outright hucksterism. For example, those who do not care about the eventual result might simply strip the seeds off some ears of corn, unconcerned that a field of cow corn grew right across the road from the popcorn, and that the plant will not come true.

Certainly we can expect prices to rise dramatically, which may be difficult for low income families who most need to grow food. By year three or even four or five, depending on the severity of the crisis and the rate at which new gardeners are added, we could expect both an easing of constraints and a better seed supply, but in the short term, it might limit gardening.

The best and most important solution is for more people to take on the project of maintaining seed of one or several varieties of plants. There are both national and local seed saving organizations that can help you learn how to save seed, and get you access to a variety that needs preservation. The more home gardeners and small farm seed savers and producers we have, the more secure is the future of our food.

The two most useful books for seed savers are Suzanne Ashworth's *Seed to Seed* and Carol Deppe's *Breed Your Own Vegetable Varieties*. I strongly recommend that these be part of every gardener's library. The second one may sound intimidating, but even if you have no intention of breeding, it is full of fascinating and useful information about plant genetics, presented in an accessible and fun to read way (I know that sounds nuts, but it's really true). The reality is that seed saving truly is plant breeding — each subsequent generation becomes better adapted to your region and its conditions.

I also recommend that you join Seed Savers, the national seed saver's organization and any local or regional seed saving groups you can find. They will have a lot of friendly advice, as well as wonderful varieties to grow and explore.

Storing Seeds

Whether you are buying seed from a good seed company (and there are many listed in the link vault on my website) or using seed you've grown and saved yourself, storing your seed so that it will remain viable as long as possible is essential.

If you want to store seed for more than one year, you have several options.

1. **Keep them in a cool, dark, dry place.** This will enable your seeds to have about the usual storage life. Some seeds, such as onions and parsnips last only one year, two at most. Others, like beans, can last for decades or even centuries and remain viable. So do some research into seed storage life. I would note, however, that this is one of those things that varies a lot — I've had no trouble keeping spinach seed for several years, for example. If you have a fridge, are very, very careful not to let your seeds get moist (use silica gel and package them carefully), you can keep them in the fridge. Me, I've got way too many seeds for that.

2. **Vacuum pack them.** Lack of air exposure will extend seeds' life a bit. You can buy pre-canned and vacuum packed seeds or pack

them yourself with a food saver or a straw. Remember, they still have to be cool and dark. This should add at a minimum one year to their lifespan.

3. **Freeze them.** Obviously, this only works while the power is on, but will substantially extend the life of your seeds while the freezer is working. I keep and use too many seeds to do this with all of mine, but I plan to use this technique for short lifespan seeds, such as onions, parsley and parsnips.

My friend Pat Meadows double packs her seeds in two layers of plastic and allows them 24 hours to come to room temperature before opening the packages, so that any condensation forms on the outside of the packet, not where it could hurt the seeds. Before you do any storing, however, make sure that any seed you grew yourself is completely dry and ready to be stored.

And remember, never plant all your seed if you can avoid it. Even the best gardeners have crop failures, and the best laid plans of mice and men gang aft agley. The reality is that seed varieties are lost all the time. It is never wise to assume that there will always be more of a particular variety. So save a little extra, and store it carefully for next year.

 Recipes

Thai Salad

This is one of our favorite uses for hard-boiled eggs, and a great use for eggs that have been stored a while (eggs keep up to two months at room temperature). Fresh eggs don't peel well, but slightly older ones do. Serves 4.

Salad Ingredients
Whatever greens and vegetables are fresh and in season. Lettuce and tomatoes in the summer, but don't let that limit you—bok choy and peas are great in spring, and fall broccoli and arugula are terrific.

- 1 small bunch broccoli, lightly steamed (good optional choices are lightly steamed carrots or green beans or sliced kohlrabi or grated beets — whatever you have)
- ½ cup pineapple chunks, fresh or canned (you can use seasonal fruit too)
- 6 eggs, hard boiled, peeled and quartered

Dressing Ingredients

- 1 can coconut milk
- ½ cup peanut butter
- 1 tbsp rice vinegar
- 2 tbsp sugar
- 1 tbsp Thai or Vietnamese fish sauce (you can substitute soy sauce)
- 1 teaspoon Southeast Asian chili sauce, such as sambal oelek (optional)

Assemble the salad, including all vegetables and quartered eggs.

Heat the coconut milk in a small saucepan over low heat until warm. Add the peanut butter, fish (or soy) sauce, rice vinegar, sugar, and chili sauce (if using).

Divide the salad into individual portions and serve with warm peanut dressing spooned over it. This dish goes nicely with a bit of white or brown rice on the side, also with peanut dressing on it.

Bamboo Shoot Soup

Bamboo is a remarkable plant, and one that can provide a host of needs — food, stakes, wood for building, windbreaks. Many people avoid bamboo because it can be invasive, but in her profoundly useful book *Food Security for the Faint of Heart* Robin Wheeler observes that this is partly due to our failure to make full use of plants. She writes:

> Like most people visiting Asia, I have experienced the constant dripping of a rain of epiphanies during my stays. One of these occurred on a trip to Northern Thailand, as I was standing on the edge of a new friend's yard. I admired the grove of towering

bamboo that edged her garden boundary, in a row so straight I could have marked it off with a piece of thread, with not a single trace of bamboo growing out into the road.

"How do you do that?" I asked her. "How do you keep the bamboo from growing all over the place, outside of your yard?"

"Well, that's easy," she replied. "Everyone knows how good bamboo shoots are in their dinner. The minute one shows its head outside of my garden, someone takes it home."

"Oh," I said, "In Canada we hack down the bamboo and throw it in the bushes and buy bamboo shoots in a can at the store."

But that is what North America is all about. We have been trained that if it is right in front of our face (e.g. free, accessible) it is somehow inferior, and that the only really good stuff is at the store. The more abundantly and freely something grows, the more reviled it should be.

So much of what is needed to ensure food security for everyone is just the capacity to use what we have. This soup is a favorite way of using bamboo. Serves 4.

• 6 cups vegetable stock (or chicken)	• 3 tbsp light soy sauce or to taste
• 1 cup diced carrots	• 1 cup sliced onions
• 1 cup sliced mushrooms	• 1 tbsp sugar
• 1 cup dried tofu sheets (available at Asian grocers), broken into bite sized pieces	• 2 cups julienned sliced bamboo shoots (you can used canned too, although the taste is inferior)
• 3 tbsp cornstarch	• 1 tsp white pepper
• ¼ cup hot sauce (or to taste)	

Bring stock to a boil. Add soy sauce, sugar and vegetables and cook until vegetables are tender. Dissolve cornstarch in ¼ cup cold water, and stir into soup. Keep stirring until mixture thickens, about 5 minutes. Adjust seasonings to taste. Serve with hot sauce and fresh cilantro, if available.

Human Hands

I was once asked to contribute to one of those "mildly famous people tell you their opinion" things about what my favorite kitchen tool was. My choice, hands down, was, well, my hands. I do a lot of things in the kitchen barehanded — for example, when I open up a jar of canned whole tomatoes, I find the easiest (and most fun) way to break them into pieces is to simply squeeze them in my hands. I love to get my hands into bread dough, or cookie dough. There are things you can tell from texture and feel that measurements can't help you with — one egg might be a little bigger than another, and thus add more moisture. The way I know when the dough is ready is that it feels ready.

Human hands and human powers are more remarkable than most of us really understand. We live in a world that systematically devalues human power, even as that power moves to become among the most abundant things on the planet. We create fossil-powered tools to replace even things that human hands and energies can do quite easily, and we let the tools tell us by their presence that we cannot do things as well without them. The very presence of the bread machine stands as a silent assault on the efficacy of human hands in dough.

That's not to say that I don't use a lot of specific tools. The next chapter will explore some of them. Most of us probably don't want to go back to hand threshing grains or grinding corn in a metate. But it is useful to know that you can — that it isn't always worth mortgaging one's future for a car or a grinder. If you need to, human power will get you many of the places you want to go.

The issue, of course, is always time. Most of us have so little that the siren call of every labor-saving device sings out to us. But few of us actually calculate the real time involved. For every expensive powered tool, one must work the hours to pay for it, to pay for the energy to run it, to repair or replace it when it breaks. There is time spent cleaning and time spent making space for it. In some cases, even many cases, it turns out that the time we invest in our tools is good time — it saves us energy and time in the end. But often enough, it doesn't. Though we tend to assume that labor-saving devices save labor, they often don't. Vacuum cleaners, when introduced, led to more time spent cleaning floors because of the advent of wall-to-wall carpeting and higher standards of floor cleanliness. By the time I get out, set up and then clean the bread machine, which bakes me one loaf of inferior texture, I can make three loaves of better tasting, better textured bread — because I am practiced at using my hands.

I don't in any way criticize anyone for the judicious use of tools, but I do believe we should approach our tools with more care and attention, and really ask whether, when we add up all the costs and benefits, they are worth it. And I believe homes preparing for a time when we may have to live with less energy should probably emphasize a wide range of simple human-powered tools.

Putting Tools in Perspective

The higher the artist, the fewer the gestures.
The fewer the tools, the greater the — imagination.

— Ben Okri —

A LOT OF YOU reading this book are probably really worried by now about all the new things it has given you to spend money on. Right as the economy is getting unstable, now you've got this big new shopping list. Not only do you need food in a time of rising food prices and rapidly increasing job losses, but you should go out and buy a grain grinder, pressure canner, dehydrator, freezer, etc. This runs rapidly into money that many of us do not have to throw around.

So let's put this shopping list in perspective. Let us first start with the assumption that simpler, cheaper tools are better. Let's note that most of these tools have existed in their current forms for less than 150 years. Canning is of comparatively recent vintage, and most of the world's population still eats few canned foods. Through most of history grain grinding was either done in large mills on a community scale or by hand, using a metate or other manual grinding process. Often the grains were not ground at all. They were eaten whole or processed for beer or alcohol and then drunk after fermentation. Dehydrating was usually done by laying food in the sun. Root cellars weren't fancy basements, they were holes in the ground.

The thing is, human beings did just fine without many expensive food preserving tools. That's not to say that the tools we use aren't extremely valuable, but I think it is important to remember that many of us are stockpiling for a time when we expect to be unemployed. Most of the tools we're talking about save time and human labor, but in a world where time isn't quite at the premium it is for many of us, and when a lot of people are around to share the work, it really won't kill anyone to use older techniques. We tend to look back at the recent past and see it as *the* past — and the home grain grinder really is an improvement over the metate, in some ways. It certainly relieves us of time spent grinding grain. It also changes the texture of the grain, the flavor of the food and means we have to find work for those who used to grind it, but in terms of time saved the net is probably positive. It just isn't the whole story.

If you are reasonably healthy, or have healthy family members, and not much money, maybe you don't need a lot of these tools. Maybe you can dig a hole in the ground to store food when the time comes, and grind your grain in a manual coffee mill or with a mortar and pestle or not at all. You could, for example, simply not grind grain. Instead, you could store more rice, whole corn to be made into hominy and already rolled oats and wheat berries to be eaten as porridge or whole in salads. Remember, much of what we're storing is to enable us to keep our diets as similar to the ones we have now as possible, and that's a fine goal. But we should never confuse our desire for familiarity with necessity.

Some of us foresee a need for these things, not so much to create many little self-sufficient households, each with its own grain grinder and pressure canner, as suburban homes now each have their own washer and vacuum cleaner, but as part of a larger community.

What do I mean? Well, the thing is, everyone doesn't need a grain grinder, but someone in the neighborhood might need one to keep everyone comfortably in bread. Everyone in the neighborhood doesn't need a pressure canner — a couple will do, to be shared around. A lot of us who have middle class(ish) incomes know that we're the ones who better buy these things because our neighbors don't even know they want them yet. We're buying for our extended families and friends and neighbors and frankly, I think this is a good use of our money, if we've got it.

For those who don't have money, though, it is OK to say "I'm not going to be able to provide all the tools." Those of us who can buy them are lucky, or privileged, often because we started early, when things were cheaper and worked hard at it. Those starting later in the process with fewer resources simply may not be able to keep up. And that's OK for two reasons. The first is that, as mentioned, you can get along without a grain grinder. Sooner or later in difficult times milling will pop back up, however it is powered. It always does. And until then, even if you don't have the grinder, you have the knowledge to say, "OK, here's how you cook whole wheat berries." That's a gift too, just like the grinder.

I think it would be easy to panic if you imagine that you have to prepare your household for a future in which you have to meet every one of your needs in isolation. It might be possible for wealthier households to approximate this in some ways (not all), but poorer ones would be in deep trouble. But the reality is that we need each other. We're building villages now. Those of us with enough money should contribute what we can to the future and the village. And those without it should contribute what they can — whatever that is, for knowledge and courage and enthusiasm are vast and important things.

What You Need, What You Don't

This depends a lot on the individual. First of all, there are personal and physical issues. I find it rather pleasant to grind grain manually, and I have healthy young children willing to take a turn. An elderly person with arthritis might find it unbearable. Six-gallon buckets full of 40 pounds of wheat aren't that big a deal for six-foot me to hoist around. But a five-foot-tall woman might want to store her grains in smaller containers.

Then there are issues of taste and skill. The good thing about powered tools is that they generally don't take any skill. Someone with weak knife skills might find it much faster to chop a couple of onions in a food processor, whereas someone with good knife skills might find that the time to get out the processor and clean it takes longer. Some people have strong opinions about taste and texture. They may find the texture of the food-processed chopped liver unacceptable, and the manually chopped better, or vice versa. A job you hate always seems to take longer, so it might be worth a powered tool to grind sausage, if that's one of your hated chores, but not so much if you find sausage making relaxing.

Then there are space issues. Someone in a tiny galley kitchen is going to have to limit himself to fewer kitchen tools than someone with a huge farmhouse kitchen. Even those of us with tolerable amounts of space (and while I have a lot of storage space, my actual counter space is quite limited) will have to make choices about which appliances are kept out and which are moved to less accessible places.

My own feeling is that we should make the best choices for ourselves, but we need to think our use of tools through carefully. A lot of us simply assume that because a powered tool exists, it is preferable to the non-powered one.

I don't at all object to people making a compelling case for a tool I don't want or use — what drives me crazy is the automatic assumption that we need all the tools, we should spend a lot of money on them, and that a good kitchen has them all in it.

Grain Grinders

If you are storing whole grains and you can afford it, you'll probably want a grain grinder, and probably one that works without power, so that you can use it even if the power is off. If you want an electric mill too, for daily grinding, the only one I have any personal familiarity with is the Whisper Mill, which several people I know recommend. It is now available as the Wondermill. I'm told it is the quietest of the bunch (although it sounds like elephants trumpeting, so take that for what it is worth). If you are grinding a lot of grain for a large family or for a business, and want to cook entirely with whole grains, an electric mill is well worth the money. If you are concerned about power outages, you will also want a manual grinder — and the two together get into money. An electric grain mill runs about $300–500, while most good manual ones are over $100. So I'm going to assume that most of us are going to get a manual grinder, either in addition to an electric one, or instead of one.

We have a manual grain grinder and use it almost daily, and don't mind not having an electric one. I rather enjoy grinding grain. It is also sometimes possible to electrify a manual mill if you are good at that sort of thing, or even to hook one up to an exercise bike. Grain grinders vary quite a bit in quality, ease of use and cost, so you should do some research into your choice.

There is a fair range of options. The Corona Mill was designed for poorer nations where corn is the primary grain. Corn is an easier grain than many others to grind, and if you have more time than money or are willing to mostly eat tortillas rather than wheat products, a Corona Mill is a good, cheap grain grinder. New, they cost under $50, and even better, there are tons of these around used. I've seen several at yard sales for under $5.

On the other end of the cost spectrum the Country Living Mill or Diamante Mill are both above $400 and are wonderful ways to grind. Both are very smooth and easy, particularly if you are grinding a lot. Either one might be a great neighborhood or group investment.

I own a Lehmans Best grain mill which is priced at around $160. Ours has gotten a great deal of use over the years without any signs of wear. There are several other mid-priced mills that you might want to consider, though, so do your research.

I find that a grain mill is one of the few tools I really don't want to live without. It opens up the range of things I can cook and store enormously, and extends the storage life of my favorite foods by allowing me to store them whole. It is the one single tool that a person seriously into food storage and local eating might definitely want.

How to Cook When the Power's Out

How will you cook dinner when the power goes out? We've spent some time on discussing what you might do to dehydrate or grind food without power, but how are you going to cook? This may or may not be an issue. If you have a gas stove that can be lit manually, you may not need to worry much about it — unless, of course, there is ever a problem with the gas main or with your ability to pay the gas bill. Only you can evaluate how serious a concern this is.

If you are going to store something better than surplus MREs (yuck!), you need a way of applying heat to food. In the simplest sense, you could store a hibachi and some charcoal, build a cement block fire pit and store some wood or cook over an open fire. But if you'd like some alternatives that don't involve trying to light an open fire outside during a torrential rainstorm or blizzard, you might want to think about an alternative cooking method.

The most traditional emergency backup method would be a camping stove of one sort or another, available at most camping stores. They use various fuels — usually propane, kerosene or alcohol — to heat food. These are an interim solution, because they don't use renewable fuels and because they still put you outside in the thunderstorm — most can't be safely used inside. Still, they are an inexpensive way to get cooking done in a crisis.

You may already have a fireplace, wood stove or wood cookstove. These all can be cooked upon, using various techniques, but all but the most basic things will require some practice. First of all, if they are infrequently used, make absolutely sure that you have the chimneys cleaned regularly and have a fire extinguisher that you know how to use. There is no point in having a hot dinner and a burned down house, and fires always proliferate when people are using unfamiliar equipment in an emergency.

Our family has both a heating wood stove and a wood cookstove. The cookstove has a smaller firebox and an oven and flat surface designed to be cooked on. If you have a small house and need a back-up source of wood heat, a cookstove allows you to bake, simmer and fry all at once while also heating your house. We love ours, and it gives our home a comfortable security. It does take some practice to manage. If you get one, we recommend Susan Restino's book *Mrs. Restino's Country Cooking* which covers wood stove cookery quite thoroughly. One other advantage of a cookstove is that in a power outage you will be able to pressure can meat and other high-value foods in your freezer during a crisis.

Regular wood stoves can also be used for cooking. It is easy to put a pot on the back of the heater to simmer, and if you make an oven out of sheet metal (I've seen someone convert an old metal breadbox to one), you can bake cookies or biscuits on top of it. The best wood stoves are more efficient than the best cookstoves, and can hold a fire overnight, whereas most cookstoves can't. So you may decide if you are buying a wood stove that this makes more sense, and be prepared to rely mostly on stews and soups during a power outage.

Fireplace cooking is very different than stove top cooking, but fascinating in its own way. You need some tools here — something to hang a pot from, a grate and some cast iron Dutch ovens. Again, it is an art that requires practice, so if you are going to rely on your fireplace, make some time in the evenings to practice cooking there as a family project.

There are also strategies you can use to reduce the amount of cooking energy you need. Keeping pots covered, placing hot food in an insulated, sealed container (known as a haybox cooker) to keep heat, and using a pressure cooker are some good options.

Rocket Stoves

You can also make a very small biomass (wood, straw, pine needles, corn) stove called a "rocket stove" that is extremely efficient, much more so than a wood stove. A rocket cooking stove is a great option if you don't need heat, just cooking power. It can be powered by twigs and makes minimal emissions. Rocket stoves are not hard to make yourself — they don't take more than a half hour and commonly owned tools and equipment. Their major innovation is that instead of wasting the heat the way an open fire does, it captures and directs it, meaning that tiny amounts of fuel can really do a great deal.

There is a video showing how to make one here: video.google.com/videoplay?docid=7974468238308334o1

And plans for one here: howtopedia.org/en/How_to_Build_a_Winiarski_Rocket_Stove

And here: cato-projects.org/ArLivre/RocketStove1.htm

Another great resource for all kinds of low-input, high-output, sustainable stoves is the Aprovecho Research Institute. They have two paper publications: *Capturing Heat* and *Capturing Heat Two* that emphasize low-input, low-emissions homemade solutions for cooking and heating. These are great publications and highly recommended.

The benefits of rocket stoves is that, unlike camping stoves, they make sense for everyday use. Reducing our cooking energy emissions is important enough that we should be looking not just for emergency solutions but for low-impact ways to cook every day. Besides, a crisis isn't a great time to be trying to figure out how to use something you've barely touched before.

An outdoor masonry oven is a great tool as well. These are made of clay, bricks or even mud, and can produce a great deal of food with small quantities of wood or other readily available biomass. They cook outdoors, but because they are sheltered and enclosed, you can cook in them even in very cold wet weather. Aprovecho has some material on this, but the most detailed resource is Kiko Denzer's excellent book *Build Your Own Earth Oven*. This project is doable even for the unhandy, and provides not just a good back-up heat source, but a low-impact way of cooking every day. Because the mass of the stove holds the heat well, it can be used for multiple cooking ventures. You can start by baking pizza and as it cools bake bread, cook a casserole and even dehydrate at the end of its warmth.

Solar Ovens

But even better than a wood cookstove or other biomass stove for many people is the solar oven. These are wonderful tools, that can be used by everyone, in every climate. If you live in a warm place, say much south of the Mason-Dixon line, and make or buy a good oven, you probably can use a solar oven for cooking any time it isn't pouring. For those of us who live in more northerly places, solar ovens may not be quite as useful, but you can use them an awful lot of the year — on sunny warmish days in January and consistently from April until October. They are great tools, and given that they make no emissions everyone should use them when they can. We try to have ours at least preheating water for tea or washing even when we aren't cooking anything.

You can make your own (I've made several, and they work very well indeed) or you can buy a commercially made one from sources listed on my website. I have both homemade versions and a commercial SunOven. Both are excellent, but in my climate the SunOven gets hotter.

Solar oven cooking is a great homeschool project and kids find it fun. There are a wide range of plans for all sorts of solar cookers that can be made with simple things you'll find around the house at solar cooking.org/plans.

Recipes

Corn Tortillas (With or Without a Tortilla Press)

The difference between these and the kind you get at the store is the difference between night and day, or between a supermarket tomato and a vine-ripened one. Don't miss the chance to try these. They are wonderful for fajitas and enchiladas, or baked to make corn chips. Makes 1 dozen tortillas.

- 2 cups Masa Harina (corn flour—this is different than cornmeal)
- 1 tsp sea salt
- 1 tbsp oil
- 1¼ cups hot water

Mix corn flour and salt together, add hot water and oil, and stir together with a wooden spoon or a fork. As soon as it is cool enough to touch, mix with your hands until fully incorporated. If crumbly dry, add another couple of tablespoons of water. Knead for two minutes. Begin to heat up a cast iron pan over medium heat, without oil. Pinch off a piece the size of a golf ball, and pat into a round with your hands. Either use your tortilla press to shape the ball or quickly roll it out with a rolling pin. When you have a tortilla-looking round, put it on the hot pan for 45 seconds to 1 minute; flip quickly and remove. Do the same with the next tortilla. Keeping them coming will require all your attention — having someone else to help with the pan can be nice.

Chili in a Solar Oven

Think of your solar oven as a slow cooker, and you can pretty much adapt any recipe used for a crock pot to it. The only exception is in very hot climates, where your solar oven may get too hot to use crockpot recipes. As always, experimentation is useful. Serves 4.

- 2 cups of soaked, precooked pinto beans (you can do the preliminary cooking in the solar oven the day before, or even earlier in the day)
- 3 medium fresh tomatoes or 1 large jar of diced tomatoes
- ½ lb ground beef, turkey or ¼ lb tvp chunks
- 1 large onion, diced
- 3 large garlic cloves, minced
- 2 tbsp semi-sweet chocolate chips
- 2 tbsp good quality chili powder
- 2 tsp ground cumin
- 2 tsp ground coriander
- 2 tbsp lime juice or cider vinegar
- 1–3 large jalapenos

If desired, briefly brown onion and garlic and meat (if using) in a little bit of oil. For the last minute of cooking, add spices and allow heat to release flavor. Put remaining ingredients in solar oven pot and combine. Cook 4–8 hours, longer if you are putting the meat in raw. Don't be weirded out by the chocolate — it adds a lovely depth of flavor to the chili.

Dutch Oven Biscuits over an Open Fire

These are great for camping as well as home fireplace cooking. The most important thing is the pot — you want a cast iron pan with a flat lid, so that you can put coals on top of the lid to heat it evenly. Remember, light, flaky biscuits are created by gentle, light handling, so mix in wet ingredients only when you are ready to form them, and handle them as lightly as possible. Serves 6 hungry people.

- 2 cups whole wheat flour or a mix of white and whole wheat, to taste
- baking powder
- 1 tsp salt

- ¾ cup buttermilk or milk that has gone sour
- 4 tbsp butter (melted) or oil
- 1 tsp baking soda

Mix dry ingredients together with a fork. Add butter or oil and stir quickly to incorporate, pour in buttermilk and mix with hands to form a ball of dough. If too dry, add a little more milk, quite gradually, until it just forms a dough but is not terribly sticky.

Dust a surface with flour and press the dough ball on. Roll to ½-inch thickness and cut out biscuits (if you don't have a biscuit cutter, you can use a water glass). Place biscuits in lightly greased Dutch oven, and use fireplace shovel to scoop some hot coals on top of the Dutch oven. Cook for 30 minutes, then remove, check and if not cooked, return to fireplace for 5 more minutes. Serve hot with jam or butter.

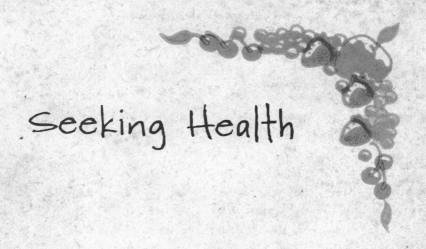

Seeking Health

In his essay "Health is Membership" the incomparable Wendell Berry writes:

> You would think also that a place dedicated to healing and health would make much of food. But here is where the disconnections of the industrial system and the displacement of industrial humanity are most radical. Sir Albert Howard saw accurately that the issue of human health is inseparable from the health of the soil, and he saw, too, that we humans must responsibly occupy our place in the cycle of birth, growth, maturity, death and decay that is the health of the world. But probably most of the complaints you hear about hospitals have to do with the food, which…tends to range from the unappetizing to sickening. Food is treated as another unpleasant substance to inject. And this is a shame. For in addition to the obvious nutritional links between food and health, food can be a pleasure…
>
> Why should rest and food and ecological health not be the basic principles of our art and science of healing? Is it because the basic principles already are technology and drugs? Are we confronting some fundamental incompatibility between mechanical efficiency and organic health? I don't know. I only know that sleeping in a hospital is like sleeping in a factory, and that the medical industry makes only the most tenuous

connections between health and food and no connection
between health and the soil. Industrial medicine is as little
interested in ecological health as is industrial agriculture.

A further problem and an equally serious one, is that
illness, in addition to being a bodily disaster, is now an
economic disaster. That is so, whether or not the patient is
insured. It is a disaster for us all, all the time, because we all
know that, personally or collectively, we cannot continue to
pay for cures that continue to get more expensive. The economic disturbance that now inundates the problem of illness
may turn out to be the profoundest illness of all. How can we
get well if we are worried sick about money?

— Wendell Berry, *The Plain Reader,* 60–61.

I have two instinctive reactions to this, perhaps ones that will seem
familiar to some of you. The first is to argue with Berry in the interest
of my family who can only survive in the world of medical technolo-
gies and high-level interventions. The second is that my first reaction
is too easy. The diabetics and thyroidectomy patients and so on are a
small percentage of the general population, and we can afford to care
for them in the land of medical technology and still offer a world of
better food, which makes managing blood sugar easier and a world of
fewer pollutants that might result in lower levels of abnormal thyroid
function.

We are embedded in one system of health care and many of us
depend upon it, which makes it hard to shift our way of thinking to
one that places the technology in a secondary place. I've got it easy —
I'm healthy, my kids and husband are healthy. I don't have to navigate
the darker shoals of this so far. But I know that for more and more
of us, we can't access either health care that has its roots in ecological
health or one rooted in technology. We can't afford the technological
one and we have been systematically denied a clean world, healthy
food, enough time to rest, and peace and quiet by the very nature of
our society. We are, to put it bluntly, trapped.

This book isn't going to get us out of the mess, and indeed I fear I have more questions than answers. But despite my emphasis in the next chapter on storing the technological elements of modern medicine, any answer to the great problem of health care must begin by asking Berry's question. Can we begin again, with technology as a reasonable adjunct to a system that emphasizes a decent ecology, decent food and a decent way of life? That's why I think of this whole book as being in part about health care — because food, the way of life that accompanies it, the limits it imposes and the freedoms it offers are a tiny gesture, I hope, in that direction. It is nothing like all we need, but perhaps it is a start.

14

Medicines, Health Care and Special Diets

Special Diets

WHEN I TEACH FOOD STORAGE, there are a lot of questions about special needs, and particularly about the special needs of young children. Even if you personally are male or past childbearing, you may end up providing a place of respite for families with young kids or pregnant women in crisis, and it is important to think about them. I have encountered many people over the years who never expected to see their children suddenly arrive back home, or to end up raising their nephews or grandchildren, or to get pregnant (or pregnant again) and did. Do not think that this information could never be relevant to most of us. Remember, plans are good — but as Robert Burns didn't quite say, the best laid plans gang aft agley more or less whenever the opportunity arises.

The first and probably most essential component here is water. I know a lot of people respond to my discussions of storing water with, "OK, we've moved into total whack-job territory." And yet, I'm going to say that this is particularly important if your household includes or might include pregnant women, infants or very young children who are especially vulnerable to disease, parasites and chemical contaminations. They also all have very little tolerance for dehydration or water stress. So if you are/have/might have anyone who falls into the above categories, please take the time to read the section in Chapter 6 on water, and have a stored reserve of water.

So if you have or might have young children, pregnant women or infants, store water, and have a way of filtering your water in the long term. If you have a limited supply of filtered or known safe water, and are worried about contamination, the last people to touch potentially contaminated water should be children or pregnant women — lifelong consequences are possible.

One issue for pregnant women may be nausea. Pregnant women can be extremely picky, not out of any malice, but because they can't eat much without throwing up. To the extent you can, accommodate women in early pregnancy suffering from nausea in any way possible. The reality is that hunger makes the nausea worse and can result in a "death spiral" of being unable to eat or keep anything down long enough to deal with hunger-induced increases in nausea. This can cause dehydration, occasionally even death. So if you are relying on food storage and have a sick pregnant woman, do the best you can to find something she can eat. If you plan to be pregnant and have specific nausea triggers you might consider storing them. Also if you plan to be pregnant, sea bands or ginger might help (nothing worked for me).

Otherwise, pregnancy doesn't require special foods. But infants do. Infants under four months (six months is considered ideal) should be exclusively breast-fed whenever possible. Breastfeeding is essential. In a crisis, it can actually save lives. Formula often becomes unavailable in a crisis, and a nursing mother can not only keep her own infant hydrated (even if she is suffering from dehydration she will continue to make some milk) but potentially other infants as well who can drink expressed milk in a bottle or cup or, sometimes, be taught to nurse. While not every woman can nurse, far more can than do, and for longer than most American women do.

But what about women who can't nurse, or those who adopt? And, for that matter, I'm going to say something that most mothers don't like to hear. We aren't immortal or invulnerable. Trust me, I know how it feels to believe that you have to be OK, because your children depend so much on you. But things happen sometimes to mothers. And the survival of our babies and children shouldn't depend on the ability of any one adult to be present to feed them. So having some kind of backup makes sense.

That backup could be another lactating woman nearby, it could be a goat (not a cow — cow's milk can cause intestinal bleeding in infants), or it could be a store of infant formula. I know that we should, whenever possible, store what we use and vote with our dollars for the world we want. But every time I've had a baby, before I gave birth my husband and I bought a six-month supply of generic, cheap infant formula. Most formula has a two year expiration date, and if unopened it is safe to use for one to two more years, although it will experience some decline in nutritional value. That decline means that you'd be better off giving a child fresh formula or breast milk, so do this only if you really need it.

I am a passionate advocate of breastfeeding — but I care much more that babies live even if their Moms aren't around, or can't nurse them, and someone be able to take care of the babies around them. Only you know if your circumstance merits doing this, but it is something to think seriously about. I think of my decision to store formula during my children's infancy as a donation to charity — most food pantries desperately need formula. In addition, it provides a measure of security to our family that has had great value for me.

Once an infant is four months old (again, six is considered optimal, but by five months my kids were always grabbing food out of my mouth at the table, so I thought they were ready), you can gradually begin transitioning them to mashed-up solids. (Actually, when I was an infant, solids were begun as early as six weeks. This is not recommended now, but if formula or breast milk are in short supply, it can be considered. Again, do it only if you have to.) Waiting longer is considered better, particularly if you have a family history of food allergies.

Babies don't need "baby food" per se, although it is good to start them on mashed-up, very simple, low-allergen foods like rice, greens, potatoes or orange vegetables. But again, they should be getting their food primarily from mother's milk, goat's milk or formula until nearly a year. Babies need a high-fat, high-protein, high-quality diet. If you think infants may come into your orbit, store for them.

Young children, under two, need more fat than most people, so storing some extra high-fat food is a good idea. Fish oil is particularly useful if you can keep it cool, because it enhances brain development. Otherwise, young children simply need a balanced, healthy diet. But this can be tough, since toddlers often are extremely picky eaters. This means that storing familiar foods and getting kids familiar with whole foods used in storage is especially important.

Toddlers' pickiness has some evolutionary advantages—as they get more mobile, they get more choosy about what they eat, which is protective. It is helpful to recognize that this is a passing stage and just concentrate on finding foods they like. Remember that toddlers often have to encounter an unfamiliar food over and over again before they will try it. Keep trying. Generally speaking, if they aren't making a complete break from familiar foods—which they shouldn't be, since we're all trying to eat what we store—kids won't generally do themselves any harm.

From raising an autistic child, I know that there are some children who have issues over and above ordinary pickiness. These kids will not eat some foods, even if they are hungry, because of intense sensory issues, and can suffer health and nutritional consequences. A good friend of mine, whose daughter falls into precisely this category, alerted me to a storable product that might be helpful for children who will eat only a small range of foods because of disability. While not a perfect solution, this nutritional supplement can be mixed into any food, since it is effectively tasteless, and provides a good degree of vitamin supplementation. The product is NanoVM from Solace Nutrition, and has formulations for children 1–3 and 4–8, although the older version can be used by older children. It has no off tastes, as many supplements do. You can get it online here: solacenutrition.com/products/nanovm/ nanovm.html.

For healthy older children, I think a low-tolerance policy towards picky eating is important. And again, kids make it extra-urgent that you begin eating out of your food storage regularly. Believe it or not, my kids think stir-fried collard greens are a treat. I know that sounds unbelievable to many readers, but the thing is, children grow up in the food culture they actually live in. A food culture where the adults eat collard greens, praise collard greens, take the time to grow them and offer them regularly to children will (mostly) produce children who eat collard greens.

First Aid Kits and Medications

Accidents and illness happen to the best of us. It is wise to have some measure of preparation for both illness and injury at home. This is simple common sense. But the kind of first aid kit you can buy in a drugstore will not be adequate to your needs. The reason for this is pretty simple — those kits are meant to provide short term relief for minor emergencies. The assumption is that anything more serious will be passed on to the professionals.

My own assumptions are a little different. In a crisis, it is perfectly possible to imagine that emergency services may not be able to reach you quickly. For example, in December of 2008 many areas of Central Massachusetts were inaccessible for several days due to downed trees from a heavy ice storm. Those who sustained injuries were often simply on their own — and injuries from ice falls, chainsaws and the use of unfamiliar heating sources rose. After Hurricane Katrina, many of the hospitals in New Orleans were closed, and the ill and injured simply had no recourse.

The second reason is this — sometimes hospitals are not safe places to go. In the event of a flu pandemic, for example, the last place you might want to take someone with a physical injury or who is in labor, for example, would be a hospital full of infected patients. In areas where there aren't enough beds to serve a community, the expectation is that people will take care of most medical needs at home, even if they are of a sort that would normally require formal medical attention.

I'll talk more in the next section about caring for someone with a serious illness or injury at home. This is a lost skill, and one that scares the heck out of a lot of us. At the same time, it is quite possible that any of us may have to provide medical care for friends, neighbors or family members in a crisis. And that means we need to know how to respond appropriately.

At the same time, it is worth reminding everyone that the most important strategies you have for dealing with medical issues are *preventative*. That is, it is always easier to avoid trauma, injury or illness than it is to deal with it when it arrives. If you are in a situation where medical care might not be available, take extra care when doing risky things, keep a close eye on children to keep them safe, wash hands and avoid sick people. Get plenty of fresh air and exercise, keep wounds clean and practice basic hygiene and safety procedures.

But for now, here are medical supplies you might want to have. Any list of medications and supplies is necessarily imperfect, and ideally you'll personalize your lists as much as possible. Only you know what allergy medications work for you or that your wife's knee is prone to going out during heavy work periods. But it is possible to meet most needs with a good, solid, basic kit.

Not all of these things are needed in a first aid kit — that is, the problem with first aid kits is that you end up searching through them for what you really need. Some of these things should be in emergency kits, while other supplies ought to be kept in the home for ongoing medical problems. In fact, I suggest you have several first aid kits — one for minor emergencies like cuts, scrapes, sprained ankles and bee stings, a larger one for more serious situations and another kit to keep in your car or evacuation kit.

- Rubbing alcohol
- Triple antibiotic ointment
- Sterile bandages
- Tums or another antacid
- Eyewash kit
- Disposable gloves, masks
- Chemical heat and cold packs
- Hydrogen peroxide
- Gauze pads in multiple sizes
- Anti-diarrhea medicine
- Anti-nausea medicine
- Suture kit
- Magnifying glass
- Space blanket
- Butterfly bandage (the best are called "steri-strips")
- Burn bandage (comes impregnated with medicated cream, one brand is Burngel)

- Vet wrap or Ace bandages in various sizes (vet wrap is the animal equivalent and is cheaper and works on people just fine)
- Triangular bandages to cover large wounds, make slings or use as a tourniquet in an emergency (make sure you know when and how to use a tourniquet, or you can do more harm than good)
- Splint (SAM emergency splints can be adjusted to support just about any limb and are reusable — well worth the money)
- Provoiodine will sterilize anything and does not sting
- Anti-bacterial, no-water handwash (wash hands before touching wounds)
- Tea tree oil relieves itching, sunburn pain, fungal infections, ringworm, athlete's foot
- Tweezers — get serious medical grade tweezers if you can, since the blunt-tipped drugstore ones don't work that well.
- Sewing needle (for removing intractable splinters — sterilize in alcohol first)
- Superglue — you can actually use this to hold wounds together. There's a medical grade "dermabond" that is expensive but sterile and better, but plain old superglue was used during triage in the Vietnam war.
- Kids' band-aids (these are important because often a character or decorative band-aid will distract a child enough to get them functioning again)
- Lollipops (to distract kids in an emergency situation or for diabetics experiencing low blood sugar)
- Painkillers (Tylenol, ibuprofen, children or infant formulas as appropriate)
- Low dose Aspirin (administer if there are signs of heart attack or stroke)
- Antihistamines (Benadryl, prescription)
- Cough syrup (adult and child as appropriate)
- Powdered electrolyte replacement
- Tampons and sanitary napkins (these are sterile and can be used as bandages, one for any penetrative wound, the other as a pressure bandage)

- Bite and sting extractor kit for bee stings and snake or spider bites
- Blunt shears for cutting off clothing
- Flashlight (for nighttime emergencies) — get small but bright LED light
- Ziploc bags for safe disposal of medical waste, making ice packs, etc.
- Duct tape and bandage tape (the latter may actually work better)
- Homeopathic Arnica (for shock and trauma)

Now this assumes you actually know what to do with all this stuff. It would be easy to read this list, go out and buy the stuff, and put the pile on the shelf and leave it. In fact, you need to know how to respond to emergencies. I strongly recommend that everyone take at least the Red Cross First Aid and CPR classes, but also consider First Responder, CERT and EMS classes. If you can't take classes, read the books I've recommended below *before* you have to deal with a crisis. Get all the adults and teenagers in your family to read them, so that everyone has some knowledge of how to deal with an emergency.

You may have noticed that there are no antibiotics on this list. It is true that in the right hands an emergency supply of antibiotics can be extremely useful. But I'm reluctant to put antibiotics on the list because people have a tendency to jump immediately to "I'm sick, I'll take the antibiotics." Since antibiotic resistance is a huge problem in our society, with nearly 100,000 cases of antibiotic-resistant "super-staph" MRSA every year (20 percent of which are fatal), I'm much more concerned that antibiotics be in the hands of people who will only use them if they have a recognizably bacterial infection, that the variety of antibiotic is appropriate to the illness, that they are certain that they or the people they administer them to have no allergies and are getting an appropriate dose, and that they have researched the antibiotic and its safe shelf life.

What about purchasing a pre-made emergency kit? These can work as the base of a modified, personal kit, but generally speaking, they include a lot of things that aren't that useful and it might be wiser to start from scratch. You might also want to include emergency pet or live-stock supplies in your kit — remember, animals have emergencies too.

Medical Care when You Can't Call the Pros

If you find yourself in an emergency where you can't get to a hospital, hospitals are not open, or they are so overcrowded or potentially infectious that you are better off at home, you may have to deal with a range of illnesses, injuries or traumas on your own.

The best way to handle this situation is to be prepared — know what you are doing, and to be ready to deal with whatever situation you are face to face with. Because of this, it makes sense to have read books that teach you how, ahead of the crisis. Here are some recommended references.

- *The American Red Cross First Aid and Safety Handbook* by Kathleen Handal, Little, Brown and Co. 1992. A basic guide to first aid, this covers the absolute minimum everyone should know. Everyone in your house must read this book and understand it.
- *Book for Midwives: A Manual for Traditional Birth Attendants and Midwives* by Susan Klein, Hesperian Foundation. The best book of its kind — safe, low technology childbirth. Several people in your community should know how to deliver a baby in an emergency.
- *The Complete Book of Dental Remedies* by Flora Parsa Stay, DDS, Avery Publishing Group, 2004. This includes conventional, herbal and homeopathic dental remedies for common problems.
- *Ditch Medicine* by Richard L. Coffee, Paladin Press. An excellent guide for dealing with serious injuries and illnesses, it covers wound closure, infection control, chest injuries, burns, etc. Not a first-aid book, it assumes basic medical training beyond the first-aid level. This is probably not a book for everyone, but for someone with some basic training who can go a bit further, this is very helpful.
- *Special Forces Medical Handbook.* This is a reprint of a US Army training handbook, and covers emergency medicine in less than

optimal conditions including emergency deliveries, sterile procedure, dentistry, trauma, chemical exposure. This is probably further than most ordinary folks will want to go, but for those with
an interest in being a local medical resource, it is very valuable.

- *Where There is No Dentist* by Murray Dickson, Hesperian Foundation. Available for sale or free download online, this covers most
basic dental procedures. No one can concentrate when their teeth
hurt — a must for every home.
- *Where There is No Doctor* by David Werner, Hesperian Foundation. Also available online, this village health care handbook
assumes that no doctor is available, and conditions are similar to
those in most third world villages. Highly recommended — everyone should own this book.
- *Where Women Have No Doctor* by A. August Burns, Ronnie
Lovell and Jane Maxwell. Hesperian Foundation. An essential
supplement to the above, this deals with sexual issues, medical
conditions specific to women, pregnancy, nursing and childbirth.

At a minimum I'd recommend that all households have the Hesperian
Foundation books, all of which are available online at hesperian.org,
and the Red Cross First Aid Handbook. This shouldn't set you back
much and is invaluable if you ever need it. (The Hesperian Foundation also has a charitable giving program — if you are downloading one
of their books for free, and can afford it, you might send a set of the
books to a poor village in the third world.)

Prescription Medications and Supplies

Before we get into the question of how to store or obtain a supply of
prescription medications, the first question we should all ask ourselves
is how necessary our medications actually are. I know we all react with
an instinctive, "But of course my medications are necessary." And they
may well be. But it is a fact that people in the US and Canada take
nearly twice as many medications as many Western Europeans do, and
yet the Europeans have comparable or slightly longer lifespans. This
suggests that many of us probably take medications that we could do

without, perhaps with some lifestyle changes. It is something to consider.

But let us suppose that you really do need your medicine. To start with, everyone who depends on a medication should keep a two-week supply, plus duplicate copies of their prescriptions, according to FEMA and the American Red Cross. In a bad crisis you may be unable to get a refill for several weeks. In fact, it is possible to imagine longer disruptions than that, and a three- to six-month supply would be ideal.

But this presents several difficulties. First, there's the cost of the medications. Additional medicines may not be covered by insurance, and, of course, many of us have no insurance. Some doctors are sympathetic to the need to prepare for disruptions, but some are not, so it can be difficult to get additional prescriptions. For those who depend on controlled narcotics, the issue is more complex still. It is impossible to get additional supplies prescribed.

Given that FEMA and the American Red Cross, along with the American Medical Association (AMA) all express concerns about emergency preparedness, and given that so many people depend heavily on prescription medication, it would be useful for some kind of comprehensive program of physician education in preparedness to be instituted, and for the US government to encourage insurance companies to cover emergency prescriptions, since the barriers to achieving basic preparations are so high here. Unfortunately no such program exists that I'm aware of.

Given the imperfect situation we have now, the first step in getting a supply of prescribed medications is simply to ask your doctor. Explain the situation, note that it is fairly common for disruptions to occur, and ask if she will support your effort to acquire an additional supply of medications. This is most likely to be successful if you have a relationship with your doctor, and if you clearly and honestly explain your concerns.

Once you have a prescription, pay close attention to rotation. Because the medicine can expire, you want to be sure you are using the oldest packages first so that your supply is always as fresh as possible. Most medications may lose potency, but are safe and reasonably useful even after many years. The federal government has sponsored a program for years known as SLEP — Shelf Life Extension Program for medications. They have found that more than 90 percent of all medications are still potent with no harmful effects 15 years after expiration. Expiration dates are more about making sure that we keep buying medications than about drug potency. There are some major exceptions to this — insulin, nitroglycerin and some antibiotics, for example. A few medications can become toxic after their expiration, while others will show low-level declines in potency.

If you don't know what the storage life and issues are with your medication, you should call the drug company that makes it and find out, but take their statements about expiration dates with a grain of salt unless they can point to a real decline in quality or increase in toxicity. Ask them how they figure out storage lives and what the potential consequences of taking out-of-date drugs are. Write the information down for all prescriptions you depend on. And if you do take a short lifespan drug, you'll need to be super-careful about using up the oldest first and keeping your supply updated.

It may sometimes be possible to shift from a short-lifespan drug to a longer lifespan one, if necessary. Only you and your doctor can calculate the advantages and disadvantages of doing so.

Most over-the-counter medications can be safely used past their expiration date, but again, this is something you'll want to research. There are simply too many such drugs, and their compositions vary from brand to brand and country to country for me to provide reliable storage lives for over-the-counter and herbal preparations. Generally speaking, dried herbal preparations lose potency quite quickly after a year, but alcohol-based tinctures last nearly forever. If you are making your own herbal medicines, basing them on high-proof vodka might be the wisest strategy for long-term security.

You should also keep up-to-date copies of your prescriptions (including, if you use them, your eyeglasses prescription) and your medical records somewhere easily accessible along with important papers so you can grab them if you are forced to evacuate. It can be very difficult to find someone to write you a prescription in a crisis, and you don't want to be without a copy of yours. The medical records are absolutely imperative if any of the medications you depend on are controlled narcotics (which odds are you won't be able to get an extra prescription for) because convincing a strange doctor in a strange place to give you a controlled substance is likely to be difficult.

Most medications are best stored in a cool, dark, dry place. You might want to double Ziploc them or otherwise store them in as airtight a way as possible to slow degradation if you are holding them for a longer period. It should go without saying that all medications must be stored away from where children can get them, in childproof containers.

What about drugs that require refrigeration? What do you do if the power goes out? In most northerly parts of the country, water comes up from the ground at fairly cool temperatures, and storing drugs in buckets of water, or in a hole you have dug in the ground will keep them cool enough for a short time. If you have a creek or other water source that is cool, you often can seal the drugs in a container and submerge the container (don't let it get washed away, obviously) in the creek. If there is no way to keep needed medications cool, having someone go for help is probably the best strategy.

In trying to build up a longer term reserve, whether to mitigate a job loss or for a protracted disaster, my own feeling is that you should take a "belt and braces" approach. The more ways you have to hold up your pants or ensure your supply of medication, the fewer chances you'll end up with your pants down. After all, your life is worth it. So make use of several of these strategies.

The first solution would be to store a larger supply. If you are taking a narcotic, or using a short-lived drug this is particularly difficult, but a friend of mine says that sometimes she is able to skip a dose, and when she does, she puts it aside. By refilling immediately and occasionally enduring quite a bit of pain, she has managed to put a small reserve aside. Only you know if that is possible for you, but it might be worth trying.

If your current drugs are short-lived, it might be worth researching whether there are alternatives you could shift over to. In fact, this

is probably worth looking into for everyone — that is, if your drug is
available in multiple forms, know what they are. One may be in short
supply when another is available. There are risks, of course, in any such
substitutions, but being able to get a functional substitute is probably
less risky than going entirely without. Make an appointment with your
doctor to discuss your options.

What happens if there is a long-term crisis and no way of getting
your drugs at all? Well, there are a couple of options.

1. First, are there alternatives? In many cases, there will not be, but
   sometimes there are. For example, those on heavy pain medication
   may be able to rely on alcohol to dull their pain somewhat (yes, this
   is risky, undesirable and yet it may be necessary). I cannot suggest
   that people engage in illegal actions, but on the Internet there's an
   essay by Michael Pollan describing the possibilities of producing
   homegrown opiate painkillers using garden poppies, and others
   have said that marijuana is an effective pain reliever.

   Some prescription medications can be substituted for with
   herbal preparations — some quite successfully, some not very. But
   it is worth noting that many drugs *are* herbs, or were originally. It
   is not worth dismissing herbal medication out of hand. Talk in advance to a naturopath or other practitioner and to your doctor. In
   some cases, such as the substitution of anti-depressants with the
   herb St. John's Wort, the two should not be taken together.

   Sometimes you can reduce your need for a medication partly or
   entirely by lifestyle changes. Many of those with high blood pressure, for example, could manage it with diet and exercise alone if
   they really had to. Giving up a Western diet, eating very low on the
   food chain and exercising a *lot* will not be pleasant if you are already
   unhealthy, but it might be better than the alternative. A friend of
   mine with type 1 diabetes tells me he can cut his insulin requirements in half by careful dietary control and extensive exercise.

2. Have a plan for ensuring supplies in your community. If you can
   imagine a crisis in which drugs continue to be manufactured in
   some places, but just aren't getting to you (what most crises have
   looked like in most of the world recently), it might be worth get-

ting a group of concerned citizens together and contacting pharmaceutical companies about ensuring supplies during periods of disruption.

That is, while one person is not a very powerful entity with a company, a city or state or regional group made up of people with medical dependencies might be able to work out supply delivery plans and direct purchasing for an extended emergency. They might not — I have not tried this. But advocacy groups are powerful.

My own suggestion would be to start at the municipal or county level and consider organizing from there, perhaps linking community groups together to contact major pharmaceutical companies directly. You might also consider starting a citizen action group that lobbied the Federal Government and the AMA directly to pass legislature that makes it easier for patients to prepare — that is, that educates doctors on the need for a reserve supply of medication, that requires insurers to pay for some non-narcotic drugs for emergency supplies and that offers incentives to communities to stockpile basic drug supplies.

3. Go Local. This is not going to be possible for a majority of drugs, but some very simple chemical combinations can be made in a college (or even a good high school) chemistry lab. I am not a chemist and I am not an expert here, but several chemistry professors and high school chemistry teachers have told me that they could manufacture a number of drugs that had comparatively simple formulae. Antibiotics, thyroid medications and heart medications were among those mentioned as particularly possible, if they had the relevant materials.

Some of those chemicals are cheap and fairly shelf stable. It is not impossible that some drugs could be synthesized locally — and make a rather good business for a chemist. My own recommendation would be to do some research into your drug. Generally, it will be possible to find the formula if it is no longer proprietary information of a single company, so if you have a choice of medications, in many cases you want the oldest form. Talk to graduate students or professors at your local university or even a high school chemistry teacher about your fears about the future and your desire to find a local solution. It will not be possible in every case, maybe even most cases, but trying is better than accepting the loss of needed medications.

4. Make sure that others know about your situation. For example, all utilities maintain lists of customers with medical issues so that power is restored to them first. Make sure your local emergency services know that you have an acute medical condition that may require them to help you evacuate.

This is not an easy issue once you get outside the short term. But it is worth thinking about, and thinking hard.

Recipes

Garlicky Oatmeal Soup

This is adapted from Sarah Leah Chase's *The Cold Weather Cookbook*. In her family it is a classic pre-Thanksgiving menu, but with a few modifications it would be ideal food for a sick person. It is quite delicious, and you don't have to be ill to enjoy it — it is the definition of comfort food that heals the sick and nourishes the well. Serves 4.

- 4 cups rolled oats
- 4 large onions, diced
- 1 tsp nutmeg
- 8 cups broth, chicken is traditional, but vegetable is good
- 12 cloves garlic, diced
- 1 bottle good dark beer
- 1 tsp cayenne

Toast oats in a hot oven for 10 minutes until light brown. Remove and set aside. Heat the oil and sauté the garlic and onions. Add remaining ingredients, stirring regularly to prevent soup from sticking. When it comes to a boil, remove from heat, cool to room temperature and then refrigerate or put in a cold place. Reheat the next day, thinning if necessary with more broth or beer to taste. Serve hot, with a little cream or goat cheese stirred in if you like.

Baked Apples with Dried Cranberries

Another recipe that even the frail or those on special diets can enjoy. This can be made entirely without sweetener, using just apple cider or butter, and for those who can't chew hard foods, the melted apples can be mashed and are delicious. Serves 6.

- ⅓ cup dried cranberries (raisins will do, or can be omitted if there are texture issues)
- ⅓ cup brown sugar (can omit if there are blood sugar issues)
- 1 tsp lemon peel or 2 tsp vanilla   • 6 whole apples
- 1 cup apple cider

Core apples, but otherwise, leave whole and place in baking dish. If cored, fill holes with lemon peel or vanilla, cranberries and brown sugar. Otherwise, pour cider over and bake for 1 hour at 400°, or until apples are very soft, but still held together by skin. Can be served with whipped cream or ice cream.

stuff

I have a very ambivalent relationship to the question of stuff. On the one hand, I'm not a big fan of consumption as our consumption of goods and resources is one of the root causes of resource depletion and climate change. I buy most of my possessions used, and as a consumer I guess I'm one of those people dragging the economy down.

On the other hand, for someone who is hostile to consumption, I have a lot of stuff. I live in a big old farmhouse full of stuff. I'm not really sure how to resolve this contradiction, or how I feel about it.

Part of the issue is that I live in two worlds. I am living now in a high-energy society, that makes use of a lot of high-energy tools that cost a lot of money. While I minimize my use of some of these, there are some I depend on — for example, my computer. In order for me to do my job, I need a computer, a phone line and the money to keep up an Internet connection.

Beyond that minimum, there are things I use because I do this other work — for example, I could hand wash all my laundry, but then I probably would have less time to write. There may come a time when I think that trade-off is reasonable, but for now, the washing machine is a necessity. .

Then there are parts of high-energy culture that I really value. I have many thousands of books, and I read and re-read them, refer to them in my writings and enjoy having them. I realize that the 14th century author Chaucer died with fewer than 50 books (a mammoth library by the standards of the day), but I'm simply not prepared to do with that few, at least as long as I live fairly far from a good library. I don't find cheap printing or the ability to get to hear long-ago recordings of classical music alongside present day hip hop to be at all bad uses of our energy abundance, and even if I should, I don't feel terribly inclined to go down to a handful of CDs or books.

At the same time, I also live a low-energy lifestyle, and am anticipating a much lower energy one, because I believe living sustainably is essential to preserving our ecology. This also requires equipment and the space to store it. For example, I grind my own grain, which means finding space on the counter for a grain grinder. I have more than 700 canning jars, which I fill with things, but which then gradually empty out and must be stored. Besides our CD player and CDs, we have a piano, a banjo, six recorders, a dulcimer, an autoharp and more, since my husband makes acoustic music. We have two wood stoves, which necessitate a large supply of wood and tools for the stove, wood chopping and managing wood.

Now sometimes I can manage the balance between these two lives by choosing to prioritize one. For example, I can decide that I'm going to get rid of the food processor to make space for the grain grinder, or to replace one of our vehicles with a bike and trailer. The clothesline has replaced the dryer, the freezer and natural cooling our fridge, solar-charged batteries our old disposable ones.

But often I'm struggling to balance the requirements of both lives. For example, several times a year we visit family in Boston or New York City. When we do this, it is awfully convenient to have a furnace to be kept at a very low temperature to keep the pipes from freezing. If we don't do this, we have to drain the pipes and shut off the water, which means that whoever cares for our animals has to haul water from the pump outside. So for now, we have both a furnace and wood stoves. We have bikes and a car. We have a manual water pump for the inevitable power outages and an electric water pump for the rest of the time. We're trying, as best we can, to balance and compromise.

I try very hard to make sure that when I acquire a lower-energy tool, I do make use of it and that it doesn't just sit around for an emergency that may or may not come. Thus, we do cook quite a lot in our solar oven, but I can't say that it has totally replaced my electric stove, even in summer.

And it all adds up to a lot of stuff. Then add in the other stuff. The kid's toys. The clothes. The tools. The books. The music. The pots and pans and furniture and things get, well…chaotic.

So my goal is to try to bring order to the chaos. But that means figuring out not just what I really need now, but what I'm likely to need in a future when going out and buying things isn't as easy, or when I no longer have the money for either luxuries or necessities. I'm attracted, at times, to the light life, where all your possessions could fit in the back of a car or even a backpack. I dream sometimes of the one-room cabin (although somehow my dreams rarely have children in them in that particular scenario). I admire people like Peace Pilgrim and Buddhist monks who had with them only what they could carry. But of course, when Peace Pilgrim rested, she rested in the homes of people who had pots and pans and blankets. The Buddhist monks rely on charity from those who have more. The minimalist aesthetic works for some, but depends on there being community and public resources, and those who have something to give.

I think perhaps that the solution lies in a balance — a balance of people who live minimally with those who have enough to share, and also an internal balance. I cannot say that there is no wasted space, no unneeded expenditures, no stuff that serves no purpose in my life. I probably will never be able to say that, but sorting and clarifying, thinking through what I need and what I do not — and remembering that the latter is as essential as the former — can get me to an imperfect balance of sorts.

15

Now What?—Making Space and Managing Food Storage

To know and not to do is not to know.

— Wang Yang Ming —

KATHY HARRISON, whose wonderful book *Just in Case: How to Be Self-Sufficient When the Unexpected Happens* goes into a great deal of detail about how to respond to a range of crises, entitles the first chapter of her book "Organize." That is, she suggests that the very first step that you take in shifting away from the just-in-time mentality should be to start thinking about your relationship with your possessions.

I think she's absolutely on-target. A lot of us look at the idea that we now have to find room for a pantry's worth of stored foods as a new strain on our capacities — and it will be, unless we are prepared to prioritize and shift our thinking. If we just try to cram the beans and rice in around everything else, we're in trouble. If we start out by sorting and making new space, we can make this work.

So taking a page from Kathy's book, I'm going to recommend that all of us start sorting and organizing as one of our primary projects. Most of us suffer from some degree of clutter in our lives, but often the connection between the clutter and our future well-being is somewhat tenuous. Sure, it would be better if we didn't have so much stuff, but it doesn't really impact our survival.

But the reality is that if we don't have a store of food, and if we don't have the skills to support and build upon local food systems, we could go hungry, we could watch our children or our nieces and nephews go hungry. Which, at least for me, is a pretty good reason to start sorting out the crap.

Making space for food storage and for home-preserved food starts by making space, period. Now someone who lives in a tiny 180-square-foot studio won't have a lot of room to store food. But the average American has 850 square feet per person. It seems safe to say that an awful lot of us could clean out a closet or two. And even if we don't have any space of our own, maybe we could find some in the home of a nearby friend or family member.

Where do you look? Well, how about under the bed? In Amy Da-cyzyn's book *The Complete Tightwad Gazette* a reader tells the story of how she reassures her children that there are no ghosts under the bed: she points out that there's too much toilet paper there for any ghost to fit.

Putting up shelving makes a huge difference. We had a fairly use-less space around a pair of glass doors that lead out onto the porch in our kitchen. We added some beautiful dark wooden shelving, and now our beans, grains, herbs and other stored foods not only have a place, but everyone who comes into the house exclaims at how beautiful they make the room look.

What about a closet? My "pantry" is actually a walk-in closet, with shop shelving along the walls. How about your basement? Remember, it needs to be reasonably dry, but a cool basement area is a terrific place to store food. Some houses have accessible crawl spaces.

Can you make use of underused areas? In houses with high ceilings, for example, there might be room for shelving above eye level. Only you know where space might be found in your house.

Sometimes we can find space simply by looking at things in a new way. I have a set of glass mixing bowls that I like very much. The bowls range from large to tiny, and they nest together. But because I'm lazy, I often put them back together out of order, and found that then I couldn't fit them all together, so the bowls were taking up a lot of a shelf. It suddenly occurred to me that the only reason I was keeping all of these bowls together was that they were a set. I really only used the two largest and one medium-sized one. What if I kept those on a shelf, and then moved the others into a less accessible place. Suddenly, I had half a shelf again.

The rule of 20 percent is pretty consistent. Experts tell us that we usually wear 20 percent of our clothes 90 percent of the time. We use the same 20 tools for 80 percent of our jobs. We use the same dozen or so bowls and pans 90 percent of the time. Now in some cases, we simply don't need the other 80 percent, or some portion of it. We could get rid of some of our clothing, maybe use the money from selling it to get something we care about more. But even if we do need the other 80 percent of the tools, maybe they don't all have to be right there in the tool box. Perhaps it would be OK to move those out to the garage, to free up some space, while we keep the most essential tools in the house where we can get at them easily.

The Chatelaine

Once upon a time, a chatelaine was a belt, on which the mistress or master of the house kept the keys to the pantry and valuable stores. Later on, it came to mean the "keeper of the keys" — that is, the person whose job it was to make sure that the store of food, herbs and spices and basic goods were organized and taken care of.

I use the word here because I think it is time to revive the tradition of the chatelaine (which is often used to mean a woman, but guys can and should do this too!). When we were stopping by the grocery store twice a week to pick up ingredients (or worse, stopping by Burger King to pick up fast food) there wasn't a lot of household management to do. When we have to prepare to live with less energy, and when there are stores to manage and seasonal preserving to do, being chatelaine is a deeply urgent job. It deserves a title, ideally the sort that makes people impressed when they hear it.

Now I hope it is clear that you don't have to be a perfect house-keeper, or a perfect person, to do this work. There are going to be some mistakes in the process. The point is that we all go into this realizing that what we're doing isn't just storing a few grains and carrots, but developing a new relationship with our food. If your experience of food management is like what mine was back before I started doing all this — buying food, stuffing it in the fridge, eating some of it and throwing the rest on the compost pile, the sheer depth to which you get involved with your food will probably surprise you.

To give you a sense of how that looks in my house, let's start with the apples. Eli is apple obsessed, and as obsessions go, it is an easy one to be supportive of. So every fall, we buy 10–12 bushels of apples (this is far more than any rational family with fewer apple-obsessed kids would need) and keep them in bins on my front porch. But, you know that saying about how one rotten apple will spoil the whole barrel — ask me how I know that it's true. As we get later into the season, one regular job involves sorting out the apples, taking out those that are getting wrinkled or showing brown spots and making them into applesauce or pie.

It isn't just the apples, though. As the winter season winds down, I'm doing this kind of work more often with the fresh foods we root cellar — roasting a squash with a soft spot and freezing the contents, cutting bits off a potato. Mercifully, the onions don't need my attention much, although a few begin to sprout. But we have to keep the potatoes in the dark so they don't turn green. The carrots are now mostly softening up, but that's OK — soup time. The sweet potatoes thankfully remain resolutely firm. I always forget a few until it is time to clean out the storage in July for replacement, and they are usually still good.

Food storage management is a cyclical process. Even bulk purchases at a supermarket, for example, have to be dealt with four times, at least. The first is when you buy the stuff, and haul it home. The second is when you repackage it for storage (you can order grains and beans packed for storage, but they will be appropriately more expensive). When you transfer things to their buckets or jars, get rid of as much oxygen as you can and *write the date on the jar, bucket or container of food before you put it away.* I can't tell you how many times I've ignored this advice, always to my regret. If you keep a marker by where you keep the food, it takes .02 seconds and you will be very glad you did it.

The third time you visit the food is when you take it out and use it. The fourth is when you reorder or buy more. The big key, I find, with knowing when you need more of things is embedding some signal in the storage process that says "time to get more" before you actually run out. That could be a rule that you put it on the grocery list when you take the next-to-last one out, or that you do a weekly survey of what you have. For larger quantities, mark a line halfway down on the bucket—when you can see the line, it is time to put lentils on the order list. Keeping a pad and pen around so that you can write these reminders down when you are thinking about them helps with the "out of sight, out of mind" problem I have.

Gardens only flourish when the "gardener's shadow" is there to make them flourish—and most food is like that even after it leaves the garden. Some foods will happily and quietly sit on the shelf for long periods without your attention, but even they deserve and need a quick scan now and then.

I try to do this while getting ready for Passover each year, since I'm cleaning anyway. I try to look at, touch and examine every jar, can and bucket. It is a good time to make large donations to the food pantry, and a good time to sort out what isn't good, or what really should be used sooner, rather than later. It would be smarter to inventory more often, but I'm not perfect.

This is also when I begin my estimates of what I'll need for the next year. I track when we run out of home-produced things. For example, we ran out of strawberry jam in January this year, and peach, blueberry and raspberry by the end of February (the fact that my kids get bigger each year somehow escapes me in my planning most of the time). We still have cranberry and black currant, but those aren't our preferred choices. OK, that means I need to put up ten more jars of each of our favorite flavors to see us through to strawberry season.

I estimate how much rice we went through last year. If I know this, I can make two or three bulk orders over the course of the year, spacing them out. I know we go through about 200 pounds of rolled oats a year, so picking up a 50-pound bag every few months will keep my stores about even. If I want to increase my stores, I might want two bags.

As I go through, I sniff the jars of herbs, to see if I need more. Every year, I grow more varieties of medicinal and culinary herbs — do I need to plant more sage or pennyroyal this year? Or just harvest more regularly? As I'm placing seed and plant orders, I think ahead to what we might need if current patterns go forward. There are plenty of things I don't grow, so those go on the list for the next time we go to the bulk herb store.

Where do we want to replace store bought with homegrown? What do we wish we'd had more of, and what could we have made do with less of? The garden and food storage are more closely tied than you'd think. For example, my root cellaring is much more effective if I grow varieties designed to store long times. So my seed choices begin with preservation in mind (see the root cellaring chapter for more details).

I check the top of the jars of home-canned food by pressing them gently. If one of them pops up, the seal has broken and the jar is no good. It doesn't happen often, but every once in a great while, it does.

The freezer too needs some checking. I don't want to find unidentifiable freezer-burned things in the bottom this year. Are we out of home-frozen broccoli? Here is where a list, made in the fall, is a huge help. We use boxes and bins in our freezer, and write down what's in them, and also the absolute number of things. If I know I have only five containers of frozen corn, it makes it easier to space them out. I make marks for them and strike each one off as we use it.

Some things shift location. For example, I buy bulk, fair-traded chocolate chips. Through the fall and winter they sit in the cool pantry. In the spring, they move (except for a few in a jar on a shelf) into the freezer. This serves multiple purposes. In the fall, the freezer is far too full to accommodate chocolate chips and it is plenty cool in the pantry closet. In warmer weather, the chocolate chips stay fresh better in the freezer, and the freezer runs more efficiently when it is full.

Dry and dehydrated foods need the least attention, but not none. Check for bugs, make sure seals are tight, and then check once a year at least.

Canned foods should be checked several times a year, to make sure that no hard bumps have broken a seal, and that they are being used regularly. They will last some years, of course, but the nutritional content is higher early on.

Root-cellared foods should be visited regularly — every few weeks in the fall, more often as the winter progresses.

Frozen foods should be checked on every few months.

I use one notebook (you could computerize it, but I'm not a spreadsheet kind of girl), to manage all my stores. I know how many buckets of rice and jars of corn relish I've got, and when I bought them. I keep running lists of things to order more of, and notes on what to do better next year. I always forget to write some things down. I always screw up and let something rot that shouldn't. I always make mistakes with food storage, and so, most likely, will you. Sometimes they are big mistakes, but as I get better, they get smaller — mostly.

You shouldn't expect to do this perfectly. Yes, it is important not to waste food. But the truth is that the best way to learn to manage stored food, to become comfortable as Chatelaine of your household, is simply to do it, and that means making mistakes. But make them now, while they are easily reparable.

Wait, Aren't I Done Yet? — Allocating Resources

OK, you've canned your heart out. You've dried everything that can be dried. You got the oatmeal, the spelt, the anasazi beans, the nutritional yeast, and put it in buckets. You vacuum packed. You built shelves. You made sauerkraut, kimchi, chutney, you name it. You built a root cellar. You did it all. Now you are all done, right? Nothing left to do but sit around and wait for dinner to get made (assuming, of course, that magic fairies, a housemate or loving partner will take care of this, since you've been working so hard.)

Sorry, but there's one more thing. You need a system to allocate everything. Think about it. If you eat strawberry jam every day (my kids' preference) for six months, you will have six months with no strawberry jam. If you froze 16 servings of broccoli, you don't want them gone by October.

And for the things you don't make yourself, well, there's shopping to do. If you want to keep a six-month supply of Earl Grey tea around, you have to go shopping when your stash drops down. How do you know what you need, when? Or how often you actually have to go into the pantry and count the boxes of pasta?

Now there are probably readers out there who have nifty spread-sheets and designed programs. I am not one of them. Me, I've got my notebook.

In my notebook, I have my actual reserves — jars of canned vege-tables, jars of dehydrated vegetables, pounds of whole wheat, etc., and my desired reserves — "desired" is what I'm shooting for. I keep a list there of "things to add next," although this is flexible. If Agway is hav-ing a sale on our brand of dog food, I might buy a couple of extra bags if I happen to be there, even if it isn't on the list yet.

Every fall, I go through and count everything, which is a pain, and I hate it, but it is useful. I make a little list to hang up in the storage closet of how many of each item (pickled beets, dried apples, etc.) I have by the jar, the bucket, etc. and I try really hard (and fail miserably every once in a while) to take .02 seconds and put a check mark next to each item. Then, once in a while, I count the checks. OK, we've used 4 jars of dried greens and have 13 left. Got it.

For stuff we have a limited amount of, I make a chart listing the months across the top divided by the number of items I have. So if I have 20 quarts of honey-lemon carrots, and I want to eat them from December to June, that means 3 quarts each month, plus a couple months with 4. When the carrots are done for the month, we don't have them again until next month.

There are a few items that are a bit hard to allocate wisely — things, for example, we all like a little too much. These I sometimes hide. It is such a treat to pull out one last jar of blueberry pancake sauce or salsa after everyone thought it was gone for good. (Of course, this only works if the Chatelaine can be trusted — in my house that's by no means a certainty). But, of course, being Chatelaine means that if something disappears it can be attributed to "spoilage."

I do inventory in the spring again. I see what we ate, what we used, what we wish we'd had more of and when we ran out. OK…double the apricot sauce, but we had more green beans than we needed and we need ten more quarts of pickles. I've also learned to add five to ten percent for the growth of four boys. They are going to eat more every year, so why not plan for it? This also gives me something important — a real sense of what a winter's worth of food looks like for us. I try to keep track of what we buy that doesn't count as storage as well, because it gives me a sense of what our totals are.

Does this sound too overwhelming? Well, when you are first starting food storage, it is easier to simply focus on a few foods, the dozen or so things that provide the basis for a monotonous but tolerable diet — beans, rice, vitamins, dried greens, canned pumpkin, rose hip tea, rolled oats, salt, spices, honey and tuna, for example, would cover most of the bases. So you can concentrate on those, if you like.

I know, I know, you thought you were done, and here I've got another project. But once you've done this, you really do get to take a nap, put your feet up and wait for the fairies to make dinner.

Minimizing Waste

In the US, we waste at least one quarter of all our food. That number should shock and horrify you. We live in a world where people are genuinely starving, and almost a quarter of our food is thrown away, of no benefit to anyone. Besides the cost to the rest of the world, this costs us a lot of money that we can't afford. We need to give our attention to minimizing wasted food. It may not be sexy, but it makes a huge difference.

If you have animals, a worm bin or a compost pile, you can at least ensure that your food waste has an upside. And you should, if at all possible, have one of these. Food waste that is thrown into landfills produces methane, contributing to global warming. But even if you do have animals or a compost pile, it is still cheaper to feed your worms on banana peels than on chocolate layer cake you let go bad, and it is better for everyone if people food gets used as people food.

So how do you handle and manage your stored and preserved food to minimize waste?

1. To the extent you can, try to minimize gaps between harvest time and preservation. The longer you wait, the lower the quality of the food, with fewer nutrients and more spoilage. The more you risk, as well, one rotten berry giving an off taste to the whole batch, not to

mention the swarms of fruit flies. If you can preserve on the same day you harvest or purchase your produce, that's ideal. The reality is that sometimes it doesn't work that way, but the shorter the time between harvest and preservation or storage in appropriate conditions, the less waste.

2. Have a back-up plan for edible parts of the food you don't want to preserve. Those lemon peels can be dried to make lemon zest, or used to flavor lemon vinegar. The apple peels can be used to make apple vinegar. Watermelon rind pickles, corncob jelly, soup stock made from peelings — these things make use of otherwise wasted food parts.

3. When you are freezing or canning, pack the food in quantities that you can eat quickly. Yes, I know it is faster to can all that blackberry jam in quart jars, not half-pints, but if there are only two of you, your jam may go moldy before you can use it up. It's the same with freezing — if you freeze all the chicken stock in one container, you then have to use it all at once.

4. Expect to have to use some things up quickly — that jar of jam that didn't seal, or the pressure canned soup that you think ought to be eaten quickly. The bits of meat that didn't fit in that last jar can make chicken salad or go into a stir fry. The soup can be dinner tonight, the extra jam can be filling for a batch of muffins.

5. Don't buy more than you can store. It would be a mistake to buy more food than you can store correctly. Don't a bushel of oatmeal until you have jars or buckets.

6. Less air and cooler temperatures are almost always better for stored things. Life isn't perfect, but it is worth making some effort on these fronts if you can.

7. Check everything regularly. Open lids, examine sealed jars, take a sniff of the sauerkraut. Remember, the Chatelaine work is part of the job.

8. In an emergency, get out the canner and dehydrator, and get to work. Sudden early frost meant you had to pull in all the berries? Power was out three days and now you have half a cow partially defrosted? Bad storm took down the cherry tree, and the cherries with it? Cold snap came too early to ripen the tomatoes? Well, it

is time to get out there with alternate methods. Throw the frozen corn in the dehydrator, get the pressure canner running and can that beef as stew, make green tomato pickles. Food preservation techniques can save you from food losses you can't afford.

9. Even in a non-emergency, food preservation should be used to extend the life of food that can't be saved any other way. We can the slightly wrinkled apples in the root cellar as applesauce, we make sauerkraut and kimchi when the cabbage is fading, dehydrate the onions and garlic if they show signs of trouble. A combination of strategies can work better than any single one.

10. Once you've preserved something, don't forget to eat it. This sounds obvious, but it isn't to a lot of people. You worked hard to preserve this food, so use it up, plan your menus around the leftovers, make sure you scrape out the jam jar (if you add a little water to a jar of jam and shake it up, you can make a popsicle out of it), and use that pickle brine to flavor your tuna sandwich or as part of salad dressing.

Recipes

Perfect White Bean and Whatever Soup

Mark Bittman is perhaps my favorite living cookbook author since the amazing Edna Lewis died, with a gift for making his recipes just perfect. Despite its perfection, I did take the liberty of amending his white bean and escarole soup to allow for a wider range of ingredients. Serves 4.

- 1 lb escarole, dandelion greens, mustard greens, or just about any other greens—you can also used dried greens, but it won't be as tasty
- 1 cup olive oil
- 1 cup any kind of dried beans, cooked until just tender
- 5 cups chicken stock, vegetable broth or water
- 1 tbsp sliced garlic
- A handful of pasta, rice or wild rice
- 2 small or 10 oz canned diced tomatoes, drained, or 6 dried tomatoes

• dried or fresh rosemary and thyme • 1 tsp chili flakes (to taste)
• salt and pepper

Put half the oil in a skillet and sauté the garlic and chilies. Stir occasionally until garlic begins to color. Add greens and tomatoes and stir; add beans and stock or water and herbs and adjust heat so mixture simmers steadily. Cover.

Cook about 15 minutes, or until greens are tender. Drizzle with reserved olive oil and extra rosemary and serve.

A Northerner's Attempt at Hoppin' John

Eating round peas and beans on New Year's is a tradition in the American south, and also among Jewish communities. I, of course, had to try and mix the two a bit, and make a Northern, Jewish Hoppin' John. Tasty, though — whether on New Year's, before you clean out your pantry as part of your new resolve, or any time. Serves 4.

• 1 lb dried black eyed peas	• 8 cups water
• 1 onion, stuck with cloves	• 5 garlic cloves, peeled
• 2 bay leaves	• chopped red onion or scallions
• 1 cup fresh parsley or other greens or sprouts	• 6 tbsp red wine vinegar (good cider is OK too, as is lemon or sumac juice)
• 1 tsp minced garlic	• 2 tbsp Dijon mustard
• 1 tbsp tahini	• ½ cup olive oil
• salt and pepper to taste	

Put the peas in a pot with water, the onion with cloves in it, 5 whole cloves of garlic and bay leaves. Bring to a boil, reduce heat and simmer 45 minutes or until just tender. Don't overcook. Drain and remove onion and bay leaves. Mash boiled garlic and reserve.

Add peas to a large bowl, mix in chopped onion and greens or sprouts. Toss. In a separate bowl combine remaining ingredients and mashed garlic cloves. Whisk together and toss over peas. Serve warm.

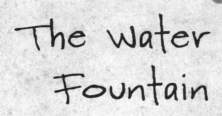

The Water Fountain

Like everyone in the rich world, I carry a bottle of water (filled from my tap, not purchased, of course) with me everywhere I go. Were someone from the past to spot us, they'd be stunned by the sight of all the people, clearly headed on long treks into the uninhabited jungle, carrying water lest they die of dehydration. Because, after all, in historical terms, at least in the US, one carries a canteen or other source of water while camping or otherwise engaged in a trek to uncertain, undeveloped lands. In populated areas, folks 30 or 40 years ago would have told a thirsty person, "Wait until we get to the water fountain."

You remember those water fountains, right? The things that meant you didn't have to buy soda or haul a bottle around, you just waited until you passed the next one, and drank your fill. You remember playing the game of squirting your sister in the nose? I do. Water fountains were in public parks and by public restrooms, in town centers and everywhere you went. They obviated the need to purchase anything when you had such a simple, basic human concern as thirst. You could trust them to be there. If you whined, "Daddy, I'm thirsty," waiting for the next water fountain was reasonable, achievable, because they were always there.

And, of course, it was this very publicness that was dangerous. Dangerous a couple of generations ago because one's lips might touch metal that had touched the lips of a person of another skin color. Then dangerous because one might get germs from them (never mind that most plastic water bottles involve drinking a big old slug of dioxin and bisphenol-a, which isn't exactly good for you). After all, they are *public,* and public is scary, because anyone can

use it. Even poor people. Even icky people. Even people we would
normally never share anything with. Thus, we magnify our fears of
other people to avoid having to find public solutions. Or we simply
get in the habit of privatizing everything, leaving the public sphere
to those who can't afford to leave it. We then call this "the tragedy of
the commons," but in fact it is the tragedy of privatization and wealth
and our rejection of both commons and common ground with other
people.

My youngest son, Asher, is in the full throes of toddlerhood right
now, and when exhorted to accommodate his brothers in some way,
he tends to shout, "I don't! I don't share!!" Most of us don't share
very much either; we have decidedly toddlerish relationships to sharing. There are two problems with this. The first is that it isn't right
to allow poor people to be screwed because we're afraid to have to
sit next to them on the bus, but in many cases it's already too late for
that. The real problem with embracing private solutions is that when
we're unable to achieve and afford them, we find that we've trashed
our infrastructure. As we began carrying our water bottles around,
we stopped maintaining our water fountains. And now that it turns
out that the bottles are bad for us and the water in them contaminated, our options are a lot narrower.

The same is true of most preparations for peak oil and climate
change. I've been accused of fatalism, because I don't think we're
going to have the money or resources to radically transform ourselves
into a society powered by alternative energies, and I don't think most
of us are going to have the money to put tens of thousands of dollars into retrofitting our homes. But what I do think we could do is
dramatically reinforce and recreate our public infrastructure, and to
create public solutions to problems we now typically examine as private. We can live in homes that are dramatically stripped down, with
low-energy infrastructure, if we have access to a few powered public
resources that we share with others.

That is, while I think it unlikely we will all have solar-powered
pumps to bring up water from our private wells, there is no reason
your town can't put solar- or hand-powered pumps in central, public

places to provide water in the increasingly likely event of power cuts and major outages. While most people will not have a perfectly retrofitted canning kitchen, there's no reason our church and school kitchens can't be transformed into public use. While we won't all have cars, there's no reason those of us who do can't put many more people in them and carpool. I may not be able to afford a solar system for my home, but my neighbors and I may be able to afford to solar retrofit a garage on our street that could be used as a school-room, a clinic for our local nurse practitioner, as a place for band practice and neighborhood parties.

It is easier to plan just for ourselves. It is easier in many ways to carry our own water bottle. It is easier not to talk to other people, it is easier not to need other people, or have to share with and accommodate them. It is easier to pick the people you want to share with, to be exclusive rather than inclusive. There are all sorts of reasons not to think in public terms, and only, I think, two major reasons to do so. First of all, if we are to break out of our isolation, we have to, and second, because we have no choice. Privatized solutions are too costly, too exclusive, too limited. Anyone who goes into tough times imagining they will be one of the rich and lucky who will always be able to afford their bottle of water is, I think, betting on winning the lottery.

16

Creating and Using
Community Resources

Light is the task where many share the toil.

— Homer —

But Won't Someone Just Take
My Food Away From Me?

THERE'S DEFINITELY a survivalist streak building in the environmental movement as times get tougher. Mainstream newspapers are running stories about survivalism and imply that everyone who stores food is living in a bunker somewhere. And so many discussions turn to the question of the potential for civil unrest in tough times and whether it is safe for us to talk to our communities about our own reserves of food.

There are many people who hear that the energy peak, a new depression or climate change is coming and believe that building up their stocks of ammo and heading for the hills is the way to go. I recognize, even if I do not share, that impulse. It is the impulse to protect your own, the panic you feel when you realize that your society, which on some level is supposed to protect you, hasn't planned ahead for this one. And so people tend to get into discussions about what happens when refugees or hungry folk come around, and a lot of times the answer is that you have to protect your own again. In many cases "protect your own" means "shoot people."

And there are clearly some times when protecting your own will be necessary — as there are today. But I also think that sometimes this is a product of reading too many science fiction novels. In these books, you always know somehow that if you don't save every single crust of bread, your loved ones will starve to death, so it is a moral choice to say no to the wandering beggars. In fact, it is fairly moral, generally speaking, to do anything but eat them because, after all, every refugee is a threat. And in these books, they usually have swords and big guns.

Well, I can't swear life will never be like this, but it is worth noting that in many hungry places in the world, including New Orleans in 2005, refugees were actually much more *vulnerable* to violence than they were aggressive. Despite the stories of rape and murder and mayhem (which turned out to be mostly nonsense), and the people who responded to rumors of unrest by getting guns and closing off neighborhoods, most of the most desperately needy people did nothing more than wait politely, weep, beg for help and maybe sing a little. And that's true of most refugees in the world. These are desperate people who race across borders, trying to escape disaster or terrible violence. They don't attack those around them — they wait and pray for a little food. And yet we're terrified of them.

During the Great Depression, thousands of young men and women took to the rails because they were hungry and had no jobs. While they did occasionally commit acts of violence and fairly often stole small amounts of food, generally speaking these young people were much more likely to be abused than to do serious harm. They were thrown out of towns into the cold with no food, because the law said no one who didn't live there could have the sun go down on them. They were raped and beaten up by other refugees and by locals. They were thrown in jail and put in chain gangs for the offense of being homeless. Writing about it later, many of them told stories of going to soup lines and being cast out hungry because the town said that there was nothing for anyone but their own. A young man tells a story in David Shannon's *The Great Depression* of traveling through the Midwest all winter without a coat of any kind, visiting relief services and asking if anyone could give him a coat. He never got one.

Now, it is possible that none of these places had a coat to give. It is possible that adding one more bone and two more potatoes to the soup pot would mean someone's child died of hunger. I don't know. But I think it's more likely that when things get hard for us, we often panic. We look at what we have and we see all the terrible things that could happen and so we hold on hard to what we have, regardless of the consequences to others.

These issues are about to gain a new currency. The estimates for climate change-induced refugees range between the hundreds of millions and the billions. The truth is that even if we act now, the world is going to be newly full of people moving about, and their survival is going to depend on our relationship to those groups. The current economic crisis is leading to a rise in homelessness and hunger that is shaking the safety nets.

Unlike in the novels, though, we'll probably never know for sure that we'll always have enough. So how do we know whether to share, whether to greet the stranger with a gun or a plate? How do we know, if things change and the world seems uncertain, how to respond to one another?

Well, the world was once much poorer than it is now, and there was a fairly universal set of rules for this: the exact opposite from the ones we tend to assume will pertain. Right now, when we in America are richer than most kings of old, we assume that our job is to hold on tightly to what we have. But in my faith (I'm a Jew), and every other religion and in secular stories, we hear the tale of the stranger in disguise. The stranger who appears in the form of someone desperately poor and in need, and who turns out to be a god, or an angel in disguise. Those who turn the stranger away are punished. Those who welcome them are rewarded.

Our society has forgotten those stories, or allowed our fear to rule over our generosity, even though our societies are safer than most of the ones the stories emerged in. I'm not arguing against prudence and care or saying that we will always have enough to give away without thought. But we are very rich now, and I think it is worth remembering that in every society and faith, the obligation to welcome the stranger and offer them something *even in the face of our own hardship* is central to our beliefs. We need to be wary of a false sense of scarcity. Yes, plan for the future, store food, create a reserve. But recognize that in many cases, that reserve is for sharing, not for holding close.

The stories aren't always religious: sometimes it is the good king who travels in the guise of the poor. It doesn't really matter. They are designed to teach us that nothing is ever certain, that we can never have *enough* for everything we need and so we must trust in others. Even in our vulnerability we are supposed to be willing to risk something for another both because it is right and also because we too have been strangers.

Jews are frequently reminded we have been strangers many, many times, but I think even in our minority culture we have forgotten what that strangeness means. None of us can be certain that we will remain privileged and comfortable. You can prepare perfectly and still lose your home to rising sea levels or lack of water; you can do everything right and have bad things befall you. There are things we cannot control.

So each of us must live in the world as though we will someday be the stranger who turns to another for a hand. And each of us must be willing to offer one, if we expect to receive it. This is much more risky than greeting the hungry with violence or indifference. It is frightening. It is hard. What if the stranger who comes to the door is angry, or smelly or frightening? What if, despite our best rational precautions, harm is done? But then again, what if *we* do harm to an innocent stranger by allowing our fear to shape our thinking too much? And what if the stranger at our doorstep is Elijah, come to see if we have the courage of those who came before us?

Thousands of people know from my writings that I store food, and occasionally someone asks me whether that makes me afraid. My answer is no — not because I know the future, not because I am a mindless optimist, but because I know that my own security depends on sharing my knowledge with others. What I fear is the day my neighbors go hungry and wonder why I am not — not that my neighbors and I struggle together to keep the wolf from our shared doors.

Talking To Others About Food Storage

One of the issues I think all of us face is that our own personal food storage can only take us so far. Ultimately, our own security in both a pragmatic and a moral sense depends on not having our neighbors go hungry either. So we're left with the oxygen mask issue — you know, it's like those oxygen masks that come down if something bad happens on a plane. First, you start by taking care of yourself, but then, you turn around and see if anyone else needs help.

Now the part about connecting with others can be tricky. How do we begin talking about food to our family, friends, neighbors and acquaintances. How do we get started? How do we approach what is obviously a fraught subject?

I think one of the most important things we can do when we get started with these conversations is to separate out how much we want people to agree with our point of view, from acceptance of the *actions* we'd like other people to take. I want people to store a reserve of food — I'm not picky about whether they store it because of peak oil, climate change, zombies, economic crisis, volcano eruption, not liking to shop, to save money or the arrival of the rapture. I think a lot of the time it is easy to think that people only act from the motives that move us, but of course, that's not true. So generally speaking, I think it is more productive to talk to people, and figure out what does motivate them, and also to offer a range of reasons for storing food, rather than one or two.

For me, a conversation about food storage might begin with a discussion of high food prices and the savings we might get if we bought in bulk together. Or perhaps if I know someone is facing a possible job loss, about how food storage has helped my family through periods when we were financially insecure.

Or it might not begin with food storage at all. It might begin with finding common ground — for example, how can we work together to save money, or to make the neighborhood more food secure? The issue might be less about visions of the future and more about finding a way to be useful to one another.

With some people, it might take a while. If you get a negative response to something, it doesn't necessarily mean that the person you are talking to hasn't heard you or will never consider an idea. A lot of us reject new ideas the first time we encounter them, simply because they seem alien or strange. One of the tools I use is to make food storage sound routine — mentioning that something is on sale and this might be a good time to stock up on it, for example.

Some of us have religious or cultural invocations we can use. For example, if your community or family has known hunger in the past, or has religious obligations to self-sufficiency, sometimes it is productive to speak in those terms. It can be useful to talk about our history. I often ask people to think about their grandparents and great-grandparents, and ask whether most of them made it through 80 years or so without hunger, war or disruption of supplies. Putting it in family terms helps people connect to an idea that seems foreign, but may not be.

Patriotism and pride are, I think, also important ways to come at this, although they should be used carefully. Many of us are not so very far removed from people who took a great deal of pride in their self-sufficiency. While we don't want to make those who need aid feel bad, there are good reasons to invoke the sense of pride someone gets when they manage to get through tough times independently. This is important in a national sense as well. It can and should be a matter of pride to be able to take care of yourself and your own, so that resources are left for the truly needy when charities or government agencies step in during a crisis. That does not mean that pride should prevent us from taking help if we need it, merely that we should do all we can to maximize our ability to take care of ourselves and to help others.

What you are about to start discussing may not be so very alien after all. Conservative columnist Peggy Noonan recently wrote about our nation:

People want to make their country stronger—literally, concretely, because the things they fear (terrorism, global collapse) are so huge and amorphous. Lately I think the biggest thing Americans fear, deep down—the thing they'd say if you could put the whole nation on the couch and say, "Just free associate, tell me what you fear?"—is, "I am afraid we will run out of food. And none of us have gardens, and we haven't taught our children how to grow things. Everything is bought in a store. What if the store closes? What if the choke points through which the great trucks travel from farmland to city get cut off? I have two months of canned goods. I'm afraid.'"

— wsj.com/article/SB123146498555866787.html)

The truth is that people are afraid, and giving them tools to overcome their fear by action is a gift.

Most of all, I think that developing a family or community or neighborhood level of food security involves keeping at it, making it part of what normal people do. You may be surprised at how people gradually evolve from, "That's weird, I don't need to do that," to "Could you show me how to get started?"

Building and Sustaining Local Safety Nets

Of all the bad news lately, what's got me maybe the most worried is the heavy burden being placed upon already under-funded safety net programs. Consider the statistics.

In 2007, 11.1 percent of American households regularly experienced food insecurity, slightly up from the year before. A full one third of all Americans experience food insecurity, in that they don't know if they will have enough food, but generally manage to make do — the 11.1 percent is the number of people who actually go to bed hungry on a regular basis. Even before the recession hit, before food prices really spiked, we were already seeing a rise in real and serious hunger in the US.

But those statistics don't tell the whole story. Between 2006 and 2007, the number of children who regularly experience hunger doubled. Think about that. Again, this was before the financial crisis.

One out of every nine Americans needs food stamps to get to the end of the month. One out of every *two* infants in the US requires nutritional supplements from the WIC program. Subsidized school lunch program rolls are rising rapidly, by as much as four percent in some localities month over month. At these numbers, we can no longer think of these programs as safety nets for unusual numbers of the hungry. These are direct government food subsidies to a nation that can no longer feed itself. It is now normal to need state subsidies to eat.

Now the good news is that the public and private safety net programs are mostly still holding at this writing, although there are signs of trouble. The folks who work for these programs and administer them generally are doing their best to get everyone who needs help under the umbrella. I come from a family of teachers and social workers, housing advocates and eldercare workers — and people who often spend their weekends at the food pantry or the shelter. I know for a fact that while some of the people who do the hands-on work of making sure people have places to stay and food to eat and a decent education are jerks, most of them are totally committed. They usually are paid badly and do difficult, stressful work because they don't want to see anyone go hungry or cold. They are trying to stem the tide of crisis — and they are failing and, in the long term, bound to fail, because no one can stop a tidal wave with linked arms.

For example, during the biggest donation season of the year, right before Thanksgiving 2008, food pantries all over the country were short of turkeys as well as basic food staples. Most charities rely on donations made between Halloween and New Year's. This is when people most open their purses and the charities know they have to make what they get now last during the long winter and spring, when people donate less. So the fact that their cupboards are bare when they should be receiving most of their annual donations bodes badly for the days to come.

Or consider the situation with state unemployment funds. Right now several states, including my own New York (which is disproportionately dependent on Wall Street for funds), Nevada, Ohio and California may well not be able to pay unemployment claims within a very few months, just as the great wave of unemployment hits. In January of 2009, state call-in registration lines all over the country actually began to crash as a massive influx of new unemployed tried to make claims.

Meanwhile, most state-subsidized social programs, including the ones that help at-risk kids, the homeless and the desperately hungry are facing budget cuts, hiring freezes and occasionally the complete axing of a program. States are cutting back radically, and will likely have to make further cuts.

It is likely that the federal aid will be brought in — and just as likely that the scale of the economic crisis may well exceed their ability to remedy the problem too. The federal government has already spent trillions bailing out Wall Street, and now comes everyone else — states, counties, social service programs, nearly every industry. They'll all want a handout, and the reality is that we can't save everyone.

That is, we are only just seeing the beginning of the wave of unemployment and the economic crisis. What has been largely a Wall Street crisis is only now really percolating down into most of our lives. And the changes that are coming are huge — changes in our culture, changes in our economy, changes in our sense of ourselves. David Brooks, a *New York Times* conservative commentator who often annoys the heck out of me but is sometimes really, really right, put his finger beautifully on the issue:

> In times of recession, people spend more time at home. But this will be the first steep recession since the revolution in household formation. Nesting amongst an extended family rich in social capital is very different from nesting in a one-person household that is isolated from family and community bonds. People in the lower middle class have much higher divorce rates and many fewer community ties. For them, cocooning is more likely to be a perilous psychological spiral.
>
> In this recession, maybe even more than other ones, the last ones to join the middle class will be the first ones out. And it won't only be material deprivations that bites. It will be the loss of a social identity, the loss of social networks, the loss of the little status symbols that suggest an elevated place in the social order. These reversals are bound to produce alienation and a political response. If you want to know where the next big social movements will come from, I'd say the formerly middle class.

I think Brooks is right on the money here — and I don't think it will just be the former middle class. All of the baby boomers, regardless of their class, who bought the idea that security comes from affluence, that their future was more about money than their ties to family, are likely to be angry and betrayed as their pensions and retirement funds vanish. The unemployed are coming not just from service industries and new jobs, but from high-paying ones in finance and insurance.

And the safety nets will break, if this gets bad enough. They've been undercut for decades, going back to the Reagan administration, and we've already allocated a lot of our wealth into the vast black hole of Wall Street. Social programs are already strained, and the financial crisis has only just begun. People will lose first their jobs, then the benefits they expect to sustain them, and finally very basic things like food security. And the community ties and social capital that could have mitigated some of that suffering are precisely what growth capitalism has spent the last 60 years ripping to shreds.

The key to mitigation in the midst of this doom and gloom is the restoration of the social and communal ties that Brooks is talking about. There are two important reasons for this. The first is that, as Brooks points out, there's a big difference between staying home and eating beans and rice alone in your chilly house and getting together with your neighbors and sharing that meal. The sense of loss and deprivation is very different. Social scientists have confirmed what the historian Timothy Breen observed: "rituals of non-consumption" can replace our rituals of consumption, if we come together. It can be a lot easier to bear tough times if you are working together with other people and feel that you are all in the same boat.

The second, and perhaps more urgent reason is that our stability as a nation depends on building layers of additional safety nets underneath the ones that break. Think of poverty as falling out a window. Right now, there is a safety net that catches a majority of the people who fall, although by no means all of them. But what's under that net? What happens if it breaks? We need those additional nets not only because protecting others from hunger, cold and suffering is the ethical thing to do, and not only because the life you save may soon be your own, but because our personal security depends entirely on our community security. In hard times, crime rates go up, and people get angry. Brooks is right to anticipate a movement of angry and frightened people, and when people are angry and frightened, we're all vulnerable.

In a rational society there are more layers to break your fall, and we're going to need them. First, there are formal structures at the community level. If your town has never needed a food pantry because people could drive to the neighboring city, now is the time to propose it at your church, school or other possible site. Think about ways you could adapt existing infrastructure. Could the schools start distributing extra school lunches to the needy after the day is over? Could your school establish a backpack program, sending food home for the weekend with the neediest kids? Could you start a local gleaning program, or a senior lunch program? If you have these programs, but they are struggling, what can you do to reinforce them? Can you make another donation? Start a fund drive? What about setting up a bulletin board system to bring families struggling to keep their homes together with people who need housing? There are a thousand good ideas — yours is probably one of them.

The next layer reaches out to neighbors and community. I know we all worry about looking like busybodies, but now is the time to start looking in on your neighbors, and offering to help. The way to do this is to talk to people, even before it looks like they need anything. That way you'll know if your elderly neighbor can no longer afford to drive to get her medication and you can offer to pick it up, or if a neighbor is out of work and might be glad to get a day's pay helping a friend of yours winterize her house. Being neighborly, and also gentle and unjudgemental, is how you are going to know if someone in your neighborhood has no food in the pantry. For every person who signs up for aid and accepts help, there are several who would rather go hungry than take institutional charity. But they will gladly come over and share a meal with their neighbor, or do you a favor and take that loaf of bread that you've got nowhere to store.

One of the most important things we can do is to spend our money in our communities if at all possible. Every dollar you can pass on to a neighbor, a local farmer or a local business that enriches your community is one that makes everyone more secure. So maybe hire the out-of-work neighbor to plant and tend a garden for your sister, or give your best friend a farmstand gift certificate.

Finally, there's family, or the people who function like one. These are the people who are standing there with their arms out at the bottom of your fall, and are prepared to risk something to catch you. These are the people you can depend on when you have no place to go or no food in the pantry. And as long as you have food and a place to sleep, try hard to be that person yourself for close friends and extended family. In fact, try hard to extend the circle a bit if you can. A lot of vulnerable people out there could use a hand up. You don't have to take in everyone, or treat everyone like family, but if each of us expands the category of people we will not allow to fall, we may be able to catch enough people in our nets to make a vast difference.

Community Food Security Centers

What about the brass tacks of how to get some measure of community food security? Most of us simply won't be able to afford to create the ideal food preservation kitchen in our homes or build large enough reserves to feed ourselves and all our neighbors. We need community resources to enable us to store food, get access to water and preserve our local abundance for the future. My proposition would be that local communities open food security centers, consisting of (ideally) a food pantry, a community kitchen for community canning and food storage, along with cooking classes, a cafeteria, a farmer's market, a grain bank and a food co-op.

Many communities have parts of this structure. A few communities have public access kitchens and community canneries. Many have food pantries. Some have co-ops. Most communities have school cafeterias and senior lunch programs, if not any way of spreading these to the general public.

Ideally, all of these organizations would work together – the co-op would get dry commodities with long storage life like grains and legumes from local farmers by purchase or barter. They could hold them in reserve and sell them at wholesale prices to the local food pantry and to the school and local community cafeterias. The community kitchen would encourage local economic enterprise, enabling people to sell their jams and jellies and other home-preserved foods, as well as encouraging food self-sufficiency.

Imagine a community that focuses on food and economic security, building institutions like those listed below that ensure that everyone eats and the local economy grows:

- Community kitchens that allow people to preserve food both for their home stores and as items they could sell as a source of income. They could also provide cooking lessons to help people adjust to the "pantry diet."
- Food banks that build up supplies of grain and staples during times of surplus and hold on to them, for sale at stable prices. This was once done by the federal government, but no longer, so communities need to take this road. This is both a hedge against bad agricultural years and a hedge against rapidly rising prices.
- Food pantries that provide the most vulnerable with food.
- Co-ops that purchase as much as possible from local farmers, as well as large quantities of bulk goods from sustainable sources to repackage and sell to the community at reasonable prices.
- Community cafeterias. Right now, institutional cafeterias serve mostly poor quality industrial food to people who can't do much about it — the hungry, the elderly and school children. But what if we were to adapt the school kitchens in many communities to make meals that families could afford, mostly from local and healthy ingredients? What if they were open on weekends, and served good food, offsetting the cost of buying more nutritious and sustainable food for the rest of the time?
- Covered farmers' markets, allowing farmers to sell directly year-round.
- Solar or manual water pumping from a safe and reliable source for periods of power outage.

Even if you can't pull a full "food security center" together, I think it is useful to think in these terms. Such an institution could be highly profitable, improve local food security, and also create a community center.

Meanwhile, bits and pieces of this can be created. Many communities have church kitchens that might add canning equipment, or they might be able to get their town board to consider purchasing a staple food reserve, given the obvious need.

There are certainly many ideas I haven't even explored. The most important part of this is that we begin thinking of our food security in collective terms, in terms, perhaps of our obligation to love one another.

Recipes

Open House Roasted Vegetables

I love to throw parties, and these are almost always on the menu in the winter, because they are so adaptable — add sweet potatoes or not, depending on what you have. Season with what herbs you've got, add what roots you have, and let the heat bring out the natural richness and sweetness. Serves 8–10.

- 5–7 lbs of mixed root vegetables — potatoes, onions, carrots, sweet potatoes, celeriac, turnips, rutabagas, leeks…whatever you've got, cut into chunks.

- ½ cup olive oil
- a bunch of herbs, fresh or dried

- 5 cloves of garlic, minced
- 4 tbsp balsamic vinegar (or other vinegar)

Chop the vegetables and put them in a long deep roasting pan. Mix the remaining ingredients and toss with vegetables. Roast at high temperatures (450ish), stirring occasionally, until caramelized and browned and tender. Serve to a huge party of hungry people.

Almond Mushroom Wild Rice

I discovered this recipe in a now-forgotten magazine years ago and have served it to great praise to many people. Serves 8–10.

- 3 cups uncooked wild rice
- 7 cups chicken, vegetable, cider or miso broth
- 6 tbsp butter, melted
- 1½ cups slivered almonds, toasted
- 3 cups sliced fresh or dried and rehydrated mushrooms
- 6 tbsp chopped green onions

Rinse and drain rice; place in a greased baking dish. Add the remaining ingredients; mix well. Cover and bake at 325° for 1½ to 2 hours or until liquid is absorbed and rice is tender.

Gingerbread for a Crowd

I love gingerbread and would happily eat it anytime. This makes enough to fill your house with neighbors and leave some for the cook to nibble. Makes 40 slices.

- 3½ cups sugar
- ¼ cup baking soda
- 4 tbsp ground cinnamon
- 4 tsp ground ginger
- 10 eggs
- 1 qt. plus 3½ cups hot water
- 3 quarts, plus 1½ cups flour (white or wheat both work)
- 1 tbsp salt
- 3 tsp ground cloves
- 3½ cups vegetable oil
- 10 tbsp soy flour
- 1 qt. plus 3 cups molasses

Combine dry ingredients and stir well to combine. Mix vegetable oil, egg whites, hot water, and molasses in a bowl until blended. Slowly add the oil mixture to dry ingredients and mix until blended. Scrape down the sides of the bowl. Pour into many greased cake pans and bake at 350° for 30 minutes or until a tester comes up clean.

JusT No

Several people sent me this story in the fall of 2008, and I was struck by my own reaction to it.

> Gerald Celente, the CEO of Trends Research Institute, is renowned for his accuracy in predicting future world and economic events, which will send a chill down your spine considering what he told Fox News this week. Celente says that by 2012 America will become an undeveloped nation, that there will be a revolution marked by food riots, squatter rebellions, tax revolts and job marches, and that holidays will be more about obtaining food, not gifts.
>
> "We're going to see the end of the retail Christmas.... we're going to see a fundamental shift take place.... putting food on the table is going to be more important that putting gifts under the Christmas tree," said Celente, adding that the situation would be "worse than the great depression."
>
> "America's going to go through a transition the likes of which no one is prepared for," said Celente, noting that people's refusal to acknowledge that America was even in a recession highlights how big a problem denial is in being ready for the true scale of the crisis.
>
> Celente, who successfully predicted the 1997 Asian Currency Crisis, the subprime mortgage collapse and the massive devaluation of the U.S. dollar, told UPI in November last year that the following year would be known as "The Panic of 2008," adding that "giants (would) tumble to their deaths," which is exactly what we have witnessed with the collapse of

Lehman Brothers, Bear Stearns and others. He also said that
the dollar would eventually be devalued by as much as 90
percent.

Reading this, this morning, my reaction was a little different than my
normal reaction to things that come into my "inbox of doom." You
see, I've just spent two years writing and revising a book, *A Nation
of Farmers*, about the food system that makes pretty much the same
arguments that Celente is making — that both the economic and material realities of our food system are so fragile and subject to disruption that we're facing hunger in our lifetimes. So you wouldn't think
this would bother me much.

Somehow, however, this hit me rather viscerally. At first I started
to write one of my usual responses — an analysis of why this might be
true and what we can do to prevent it, yada yada. I've written dozens,
maybe close to a hundred such pieces about various bits of the food
system puzzle over the years. I can do them in my sleep. Except,
today, I couldn't. I kept thinking over and over "Fuck rational — this
is not a case for rationality."

Oh, I know it actually is, but you'll have to ask Raj Patel or Paul
Roberts or Michael Pollan or Frances Moore Lappé or anyone but
me to do the rational thing about our food system. I am not in writer
mode, I am in Mom mode, and the idea that my food system could
have gotten to this point, that my world, my country, my region, my
community, my kids may have to live in a place where food riots are
the only possible response to abiding hunger pisses me off.

My reaction to the idea that the US could rapidly decline in food
security was simply, "No. I'm not having it." I know it makes good
press, a good bit of evidence supports the idea, but *we are not having
food riots!* Dammit, I'm the Mom and people are going to get fed.

OK, I realize that sounds a little insane, and obviously, I'm not
your Mom, or the economy's Mom. Nor does my Momhood con-
fer "Empress of Everything" status, much as I might wish. Heck, it
doesn't even mean I can get the boys to remember to lift the toilet lid
every single time. But I'm still not having it.

I started out exploring climate change and peak oil and their connections to our economy with a personal motive. Something along the lines of, "Dammit, my kids will not go hungry." And I did a pretty good job of ensuring that was true — in seven years we've got our land, kept out of debt, built our food reserve, and made our land fairly productive. We've got our own milk and eggs, and gardens that could feed us and other people. And as I realized that I cared just as much about my friends and extended family and their kids, well, I did some planning for them too. Maybe it won't be needed, maybe it will, but I'm not having the people I love go hungry either.

But a little ways along that trip, I realized that food security for me and mine was a slippery slope. Where does "mine" stop? It certainly doesn't stop at my neighbors' yards. First of all, they are friends, but even if they weren't, how could I be secure if they weren't. So I started talking to them — gently — and started giving out plants and helping them start gardens and talking about food storage in my neighborhood and my larger community. Is it enough? I don't know. I hope so. But I'm not the only one here working on this, and there are more people trying it every month.

And then I started writing about it, and "mine" shifted yet again. First I was just writing to other folks concerned with the same things I was, and then people starting asking if they could reprint my ideas, so I thought I ought to collect them somewhere. And that became first my blog and then my books, with an ever-expanding number of people who tell me about their experiences and report the news and argue with me and pass my stuff on to other people. Now I get enough e-mails from people saying they started a garden or bought a food reserve or talked to their neighbors about starting something that I feel like maybe we're making progress, however small.

Most of these people don't live anywhere near my neighborhood. They write me from Portugal and Sweden and Israel and Columbia and Japan and Morocco and India, and within the US from Alaska, New Mexico, California and Florida. Some of them even do live near me. But it doesn't matter, because I'm not having any of them go hungry either (I realize they can take care of themselves — I didn't say this was rational.) And yes, I know some people already are going hungry, and some places have already had food riots. We've got to deal with that too while we prevent them in our homes.

I realize that we've now run up against the practical limits of my authority (actually, we probably ran up against them with that toilet thing, but who's counting?). But the good thing is that I have a whole bunch of readers out there, many of whom are moms or dads, grandparents (the boss's bosses), teachers, honored aunts and uncles and family friends. And every one of them has probably had the experience of saying, "No. Just, no," and imposing their vision through sheer force of will, appeals to irrelevant authorities, and the mad conviction (which is sometimes true, even when it is a little crazy) that you can work and pray and love and fight the good stuff into being and the bad stuff away. Maybe the combined force of all that unreasonable conviction can be harnessed. It should be.

None of us can ever protect our families completely. There are always more of "them" than there are of "mine." The only hope is an expanded definition of "my own people" that covers as much of the world as we can manage. And while I think there are a lot of rational issues involved here, sometimes I think it is good to be a little irrational, a little crazy, at least on some issues. Because only at the point that we say *I will not have it* do we realize exactly how far we'll go to make sure the worst outcomes never happen.

How far will we go? I don't know the answer. Certainly as far as my garden, which will grow more food for the food pantry next year. As far as my animals, where I work on raising and breeding livestock suited to suburban neighborhoods. As far as my keyboard, my blog, my books and my talks can reach. As far as calling for tens of millions of people in the US to take up food production wherever they can — in their yards, on their farms, in containers on their roofs and balconies, in vacant lots, in community gardens, in their neighbor's yards. As far as encouraging as many people as I can to store and preserve food. As far as cutting my impact on the climate as hard as I can and trying to help other people to do so, and then going back and asking if I can do a little more. As far as I can with the bit of influence I've got. As far as I can, and then further, and then the rest of you will take it as far as you can, and that's pretty damned far.

This book and the others I've written have plans and arguments, analyses and figures, policy recommendations and personal actions to take. But sometimes that's not what's needed. Just as I simply will not allow my kids to go hungry, I'm not letting my country, or my world go hungry (or for those last two, hungrier). You would be perfectly rational to doubt my personal capacity to keep it from happening. But right at the point of irrationality, of the good kind of madness, is a force I cannot name or fully describe, but that is dragged into reality by forays into territory beyond the land of reason. It sounds nuts, and it probably is, but it is also a Mother thing (and a Father thing, I suspect). And I don't have to do it by myself. The world is full of mothers and fathers and non-parents with a vast capacity to love some idea, person, animal, place, life, who know that if they had to, they could do more than any reasonable person to protect their own. And the world is full of our own.

17

Bringing It All Together— Living Independently in a Better World

Man can live about forty days without food,
three days without water, about eight minutes without air,
but only one second without hope.

— Anonymous —

I RECENTLY RETURNED HOME from speaking somewhere to, among other things, a message from someone who wanted to interview me for a mainstream media source, because I'm a writer about "preparedness." The interviewer asked me to estimate the likelihood of various scenarios and to talk about the questions of preparedness as an insurance policy.

But as I spoke to the interviewer, I found myself saying, "Oh, but wait, that isn't so much just about emergency preparedness as about saving money." Or I would say, "Well, yes, it is great in an emergency, but we also use it all the time." By the time we were finished, I felt that I'd lent myself to a discussion about preparing for a hypothetical crisis that may come someday. What I actually am starting to know something about (and I'm still just starting) is living in such a way that I'm somewhat insulated (not perfectly) from a whole host of scenarios.

The thing is, I can't really afford a lot of "prepping" of things I'm not going to make regular use of. Oh, I have emergency kits and a few things I store for various scenarios, but as I began accumulating useful things, the best way to make sure I knew where they are, knew how to work them and was comfortable living with them and without other resources, was, well, to use them. Most of us don't make major purchases on a hypothetical basis like, "Well, Josie, there's a 77 percent chance that you'll get married sometime during your lifetime, so why not pick up a wedding dress and a pair of rings right now and hang on to them." Now I don't doubt that that's the cheapest way to do it (OK, the cheapest way is to do what I did — don't wear a dress and buy the rings at a rummage sale), but it requires that during the period of your life when you are thinking of other things, you begin to anticipate every possible scenario, and put money towards a future at a time when you may be struggling with a present.

So for me, while I do talk about the usefulness of a lot of items in future scenarios, I don't want people to miss the fact that they are useful right now. That is, right now my solar lantern goes along with me when I go to the barn to milk the goats, and sometimes back to the living room to read by. Right now my sun oven is cooking lima beans from my food storage, and the food storage is saving me a trip to the store. Last winter, and the winter before, warm clothes and warm blankets substituted for expensive heating energy. Right now we eat largely what we grow or get from our neighbors, even if we'd kind of like something else sometimes. Now I do some of these things from principle, or because I want to know how to do them in a hypothetical future, but I also do them because I can't afford, and don't have time to maintain the infrastructure for the whole of two lives. I can't afford to have a regular, fossil-fuel dependent life and an expensive, back-up fossil-free one. I can only have one life at a time. I can afford my solar lantern because I use it to cut my electric bill now.

I think at the back of most of our minds is the idea that we'll only use the hand grinder or the wood stove someday in a crisis, because then we'll have more time. We won't have a job that sucks up our days, we won't have all these pressures on us. But all of us need to give some thought to another possibility — what if we don't have more time and we still need to cut expenses or make use of what we have? Even during the Great Depression, three quarters of the working population had work — and others were able to work intermittently — but you had to get up every day and go where the work was and wait for it. I think a lot of us are waiting for a life of comparative free time that may never come. In fact, we may be working more and longer, at least for a time, trying to maintain, and trying to learn to integrate these new tools into our lives.

What I do find is that using this stuff today frees up money for other things and since money comes from my time, using these lower-input things takes less total time on my part than I think. The classic example of this, of course, is the bicycle. Right now, many of us think we don't have time to bicycle places, and there's some truth to that. Why don't we have time? Well, part of the reason is that, according to the Department of Transportation, we have to work an average of two months every year to keep our cars running. Dumping the car may not be easy (I haven't succeeded yet), but the time to bicycle is there, we just have to figure out a way to access it. Life with just a bike would be harder in many ways, but easier in others. And while a car-and-bike life isn't too costly or difficult, other combinations, in which the fossil fuel and non-fossil fuel options are both kept going are harder and more costly. It is extremely expensive to lay in a winter's supply of pellets or wood and install the stove as well as keeping the oil or gas heat on.

I stopped by my friend Joy's store today — she sells bulk foods — to hear her lament that two of the nearby sources of bulk and health foods are going out of business in our area, one new venture, the other after decades. Both are closing before the winter's heating bills make closing no longer optional. Joy is making it, thankfully, but she's concerned about losing business from people who come in for sandwiches and sit a while and won't want to sit at the temperature she can afford to keep her business at. She's looking into putting in a small wood stove, though, because she knows a lot of her neighbors will be at home in their cold houses. She wonders if maybe, just maybe, her small store with its source of warmth could bring people together out of their cold houses for a period of warmth and comfort.

I liked what she was doing in large part because I think that she's looking not towards a moment of disaster, but towards her life and her business's future. Sure, it will be cold, but instead of seeing that as an emergency to be navigated in crisis mode, she's going forward into a new life and way of doing things. Joy smiled at me and shrugged as I was on my way out the door, noting that they'd "just live differently." And that might be better advice than any "preparedness" expert could ever offer.

The Battle Cry

My littlest, Asher, is a head-first kind of guy. We call him "the flying squirrel" because he thinks he can fly — as long as an adult is holding his hand (we hold on *tight*). He has no fear, merely boundless enthusiasm. And when he was about 18 months old, he would yell "Bunt to the Whee!" whenever he was about to leap head first into things.

Well, it occurred to me that everyone needs a battle cry, and since "Spoon!" was already taken, "Bunt to the Whee!" would do pretty well. Just in case you don't have a battle cry, I want to offer to share mine. Because I think you might need one too. Enthusiasm and the courage to screw up are what is needed to feed yourself these days.

The thing is, there's lots of things to write about in terms of food storage and tons to consider. But it is one of those things that takes time and practice, and gets immediately clearer once you start doing it.

The thing is, starting up any big project — growing food, storing it, preserving it — it's all overwhelming at first. And despite my hubris in writing this book, I certainly haven't mastered it. Every year I mess new things up, and forget old things and make new mistakes. But every year I get a little closer to my goals — to having a reserve to share with others, to living off our own homegrown and home-preserved food, to taking fewer trips to the store and to being able to accommodate guests at any time.

The thing is, sometimes you just have to dive in to know what you don't know. Sometimes you have to make foolish mistakes so that you can figure out what it is that you are trying to accomplish, or how to adapt an idea from me or someone else to your real life. To an extent, information can help. And to an extent, it probably can't — you just have to dive in.

So I offer you my son Asher's battle cry — Bunt to the Whee! Now is the time to dive in — make that first bulk purchase, save those first seeds, start cooking one or two meals a week from storage, try the pressure cooker or canning jam, experiment with whether you can dry those things in the sun, build that solar oven and try that new lentil recipe, ask the farmer at the market about buying bulk peaches or your neighbor whether she wants to come over for a day of canning.

I hope you'll all jump in, and not be afraid to make a mess of it. The mistakes are part of the process, and the process is central to the project. What project? Well, economic security — saving money so you can do other things that matter to you, keep your house and meet other needs. Food security so that you can feed yourself and help out those in need around you. Political action so we can stop giving our dollars to industrial agriculture, and start voting with them for something better. And a little step back towards democracy, no longer beholden for the food in our mouths to corporations we abhor. The chance to depend on and trust in our neighbors and those around us building real and good food systems. Community. Better food. All those good things.

That's why we need a battle cry. This isn't just about the rice or the garden or the canning jars. This is a small but important step in making a better way of life. And I admit, it brings me a great deal of joy to know that some people out there are trying new things and making changes. I sort of think of my own efforts as a whole bunch of us holding our seed packets, jar lifters, grain grinders (the not too heavy ones — we don't want anyone getting hurt) and wooden spoons up above our heads, ready to take on the world and the screwed up food system! *Bunt to the whee!*

OK, Now What?

So now what? I feel like we're asking that a lot these days. We have a crisis, we try to fix it, it doesn't work, there's a new crisis…it seems unending. What comes next in ordinary people's lives? Sometimes things seem dark — a friend loses their job, or you lose yours, your house is on the line, your life, your vision of the future.

Well, what comes next is probably, to be blunt, another series of crises. None of the experts I know of thinks that things are going to get better in the economy or the environment soon. That doesn't mean we're doomed, it just means that the work we need to do isn't going away soon. We are living in some dark times, but that's not the end of it. What can we do about it? Protest the bad stuff and keep trying to make it right. Call and fight and be angry. Don't let them wear your anger out. Clarify — make sure that the right message about what we need gets out. Vote, of course, because even the lesser of two evils can be quite lesser.

But more importantly, to the extent it is possible, everyone out there needs to look around them and ask what small piece of the infrastructure of their lives (and the lives of their community members) they can take some responsibility for. We need to all look and ask, "What is my job in this new world we're awakening to? What the heck can I do to help mitigate the tough times and make a better future?"

Maybe you already know your job. It's what you care about, the work you do already for free or for money, in every second of your spare time or for ten hours a day. You provide health care, grow food, teach, mend what's broken, feed the hungry, fight for justice — you do good work, and now you have to figure out a way to keep the work going without as much money or energy.

Or maybe you are head down in a health care crisis, a new baby, a lifestyle shift and you haven't the time and energy to do much more than prepare and protect yourself and your family as best you can. Your job is to get through this so that later you can do the work that needs doing. That's OK — but as soon as you can, make a little time, even if it is just to check in on your neighbors or start carpooling to the grocery store.

Maybe you don't know what your role is. Maybe you do have a little time or energy that could be used to build community, fix things, help others, but you are shy, and you don't know what to do. I can't tell you exactly what you should do. You know your talents and skills best. Maybe you are a natural organizer and leader and you should get started with your community's Victory Garden movement, building the community health center or getting neighbors to pool their resources to get a shared transport network up. Maybe you are more comfortable following in some already existing role, and it is time to get out to the local food pantry and start figuring out where they are going to get enough food to help all the hungry. Maybe you care most about kids, or elders or women or the Hispanic or Black or Asian community, and that's where you should concentrate your energies. Maybe you want to work with members of your faith, your family or your friends. Great. Do it. But do it now.

We're all going to need reliable sources of food. We're all going to need good work. We're all going to need ways to keep people housed, to connect folks who need homes with those who can't keep theirs unless they rent out some space. A lot of people are going to need warm clothes and blankets. A lot of people are going to need a meal, a helping hand, help with disabled family members and elders. And folks, when the formal economy falls away, when we cannot trust our government to act in our interests, all of us have to get acting to compensate, to keep the wolf from the door. The truth is that the economic bailout, on one level, was the final reminder of what Hurricane Katrina taught us, that no one is coming with a helicopter to rescue us. Fortunately, some of us have boats, and the rest of us can build life rafts, and there's a lot we can do to rescue ourselves.

Some of us will plant gardens, or expand the ones we have. Some of us might start selling a little more food, or making bread and selling it to their neighbors. Some of us may volunteer with local food security programs or poverty abatement groups. Perhaps we'll give talks at our local church, synagogue, mosque, temple, community center or farmers' market about local food and food security. Perhaps we'll bring food to a neighbor and let them taste the lush glory of local eating.

Maybe we'll start a farmers' market or a co-op. Maybe we'll talk to a neighbor or three about the importance of local food systems. Maybe we'll run for the zoning board and change that rule about backyard chickens. Maybe we'll get some chickens this year, or rabbits or worms or bees. Maybe we'll work on preserving open space for the animals already here on the planet.

Maybe we'll join Seed Savers, pick out a single variety, and commit to maintaining it in perpetuity so that it doesn't disappear from the earth. Maybe we'll grow a new crop, or more of it, and donate to our food pantry or a local, low-income family. Maybe we'll make a donation to organizations like Heifer International that support local food systems. Maybe we'll give a little more and live with a little less and be happy.

Maybe we'll buy more local food and less from the supermarket. Maybe we'll encourage our local schools or restaurants to buy from local farmers. Maybe someone will start a seed company, microbrewery or a CSA. Maybe we'll get our town to plant fruit and nut trees instead of regular street trees, or start a permaculture forest garden. Maybe we'll start a Victory Garden campaign in our town, city, state. Maybe we'll start thinking of "Victory" as not something you get from war, but from a world where no one goes hungry.

Maybe we'll learn to cook something new from scratch, or teach someone else how to cook staple foods. Maybe we'll put up a little more than we did last year. Maybe we'll do something to promulgate the joys of a really local diet, or explain the problems of confinement meat and industrial agriculture to someone who doesn't understand. Maybe you'll run for office, and change agricultural policy in your region. Maybe we'll feast gloriously and then eat a little lower on the food chain the rest of the time.

Maybe we'll can or dehydrate something this year, ferment or preserve something we've never tried. Maybe we'll teach a neighbor, a friend, a school class how to put up food or how to forage. Maybe we'll get our kids to eat the kale this year, even if we have to disguise it somehow. Maybe we'll get our spouse to eat it too.

Maybe we'll build soil, add organic matter, and sequester some carbon this year. Maybe this year will be the one we give up the chemical fertilizers, or the gas-powered tools. Maybe this year we'll stop treating the earth like dirt.

Maybe we'll do what we've been doing all along, only more and harder, because we understand what is at stake. Maybe we'll take on a new project, marshal our time and energy a little better. Maybe we'll start tentatively and gain confidence, or take courage and go further with this than we ever have. Maybe one of us will make a difference, or all of us will.

Remember, there *are* moments that are dark — it isn't just seeming. But the light comes back every year after the solstice, and the hard times cycle around and pass. If the light comes round again, well, so can a decent life. It is all hands on deck, folks.

Resources

This book is necessarily only an introduction to a host of engaging topics that deserve much more exploration. Fortunately, most of them have been explored in depth by various writers, bloggers and on websites. Your library and the Internet are likely to bring you connections to a host of new resources. Here are some of those I recommend. For many more, including many Internet resources for bulk purchasing, please visit my website sharonastyk.com/food-storage-and-preservation-link-vault.

General Food Storage and Preservation Books and Internet Resources

Emery, Carla. *The Encyclopedia of Country Living: An Old Fashioned Recipe Book*. Sasquatch Books, 2003. As if there were another book I could start with! Carla put together the most comprehensive book about food ever, including many, many ways of preserving and storing food. Well worth the money and now in its 10th edition.

Chadwick, Janet. *The Busy Person's Guide To Preserving Food*. Storey Publishing, 1995.

Green, Janet, Ruth Hertzberg, and Beatrice Vaughan. *Putting Food By*. Penguin, 1991.

Hupping, Carol. *Stocking Up: The Third Edition of America's Classic Preserving Guide*. Fireside, 1990.

The National Center for Home Food Preservation is the most current and complete source on the Internet, with wonderful links and information: uga.edu/nchfp.

If you don't know the incomparable Jackie Clay, take a romp through her advice columns and essays on food storage and related topics in *Backwoods Home*. She writes a monthly column on food preservation and many essays. If Jackie wrote a book, you can bet I'd buy it! She's the best there is on practical food storage: backwoodshome.com/advice/advice.html.

Food Storage Information

The resource on this subject is Alan Hagan's exhaustively researched and detailed Prudent Food Storage FAQ. It is a bit of a dry read, but it will answer questions you didn't know you had about storage life, how to pack things, etc: survival-center.com/foodfaq.

If you are trying to figure out how much food to store, a good starting place is this Mormon food calculator. There are some items that I wouldn't eat, and that don't go with the local and sustainable model, but they offer a starting point, with some nice basics on how much food actually is required for a family for a year: lds.about.com/library/bl/faq/blcalculator. Everyday Food Storage is a very user-friendly, basic food storage site, which includes handouts and plans for getting started: everydayfoodstorage.net.

Tools for Food Preservation and Sustainable Living

Lehman's sells all sorts of non-electric and manual tools for food preservation, from cherry pitters to dehydrators. Not cheap, but superb quality: lehmans.com.

The Local Exchange is a great source for a lot of useful stuff: thelocalexchange .org.

Sustainable Choice sells sun ovens and grain grinders: sustainablechoice.net.

Dehydration

Dry It, the creation of Gen McManiman, is an amazing online resource for both dehydrators and dehydration recipes: dryit.com.

We modeled our solar dehydrator on this one at Sue Robishaw's wonderful website. You might also check out her solar oven plans: manytracks.com/ Homesteading/SolarFoodDryer

Canning

I strongly encourage everyone to either print canning information from the Internet or to purchase a canning guide, ideally *The Ball Blue Book*. Canning from memory is potentially dangerous, so have the recipe and all information in front of you while you are doing it.

Ball Company. *The Ball Blue Book of Preserving*. Altrista Consumer Products, 2004.

Fermentation

Katz, Sander. *Wild Fermentation*. Chelsea Green, 2003. This is the definitive book on lactofermentation, and has wonderful recipes. Katz has a website full of information and recipes: wildfermentation.com.

Ziedrich, Linda. *The Joy of Pickling*. Harvard Common Press, 1998. Covers fermented as well as vinegar pickles — wonderful stuff!

Root Cellaring and Season Extension

Coleman, Eliot. *The Four Season Harvest: Organic Vegetables From Your Garden All Year Long*. Chelsea Green, 1999.

Bubel, Mike and Nancy Bubel. *Root Cellaring: Natural Cold Storage of Fruits and Vegetables*. Storey Publishing, 1991.

Living and Eating Frugally

Dacyczyn, Amy. *The Complete Tightwad Gazette.* Villard, 1998. A great read, with lots of wonderful information.

Best Cookbooks

The More With Less Cookbook. Doris Janzen Longacre. Herald Press, 1971. If I had to choose only a couple of basic cookbooks, this one and its sequels, which include the wonderful children's cookbook *Simply in Season* would be the start of my library. Its simple, staple food recipes are wonderful and delicious. We eat their apple-cinnamon crunch as a snack regularly, or mix it into yogurt, and it was where I got the idea of serving not-too-sweet rice pudding for breakfast.

Please to the Table: The Russian Cookbook. Anya von Bremzen and John Welch. Workman Publishers, 1990. Despite its name this is really a cookbook covering the food of the whole former Soviet Union. While it has plenty of fancier recipes, it emphasizes the staple foods of Eastern Europe — lots of roots, whole grains and very simple, inexpensive foods. The recipes are delicious as well. In college I lived on cabbage pie (which is really bad for you but spectacularly delicious), lentil and dried apricot soup and pumpkin fritters, and they are still part of our regular food rotation. Great borscht, too. I can't say enough good things about this book.

Down to Earth: Great Recipes for Root Vegetables. Georgeanne Brennan. Chronicle Books, 1996. Brennan is one of my absolute favorite food writers (among other things, she's the author of my son's favorite cookbook, *The Dr. Seuss Cookbook*). Rutabaga and barley soup, deep-dish turnip gratin, green onion and gruyere bread pudding and salsify fritters are all favorites here. Winter in the Northeast is time to devour the delights from the root cellar, and Brennan's book makes them enticing.

Mediterranean Grains and Greens. Paula Wolfert. Harper Collins, 1998. One of my favorite all-time cookbooks. This is where I learned the easy way of making polenta without all the stirring (it works on American-style mush as well). Eric and I eat pasta with bitter greens and tomatoes all summer long, particularly as the greens start to bolt, and my favorite bean and grain soup ever is her Greek-style medley of lentils, herbs and grains. Spiced barley bread is also one of the best things I've ever eaten, especially dipped in Harira. The best way to adapt to eating whole foods is to go back the cuisines that have been doing it for hundreds or thousands of years.

The Winter Harvest Cookbook. Lane Morgan. Sasquatch Books, 1990. I discovered this book through Carla Emery. The emphasis is on foods available in the Pacific Northwest in the winter, which means, roots, beans and greens. Very nice recipes — how many other cookbooks have more than a dozen parsnip recipes, or seven for daikon? My kids love her teriyaki beets (me too) and we like her broccoli dal as well.

Seductions of Rice. Jeffrey Alford and Naomi Duguid. Artisan, 2003. This cookbook is fascinating and wonderful. It explores authentic rice recipes (and foods served over rice) from all over the world. Their *Flatbreads and Flavors* did the same for wheat and flatbreads of other sorts. The risotto al birra (risotto with beer), which sounds weird, is spectacular. We eat beef and lettuce congee anytime we can get it, and we make khao ped (Thai fried rice) all the time. Yum.

Sundays at the Moosewood. The Moosewood Collective. Simon and Schuster, 1990. All the Moosewood cookbooks are good, of course, but for diversity of staple food recipes this one, which focuses on their Sunday ethnic days, is probably the best. Some of the sections are better than others. The sections on Japan and Finland are terrific. Some of the recipes need a bit more seasoning. But they are still very good and very creative. We make their sweet potato paratha quite often, and the tomato, lime and tortilla soup is a summer staple.

Soup and Bread Cookbook. Crescent Dragonwagon. Workman Publishing, 1992. This book has the remarkable utility of offering ways to make just about everything (I mean everything — she has a section on nut soups!) into soup. The recipes are great — flavorful and accessible — and she's a fun writer. I have no southern credentials at all, but I like her green gumbo a lot, and the broccoli and potato curry soup is a winter staple here, as is her split pea soup with caraway.

From the Earth: Chinese Vegetarian Cooking. Eileen Yin-Fei Lo. MacMillan, 1995. I've never made a bad recipe from this cookbook. The sizzling rice soup is incredible, and the many congee recipes are wonderful. Lima beans with soybean cake sounds beyond weird but is delicious, and lemon noodles with mushrooms are spectacular. I don't think I can say enough good things about this cookbook.

Foods of the Southwest Indian Nations. Lois Ellen Frank. 10 Speed Press, 2002. This has a fair share of foofy recipes for people with lots of money, but also a ton of great recipes for staple foods, southwestern style. The posole is great even without the meat and in the fall we eat sunflower cakes as a snack or as a breakfast. I wish I lived where I could try the recipe for tumbleweed shoots with pinto beans and wild rice, but we make pumpkin corn soup often.

Index

RECIPE INDEX

mushrooms: Almond
Mushroom Wild Rice,
319; Homemade Cream
of Mushroom Soup Base,
97–98; Stuffed Cabbage
with Dried Fruits, Mush-
rooms and Wild Rice,
172–173
Mustard Seeds, Potatoes,
Peas and Onions with
Tomatoes and, 110–111

O

Oatmeal Soup, Garlicky,
282–283
onions: Balsamic Glazed
Onions, 174; Potatoes,
Peas and Onions with
Tomatoes and Mustard
Seeds, 110–111
Open House Roasted Veg-
etables, 318

P

Pancakes, Pumpkin, 97
Pancake Syrup, 96–97
Peanut Butter-Banana
Balls, 187
peppers, Pickled Jalapenos
(or Other Hot Peppers),
155
Perfect White Bean and
Whatever Soup, 299–300
Pickled Jalapenos (or
Other Hot Peppers), 155
Pickles, Bestest Everything,
206
Pork, Salt, 225
Posole Verde, 132
potatoes: Mashed Potatoes
with Garlic and Olive
Oil, 173; Potatoes, Peas
and Onions with Toma-
toes and Mustard Seeds,
110–111
Preserved Lemons, 224
Pumpkin Leather, 156
Pumpkin Pancakes, 97

Q

Quinoa and Butternut
Squash, Creamy, 132–133

R

rice: Almond Mushroom
Wild Rice, 319; Golden
Coconut Rice, 133;
Stuffed Cabbage with
Dried Fruits, Mush-
rooms and Wild Rice,
172–173
Root Vegetables Massa-
man Curry, 174

S

salads: Japanese-Style Rice-
Fermented Greens, 223–
224; Thai Salad, 246–247
Salmon Cakes with
Chipotle Mayonnaise,
42–44
Salmon Jerky, 188
Salsa Verde, 206
Salt Pork, 225
sauces/dips: Beets with
Tahini Sauce, 157–158;
Black Bean Dip, 73; Salsa
Verde, 206
Sauerkraut, Wine, 222–223
Scalloped Corn, 24
soups/stews: Bamboo
Shoot Soup, 247–248;
The Best Beef Stew, 208;
Canned Meat Broth,
207; Chili in a Solar
Oven, 260; Garlicky
Oatmeal Soup, 282–283;
Homemade Cream of
Mushroom Soup Base,
97–98; Kimchi Tofu
Soup, 222; Perfect White
Bean and Whatever
Soup, 299–300; Posole
Verde, 132
Soybean Succotash, 189
Squash, Creamy Quinoa
and Butternut, 132–133

strawberry: Sunshine
Strawberries and Cherry
Preserves, 23–24; Vanilla-
Amaretto Strawberry
Jam, 205
Stuffed Cabbage with
Dried Fruits, Mush-
rooms and Wild Rice,
172–173
Succotash, Soybean, 189
Sunshine Strawberries and
Cherry Preserves, 23–24
syrup: Apple Cider Syrup,
207; Pancake Syrup, 96–
97

T

Tex-Mex Millet, 134
Thai Salad, 246–247
Tofu Soup, Kimchi, 222
Tomatoes and Mustard
Seeds, Potatoes, Peas and
Onions with, 110–111
Tortillas (With or With-
out a Tortilla Press),
Corn, 259–260
types of, 35

V

Vanilla-Amaretto Straw-
berry Jam, 205
vegetables: Grilled Vege-
tables in Oil, 225–226;
Open House Roasted
Vegetables, 318; Root
Vegetables Massaman
Curry, 174
Very Basic Wheat Bread,
73–74
Vodka, Grandpa Orlov's,
226–228

W

Wine Sauerkraut, 222–223

Y

Yogurt, Homemade, 156–
157

About the author

SHARON ASTYK is a writer, teacher, blogger
and small farmer. A former academic, her
unfinished doctoral dissertation focused on
the ecological and demographic catastrophes explored in Early Modern Literature.
Abandoning Shakespeare to work on the
ecological and demographic catastrophes
of the 21st century, she began by running
a small CSA and right now seems to write
books, including *Depletion & Abundance:
Life on the New Home Front* (New Society
Publishers 2008). In her copious spare time,
she raises vegetables, fruit, livestock, children and havoc with her husband in rural
upstate New York.

If you have enjoyed *Independence Days*, you might also enjoy other

Books to Build a New Society

Our books provide positive solutions for people who
want to make a difference. We specialize in:

Sustainable Living ♦ Ecological Design and Planning

Natural Building & Appropriate Technology ♦ New Forestry

Environment and Justice ♦ Conscientious Commerce

Progressive Leadership ♦ Resistance and Community

Nonviolence ♦ Educational and Parenting Resources

New Society Publishers
ENVIRONMENTAL BENEFITS STATEMENT

New Society Publishers has chosen to produce this book on recycled
paper made with 100% post consumer waste, processed chlorine free,
and old growth free.

For every 5,000 books printed, New Society saves the following
resources:[1]

36	Trees
3,297	Pounds of Solid Waste
3,628	Gallons of Water
4,732	Kilowatt Hours of Electricity
4,732	Pounds of Greenhouse Gases
26	Pounds of HAPs, VOCs, and AOX Combined
9	Cubic Yards of Landfill Space

[1]Environmental benefits are calculated based on research done by the
Environmental Defense Fund and other members of the Paper Task Force
who study the environmental impacts of the paper industry.

For a full list of NSP's titles, please call 1-800-567-6772 or check out our web site at:

www.newsociety.com

NEW SOCIETY PUBLISHERS